PRAISE FOR *THEY CALLED ME A LIONESS*

"A passionately argued, profoundly empathetic, and deeply informed examination of [Ahed Tamimi's] country's occupation. Her circumspection and clarity of thought are matched only by her vulnerability. An expertly crafted, trenchant memoir from a formidable activist."
—*Kirkus Reviews* (starred review)

"Unflinching . . . The memoir provides an intimate look into daily life for Palestinian civilians and serves as an insistent call for people worldwide to take up the Palestinian cry for freedom. . . . [Tamimi's] story, though heavy and heartbreaking, provides an important perspective, a counternarrative to many Israeli viewpoints and an inspiring account of everyday, persistent activism." —*Shelf Awareness* (starred review)

"An accessible book that is both deliberative and didactic . . . Through emotional and expository writing, the authors show us how history is and has always been deeply political and personal. . . . The authors impart a message of both urgency and hope. . . . The discourse on Palestine is finally shifting for the better, and the publication of this book, as well as the traction it has gained and has yet to gain, is a testament to that." —*+972 Magazine*

"A vivid unfolding of personal recollections, *They Called Me a Lioness* . . . zooms into the collective Palestinian experience of living under occupation and highlights the never-dying, cross-generational hope of the resilient Palestinians subjected to continuous torment by Israel. . . . [A] love letter to resistance, a love letter to Nabi Saleh, and most importantly, a love letter to a free Palestine." —*Jordan News*

"Seamlessly blends a deeply personal story with the history of an apartheid state and the constant humiliation and cruelty endured by the indigenous Palestinians . . . Somehow, through it all, love, laughter and strength triumph, uplifting the reader. . . . It's urgent for all of us to read *They Called Me a Lioness,* and gift copies to libraries, classrooms, newsrooms and legislators' offices." —*Washington*

"I cannot even begin to convey the clarity, photographic storytelling of *They Called*

T0042962

and Dena Takruri lay bare seemingly every terrifying aspect of Israel's apartheid against Palestinians, and the relentless freedom fight of Palestinians and their Israeli allies. Read and bear witness."

—Ibram X. Kendi, internationally bestselling
author of *How to Be an Antiracist*

"With more courage than any child should ever have to possess, Ahed Tamimi showed the world more than once what it looks like when you refuse to consent to your own obliteration. In this gripping, painful, and inspiring book, she tells the parts of the story that the cameras always miss: the slow and grinding humiliations of the occupation, the heartache of losing loved ones to Israeli prisons and guns, the cruelties of imprisonment, the love, laughter, and strength in solidarity that are necessary to keep living, breathing, and fighting against enormous odds. For anyone planning to stay alive on this planet in these perilous times, *They Called Me a Lioness* is urgent and essential reading."

—Ben Ehrenreich, author of *The Way to the Spring*

"This passionate memoir shines a floodlight on a people, a place, and a problem that the world too often discounts. Beautifully written, *They Called Me a Lioness* humanizes the daily headlines of occupation and resistance. Tamimi's story will rattle your soul and ignite calls for justice, equality, and peace."

—Mona Hanna-Attisha, author of *What the Eyes Don't See*

"This book soars. *Lioness* divulges an intimate portrait of a kid growing up in a political family in occupied Palestine, offering a succinct history of how Palestinians were expelled from their homes in 1948 and since *and* sharing a deep snapshot of Tamimi's own charged learning experiences in jail with other female political prisoners, some of whom were children like her. It's a book to absorb and sob through—while being informed and ignited by Tamimi's hard-won exuberant hope that state violence can be defeated by a strong and joyous refusal, accompanied by an unswerving belief that Palestine one day will be free."   —Eileen Myles, author of *Chelsea Girls*

"A powerful, moving combination of a memoir of personal resistance with a panoramic overview of the history of Palestine that leaves the reader with a detailed understanding of the daily realities of life under Israeli military occupation."

—Omar Robert Hamilton, author of *The City Always Wins*

THEY CALLED ME A
LIONESS

A Palestinian Girl's Fight for Freedom

AHED TAMIMI AND DENA TAKRURI

ONE WORLD
NEW YORK

Library of Congress Cataloging-in-Publication Data
Names: Tamimi, Ahed, author. | Takruri, Dena, author.
Title: They called me a lioness: a Palestinian girl's fight for freedom /
Ahed Tamimi and Dena Takruri.
Description: First edition. | New York: One World, [2022] | Includes bibliographical
references. Identifiers: LCCN 2022001373 (print) | LCCN 2022001374 (ebook) |
ISBN 9780593134597 (trade paperback) | ISBN 9780593134603 (ebook) Subjects:
LCSH: Tamimi, Ahed, 2001— | Palestinian Arabs—West Bank—Biography. | Political
activists—West Bank—Biography. | Government, Resistance to—West Bank. | Arab-
Israeli conflict—1993—Classification: LCC DS110.W47 T35 2022 (print) |
LCC DS110.W47 (ebook) | DDC 956.94/2092 [B]—dc23/eng/20220429
LC record available at https://lccn.loc.gov/2022001373
LC ebook record available at https://lccn.loc.gov/2022001374

TO MY GRANDMOTHER FARHA,
WITHOUT WHOM THIS STORY WOULD NOT EXIST,
AND TO THOSE WHO ARE YET TO BE BORN

CONTENTS

The Spotlight

The Slap

Prison

Homecoming

Postscript

Acknowledgments

Notes

INTRODUCTION

I SIT SHIVERING IN the tiny, freezing cell of an Israeli interrogation center, my wrists and ankles sore from the tightly clasped shackles digging into them. I inhale deeply, trying to suppress the flow of tears streaming down my cheeks now that I finally have a moment to myself, away from the taunts and jeers of the soldiers who've been harassing me for hours. Here, I allow myself to momentarily let down my guard. I'm all alone in this cell, but I feel no privacy. I spot cameras above me, on two opposite corners of the ceiling, pointed right at me. One seems to capture the cell's bathroom, which has a partially exposed ceiling. I've been dying to empty my bladder for hours, but with the risk of being filmed, I have refused to go.

For a second, I ask myself how I ended up here. How did it come to this? But I know better than to agonize over this question. This moment was inevitable, something I expected my whole life. Getting arrested by the Israeli army was always a matter of when, not if.

Days earlier, I slapped a fully armed Israeli soldier in the face in front of my house, a slap that reverberated around the world. It wasn't the first time I hit one of them; nor was it the first time it was captured on film, but it was certainly the most noticed. In a state that controls every aspect of my life, I have become the object of widespread enmity. Some even want me dead for daring to insult the central symbol of their occupation. But what I did was a natural reaction to seeing belligerent foreign occupiers on my family's land, an immoral army that had just nearly killed my cousin and was now shooting at children from the entrance of my home. And now I must pay for what I did.

Still, I ask myself, *Why now?* I'm only sixteen years old and in my senior year of high school. I should be taking my English final exam today, and I worry how much I'll fall behind by missing it. How long will I be forced to be away from school? I've worked so hard to get to this point, and my entire future rides on the test scores I pull off at the end of the year. I'm supposed to be studying right now, not sitting here under arrest. I'm supposed to graduate in a few months, not be locked up in prison. This thought makes me cry even more.

I close my eyes to try to plug the tears now pouring, but also because I can no longer bear the sight of the feces-stained walls surrounding me in this repulsive cell. Instead, my mind flashes back to the inflection points that brought me to this moment. The memories I'll never be able to shake, no matter how hard I try, now revisit me in an ambush. There I am, a five-year-old, sobbing in the middle of the night because Israeli soldiers have once again barged into our house to arrest my father. I see my mother falling on the concrete road after being shot by a soldier in a jeep; my younger brother pinned to the ground by another soldier, who is squeezing his little neck in a chokehold; my favorite uncle bleeding to death on the rocks behind our home.

This was the price my village paid for the unarmed resistance movement we dared to wage against our occupiers, the violent punishment we incurred for holding weekly protests to defend our rights and our land. I see the water cannons, the tear gas, the rubber-coated steel bullets, and the live rounds I grew up constantly having to dodge, sometimes more successfully than others. I replay all the visits to the hospital and all the funeral processions we marched in when the army killed one of our own. I hear the wailing sobs of our mothers and aunts in anguish and the defiant chants of our grieving loved ones demanding justice. I think about all the stories I've heard from my relatives, young and old, who were held captive in Israeli prisons. There are far too many of them for me even to attempt to count. Being arrested by Israel's army has always been a fact of life for us, practically a rite of passage that's impossible to avoid.

And now my turn has come.

THEY CALLED ME A
LIONESS

CHILDHOOD

I GREW UP IN a tiny village in the West Bank called Nabi Saleh. It's a twenty-five-minute drive northwest of Ramallah, the vibrant, booming city that's a cultural and commercial hub for Palestinians. Nabi Saleh, by contrast, is small and simple. We have a school, a mosque, a little market, and a gas station. Most important, we have each other. The six hundred residents of my village are all related by blood or marriage, part of the extended Tamimi family. My classmates and friends were also my cousins. It's a tight-knit community where everyone looks out for one another. And it's been that way for hundreds of years.

At first glance, Nabi Saleh appears to be a peaceful place. It's a quiet, idyllic village, home to endless hills dotted with olive trees between which wild horses and donkeys often roam. Unobstructed sunsets cast magical hues of red, purple, and gold in the sky. Children play outside freely, running from house to house, usually finding a welcoming adult to fill their bellies with a home-cooked meal.

But first impressions don't tell the whole story. To get that, you'd have to look across the main road of our village, to the hill on the other side of the valley. There sits the Jewish Israeli settlement of Halamish, a gated community with neatly arranged red-tile-roofed homes, manicured lawns, playgrounds, and a swimming pool. But Halamish wasn't always there. It was illegally established on our village's land in 1977. It's one of hundreds of Israeli settlements built on Palestinian land in violation of international law. These settlements are essentially Jewish Israeli colonies, and they continue to multiply at the expense of the indigenous Palestinian population. Over the years, we've watched the creeping expansion of Halamish, its settlers confiscating more of our land and resources with the full approval of the state of Israel. Not just approval, but facilitation, too. Israel installed a military base right next to the settlement, to protect its residents and to make our lives in the village a living hell.

But Nabi Saleh is just a microcosm of Palestine. For the past century, the Palestinian people have been fighting Zionist efforts to take more and more of our land. Zionism is a nationalist movement that began among some European Jews in the late nineteenth century. Its founders believed that the answer to mounting anti-Semitism in Europe was for Jews to settle in Palestine, which was still a territory of the Ottoman Empire at the time, populated by Arabs who were majority Muslim, with Christian and Jewish minorities, too. Only a handful of Jews took up the call then, but during World War I, the Zionist movement secured significant help from the British Empire. In 1917, the British issued the Balfour Declaration, which pledged to establish "a national home for the Jewish people" in Palestine. By the time World War I was over, the British had taken control of Palestine from the Ottomans. Under their colonial rule in the years that followed, a period known as the British Mandate, they made good on their 1917 promise by facilitating the immigration of thousands more European Jews to Palestine. In doing so, the British gave away land that wasn't theirs, with no regard for the indigenous-majority population living there: the Palestinians.

They'd eventually come to pay a price for the mess they

created. From 1936 to 1939, Palestinians waged a massive nationwide uprising against the British and their pro-Zionist policies. It was called the Arab Revolt, and while the British managed to violently suppress it, their troubles didn't end there. Beginning in 1944, several armed Zionist groups comprised of European Jewish settlers launched violent attacks against the British, who by then were trying to limit Jewish immigration to Palestine. The Zionists wanted the British gone and made it increasingly dangerous and costly for them to stay. By 1947, the British decided they had had enough and handed over the problem of Palestine to the United Nations.

Meanwhile, the Holocaust, during which up to six million Jews were savagely murdered by Nazi forces in World War II, devastated European Jewry but also changed Palestine forever. The Holocaust resulted in hundreds of thousands of survivors, traumatized and imperiled, fleeing Europe—tens of thousands of them to Palestine. Ashamed by their failure to protect Europe's Jews from Hitler's camps and ever reluctant, for domestic political reasons, to allow large-scale immigration of the survivors, much of the international community recognized the Zionist demand for a state of their own in Palestine. In 1947, the United Nations approved a plan to partition Palestine into a Jewish state and a Palestinian Arab state, with Jerusalem remaining under international control.

The partition plan gave 55 percent of the land of historic Palestine to the Jewish state and only 42 percent to the Palestinian Arab state. But Palestinians at the time made up 67 percent of the population and owned the vast majority of the land, while Jews made up 37 percent of the population and owned only 7 percent of the land. Palestinians rejected the plan outright—how could they accept what they could see only as the Zionists' colonial theft of their land? The Zionists, for their part, celebrated that they were finally getting the Jewish state they had dreamed of. Violence erupted between the two groups immediately after the plan was approved.

Israel declared its statehood on May 14, 1948, but not on empty, uninhabited land. The state was established on the land of my grandparents: historic Palestine. European Jews created a state on territory where the majority of residents were the indigenous Palestinian population. And in order to achieve this state in which they would be the majority, the Zionists had to violently evict the Palestinian majority. Even today, many Zionist thinkers freely admit that without the ethnic cleansing of 1948, they would not have had their Jewish state.

Palestinians painfully commemorate the events of 1948 as Al-Nakba, or "the Catastrophe." That's because, upon declaring its statehood, Israel unleashed its militias to force 750,000 Palestinians to flee their homes and destroyed more than 400 Palestinian villages. Some Palestinians managed to stay, retaining their land and houses inside what would become modern-day Israel. Meanwhile, the Arab countries that went to war with Israel in 1948 couldn't defeat the newly established Zionist state, which had secured millions of dollars in aid from donors in the United States. Jordan managed to capture East Jerusalem and the West Bank (where Nabi Saleh is located), and Egypt took control of Gaza. But in the end, Israel had seized way more of Palestine than the United Nations' partition plan ever gave it.

Israel's campaign to ethnically cleanse the land of its native Palestinian population didn't stop in 1948. It has never stopped. Today, generations of Palestinian refugees, more than seven million of them and their decendants, live across the globe. It's the longest unresolved refugee crisis in the world. Some Palestinians still hold on to the old iron keys of the houses from which they were expelled, in the hope of finally being granted the right of return—a right that is supported by international law but vehemently denied by the state of Israel.

Israel captured even more Palestinian land in the 1967 Arab-Israeli War. After swiftly defeating neighboring Arab armies in a matter of days, Israel seized Gaza, the West Bank, and East Jerusalem and began a military occupation of these Palestinian territories that, to this day, has no end in sight.

Growing up under a foreign military occupation means living under the constant threat of state-sanctioned violence. It also means living with the total absence of freedom, which is the case for more than five million Palestinians in the occupied territories today. We're not citizens of Israel; nor do we have a say or any political rights in the state that controls every aspect of our lives. We're stuck with the inability to plan for our futures, to travel freely, or even to move about our territories from city to city without having to cross military checkpoints. We need permission to build our homes, to travel, to work—all the basic rights and freedoms you might take for granted living in a civil society simply don't exist when you're living under military occupation. It's not an easy life, and yet, it's the only one I've ever known.

Israel justifies controlling us and denying us our rights by claiming it's about security. It has succeeded in convincing its own people and its supporters around the world that it needs to do so out of fear of existential elimination. But the facts tell a different story. Israel is a nuclear-armed country. It has had peace treaties in place with its neighboring Arab countries Egypt and Jordan since 1979 and 1994, respectively, and has normalized relations with a host of other Arab countries in recent years. Despite this, Israel continues its land confiscation, erasure of Palestinian life, and domination over us.

One of the most egregious ways Israel carries this out is by imposing an apartheid regime. The word *apartheid* originated in South Africa in 1948 to describe a system of white-minority rule. It refers to legalized segregation and discrimination whereby people living in the same territory are subject to different policies and protections by the state. Israeli apartheid is characterized by Jewish Israeli supremacy over the indigenous Palestinian population. Jewish Israelis, including the ones living in illegal settlements on occupied Palestinian territory, all enjoy full democratic rights and the privileges of citizenship. But as Palestinians in the occupied territories, we get none of that. While they're governed by Israeli civil law, we're ruled by Israeli military law. There's even a color-coded identification system to help facilitate this apartheid. We're forced to carry green identification cards at all times, which dictate the limited possibilities of our lives. The white license plates that Israel assigns to our cars stipulate which roads we're allowed to drive on. The smoothly paved bypass roads—built exclusively for settlers, of course—are off-limits to us. Only Israeli cars with yellow license plates can drive on those.

But we Palestinians have never accepted this life on our knees. Patriotism and activism course through the veins of the Palestinian people, particularly the ones from my village. We fought against the British when they occupied Palestine. We fought in the 1948 war. And when Israel's illegal settlement construction made its way to our village, the people of Nabi Saleh resisted that, too.

After the 1967 Arab-Israeli War, Israel saw the birth of a Jewish settler movement made up of religious-nationalist zealots who claimed that the West Bank was their God-given land dating back to ancient biblical times. My father, Bassem, was a young boy in 1977, when Jewish settlers came and started building on our village's land, but he, too, joined the effort to protect Nabi Saleh from theft and colonization. He was tear-gassed for the very first time before he even turned ten. But that didn't deter him from devoting his life to activism in the hope of freeing Palestine—something he has paid a heavy price for. Between 1988 and 2013, Israel arrested him nine times, and most of the sentences he served were under "administrative detention." Israel uses this designation to imprison Palestinians for up to six months without having to charge them or give them a trial. After six months, the state can renew the detention through a military administrative order. Some Palestinians end up serving years under administrative detention without ever knowing why they're being held. I have just as many memories of my dad being absent in my childhood as I do of him being around. You can never really get used to growing up without a father, but we had no option but to get accustomed to the reality that Baba was in prison and would be missing another one of our birthdays, or the Eid holidays.

One of my earliest childhood memories is visiting my father in an Israeli prison in the Naqab (Negev) Desert. I was three years old at the time. Back then, the Israeli authorities allowed family members to bring home-cooked food for their imprisoned loved ones. My mom would wake up in the middle of the night to cook stuffed grape leaves or bake small savory pies either stuffed with spinach or topped with ground beef and spices. Then she'd wake me and my older brother, Waed, before dawn and get us dressed in time to catch the long bus ride to the prison. We'd be strip-searched upon arrival and made to sit in a waiting area outside. When it was finally visitation time, we'd sit across a table from my dad, separated from him by a metal fence with small holes. I remember poking my little fingers through the holes and feeling delighted at being small enough to be able to touch him.

I WAS THE SECOND born out of four children, and the only girl. My brother Waed is three years older than me. Growing up, I considered him my hero and confidant. I have fond memories of walking to school together, before my two younger brothers were old enough to join us. I daydreamed constantly as a young girl, especially on those early morning walks to school, when I still wasn't fully awake. My mind meandered, and my legs dawdled, as if I had all the free time in the world and nowhere to be. Waed would drag me along by my backpack, yelling at me to wake up and walk faster. But on our way home from school, he'd toss over his own backpack for me to carry and then ditch me to run off and play with his friends.

In the times we did play together, he treated me no differently from a boy, which no doubt helped toughen me up. He often exercised his clout as the oldest sibling and ordered me and my younger brothers to carry out his chores around the house. But I didn't mind too much. Waed is persuasive and oozes charisma. Anyone who meets him instantly falls under his charming spell. He's lighthearted and jokes constantly—an overall delight to be around. I, however, have always been reserved in a way that's often misread as shy or standoffish. I don't have a magnetic personality and am not very social. Though I have a few close friends, I've always been most comfortable keeping to myself.

Almost three years after I was born came my younger brother Abu Yazan, whose name translates to "father of Yazan." If that sounds like an odd name for a young boy, it's because it is. His real name is Mohammad, but because there are so many other Mohammads in the village, we almost ex-clusively call him Abu Yazan. The story of how that nickname came about is a rather funny one. When he was a toddler, my little brother waddled around in a way nearly identical to an old man in a neighboring village named Abu Yazan. So, natu-rally, we started calling him that, and the name stuck. He never seemed to mind it, even though Abu Yazan is the most short-tempered one of us all. He's moody and stubborn, and you certainly don't want to get on his bad side. But I under-stand him better than most people. Neither of us takes our-selves too seriously, which is one of the reasons we get along so well.

Salam was born a couple of years after Abu Yazan. He's the baby of the family and has always been adored by all. His round, cherubic face is matched with a personality just as sweet. He's the only one of the siblings who never gave my parents any trouble, partly because he's always been a sensi-tive child who hates to disappoint anyone. But when he was six years old, Salam famously threw a fit and cried nonstop to my parents, telling them he hated his name and wanted to change it. "Why did you give me this awful name?" he bawled, throwing his hands up in the air in exasperation. Salam, in Arabic, means "peace," and he was sick of constantly hearing all the adults around him curse peace as they discussed failed negotiation after failed negotiation between Israeli and Pales-tinian leaders. We cursed these so-called peace talks because they served only to legitimize Israel's theft of our land and oppression of our people. Every Palestinian knows that there can never be peace in the absence of justice—so this false concept of "peace" wasn't just elusive; it was farcical. For my poor little brother, his entire existence was regrettably at-tached to our collective frustration over this abused word. And so, he begged for a new name.

My mother, Nariman, has always been the glue that holds our family together. It wasn't easy to bear the brunt of raising four children alone because her husband was usually either in prison or sleeping away from home to evade his next inevitable arrest. But Mama made it look easy. You'd never know about all the hardship she has endured in her life because her sense of joy and hope has always remained fully intact. She has a spirit that's impossible to crush and a heart that thrives on giving to others. It's one of the reasons she's so loved and respected by everyone who knows her. Growing up, I'd beam with pride watching men and women of all ages coming over to our house to seek my mother's advice and to confide their secrets to her. Mama has always been the strongest person I know, and watching her has taught me a lot about how to be self-reliant and independent.

As a child, I loved nothing more than to play outside in the street or on the many hills in our village. On the weekends, I'd sometimes go out to play as early as 7 A.M. and stay out until midnight, along with all the boys and girls in Nabi Saleh. As with other Palestinian children, our favorite game was *Jaysh o 'Arab*, or "Army and Arabs," which is basically the Palestinian version of cowboys and Indians. We'd divide ourselves into two groups: one group was the Israeli army, and the other group was the Palestinians. Within the Palestinian group, we assigned ourselves the roles of medics, journalists, and, of course, protesters. Those playing the role of Israeli army soldiers carried long pieces of wood shaped like rifles or, if they were lucky enough to own them, toy guns.

As soon as the game officially began, the two sides would clash, mimicking the scenes we'd seen on the news and, eventually, on Fridays during our village's resistance marches. The Palestinians in the game threw small rocks at the army, who responded by "shooting" them with their toy guns. Sometimes the kids playing the soldiers threw rocks back at their rivals, to ensure they fell. Usually, though, they just chased the "Palestinian" until they got them to fall to the ground. The "Palestinian" would of course fight back with all their might, but the "soldier" would beat them either until they were arrested—old shoelaces made excellent makeshift handcuffs—or until they gave up and cried out, "I've been shot!"

I usually played a medic along with the other girls. When I'd hear a kid cry out that they'd been shot, I'd run over to my wounded compatriot to treat their injuries and, eventually, take them away in a make-believe ambulance. But when I wasn't tending to the wounded, I also partook in the resistance by throwing stones myself. Meanwhile, the "soldiers" proceeded to chase down and arrest whomever they could. The children who were playing journalists pretended to document it all, occasionally grabbing one of the Palestinian protesters for an interview. It was great fun.

The rules of the game stipulated that anyone who was arrested was disqualified and that anyone who was killed and became a martyr got to come back to life and play another role. Sometimes, though, we'd bend the rules and pretend that one of the kids who was arrested had served a year-long prison sentence and was getting released. We'd take a break from the fighting to give him a hero's welcome, complete with celebratory singing and chanting.

We played *Jaysh o 'Arab* any chance we could, sometimes starting in the morning and wrapping up past our bedtimes, long after the sun had set and our parents had tired of calling us to come home. More often than not, we were so dedicated to our roles and committed to our battle that we truly roughed each other up. We played with such passion and conviction that we felt we were actually freeing Palestine. In hindsight, I recognize that this wasn't the healthiest game to play. The trauma we regularly endured under occupation was so inescapable that it even manifested in our time meant for fun. Perhaps it was our way of coping.

A less violent game we played regularly was *bayt byoot*, the Palestinian equivalent of playing house. If *Jaysh o 'Arab* reflected our trauma and goals to liberate Palestine, playing house expressed our dreams of a normal life. We played on the hilltop behind my house, pairing off as husbands and wives, with each couple claiming an area of the hill as their home. We collected and arranged stones to section off each house, always leaving a gap for an entryway. We'd steal empty yogurt and labneh containers from our mothers' kitchens and fill them up with soil, pretending to cook. We'd look out at the Halamish settlement across the road, with its neatly arranged homes covered with red-tile roofs, and call it "another country." Sometimes one of us would pretend to travel there and then return to tell splendid tales from the faraway land.

When I was around six years old, our game was suddenly interrupted by an Israeli army incursion into our village. This was before the weekly marches that Nabi Saleh became famous for, which means we were all still unaccustomed to regularly seeing soldiers. Until then, we'd see them only from afar, and if they did enter the village, it was for a specific purpose, like to arrest someone, which often occurred late at night.

There were about ten of us playing, including my cousin and best friend, Marah, her siblings, and me and Waed, when we saw three army jeeps race up the road toward us. In a matter of seconds, soldiers began pouring out of the jeeps and running in our direction. Terrified, we bolted down the street and into Marah's house to hide. Without thinking, we sprinted straight to her and her older sister Bisan's bedroom and piled into the closet. Waed and Anan, Bisan and Marah's brother, managed to climb onto the top shelf of the closet and squeeze themselves in there. The rest of us somehow packed ourselves in like sardines between all the hanging clothes. We stood trembling in fear, none of us daring to make a sound. From our hiding place, we could hear that soldiers had entered the house and were aggressively speaking Hebrew, which none of us understood. As their voices got closer, we knew it was only a matter of seconds before they entered the bedroom and possibly discovered us.

Before we knew it, one of the soldiers opened the door to the closet, and we all came tumbling out, landing on top of the soldiers' combat boots. Bisan, who was the oldest among us, mustered the courage to get off the floor and stand up. She looked up at the soldier with pleading puppy eyes.

"Ammo," she said, thinking that calling him "uncle" in a show of respect might somehow save us. "You're not going to kill us, are you?"

For his part, the soldier looked wildly amused at the sight of us all now lying on the floor. He didn't kill us. But at that point, it was the scariest day of our lives.

ULTIMATELY, MY FAVORITE GAME was (and still is) soccer. It was more than just a hobby. My big dream in life was to grow up and play professionally for Barcelona. I was determined to get really good. I practiced every single day, including during my recess and lunch breaks at school. I memorized every fact about the sport. There wasn't a player I didn't know, and there wasn't a match I missed, even if it meant staying up all night. For a while, Messi was my idol. But once Neymar joined Barcelona, when I was twelve years old, all bets were off. I admired everything about him—his skill on the field, his striking looks, and his charming smile—and all these traits earned him the status of first official crush. Crush is probably an understatement; I was completely obsessed. My computer was full of pictures of Neymar. I also hung his picture above my bed, next to Messi's. In time, I converted my younger cousin Janna into a die-hard Neymar fan as well. On one of Neymar's birthdays, we baked a cake in his honor and messily spelled out his name with pink frosting. I wanted to meet him *and* become as good a player as him. But with time, the sobering reality of what it meant to be a Palestinian child growing up under occupation forced me to give up both those dreams.

MUCH OF MY EARLY childhood was shaped by the influence of my paternal grandmother, Farha, with whom I shared my bedroom growing up. Before my days in prison, she was the first and only roommate I ever had. Her bed was much softer and warmer than mine, and I often pretended I had had a nightmare, just to be able to snuggle next to her and doze off into a cozier slumber. I loved Tata Farha dearly. She was kind and caring, and she always put everyone else's needs before her own. Anytime the other kids and I played outside, she'd chase us around with a big bottle of water and disposable plastic cups, insisting we take breaks to stay hydrated.

She was also the best storyteller I'd ever met. Living with her meant my brothers and I got treated to nightly bedtime stories. But they weren't the kind involving fairy tales or magical far-off lands or anything remotely soothing. Tata Farha's bedtime tales were all real-life stories that taught us the history of our family, of the village, and of Palestine. Many reflected the hell and heartbreak she and our people had lived through. All of her stories were educational. They not only shaped my imagination, but also revealed to me the generational trauma that's embedded in our DNA.

Tata Farha's name translates to "joy," which I always found ironic because life had robbed her of so much of it. She had only two children: my father, Bassem, and his older sister, Bassema, who was killed tragically in one of Israel's military courtrooms. This happened in 1993, before I or any of my brothers was born, but my grandma told us the story so many times, I feel like I was there. My Amto Bassema had gone to the court to attend the trial of one of her sons, who was imprisoned by Israel. There, a female military officer pushed her so hard she fell down a flight of stairs and hit her head. She died from a brain hemorrhage days later. Amto Bassema was the mother of five children, three sons and two daughters who would have to grow up without her. At the time, my father was also in prison. Israeli intelligence officials tortured him so badly during his interrogation that he fell into a coma for over a week.

Imagine Tata Farha's agony at that point: Her only daughter was suddenly killed, and now her only son was on the brink of death as well—both at the hands of the state of Israel. My father's survival can only be described as a miracle. Even the doctors didn't anticipate he'd live. He awoke from his coma only to learn that his sister was dead, and he was taken straight to her funeral. It was a tragedy from which neither he nor my grandmother ever recovered, although it did not defeat them. Despite her trauma, my grandmother tried her best to infuse levity into the story whenever she told it. She said that when my father came home with thirty-six stitches in his head, it was so swollen he appeared to have two heads. "One head here and one head there," she'd say, gesturing as though holding two balloons up with her hands. My imagination often kicked into overdrive trying to picture my two-headed Baba. Still, any attempt at humor could never mask the pain my grandmother carried with her for the remainder of her life, up until she died in 2011. Sometimes, I'd hear her weeping in her slumber and calling out "Bassema!" to her long-deceased daughter.

There were happier stories, too. My favorite one centered on our village's natural freshwater spring, called Ayn Al Qaws, or "the Bow Spring." It's located on the main road, at the bottom of the hill, in the small valley that separates our village from Halamish. Tata Farha described how every day when she was growing up, the villagers would wake up at 5 A.M. and carry their jugs down to the spring. Once they filled them up with springwater, they'd trek back up the hill to give their goats and sheep some water and feed them, along with the chickens. Then they'd make the journey back down to collect more water before returning up the hill. They didn't have sinks or coolers to stock up on water, so the spring and their old clay jugs were essentially lifelines for them.

Village life back then, as my grandmother described it, was simple yet vibrant, and it continued to be that way even as I grew up—albeit with some obvious advancements in infrastructure and technology. As a young girl, I relished playing by the spring. On hot days, my cousins and I would splash one another with its cool water and giddily chase one another around the olive, fig, and citrus trees in the surrounding farmland. That land, including where the spring is located, is owned by one of the elders of the village, Bashir Tamimi. It was passed down to him by his father, who inherited it from his grandfather. But generations of family ownership didn't matter to the Israeli settlers, who were determined to seize as much of the land as possible without letting anything or anyone stand in their way.

By 2008, they had built an additional fence around the settlement that took in even more of our land. Palestinian farmers were cut off from their crops and grazing pastures,

jeopardizing their livelihoods. Although the Israeli government protects the settlers and treats the land they steal as if it
were part of Israel, this time an Israeli court actually ordered
the fence to be taken down. It was, but the courts did nothing more to stop the settlers of Halamish. Undeterred, they
took our precious Ayn Al Qaws spring and built a pool to collect the springwater. They added a shading structure, benches,
and a swing set. They put up signs around the area that read
MEIR SPRING, renaming our centuries-old water source after
one of their settlement's founders. And they could do this
all because they were protected at every step by the Israeli
military—after all, the Israeli military, the settlers, the courts,
and the government are all part of the same system.

Attempting to go down to the spring became an increasingly dangerous venture. It meant risking harassment, intimidation, and even physical violence both from the settlers and
from the Israeli soldiers stationed there to protect them.
Sometimes, the settlers brought their dogs and threatened to
use them to attack us. Other times, they attacked us themselves with the weapons they constantly carried. Suddenly,
trying to visit our own property meant having a gun drawn on
us. The situation became extremely hostile and provocative,
as some of the settlers occasionally bathed naked in the pool
by the spring—a taboo in our society. Our parents ultimately
stopped letting us go down there. Everyone in the village was
disappointed at the loss of our spring, but more important,
we were fed up.

This chain of events was the impetus for the start of the
unarmed grassroots resistance movement for which our village would eventually become famous. My father, along with
my Ammo Naji (Marah's father) and a few others in the
community who had a history of activism, formed a popular
resistance committee and strategized about how to most ef-

fectively protest not just the settlers' confiscation of our land and resources, but the entire occupation and the countless injustices it regularly inflicted on us. They decided it should happen through sustained organized marches. The plan was for the people of Nabi Saleh—men, women, and children alike—to attempt to march down to the spring to affirm our right to the land our families had owned for generations and on which we relied for our survival. They picked a Friday in December 2009 to hold the first march. Friday is the start of the weekend in Palestine and the day on which communal afternoon prayers are held across the mosques. Once the Friday afternoon prayer ended in Nabi Saleh, everyone gathered outside the mosque in the village square and began marching down toward the spring.

I was a couple of months shy of my ninth birthday at the time, and the violence that had been threatened during earlier attempts to visit the spring had been enough to scare me into staying at home. And I was glad I did. That day, armed settlers and soldiers confronted the villagers before they could even make it to the spring. The settlers threw stones, and the army fired tear gas and rubber-coated steel bullets, injuring twenty-five people. Back at home, I panicked when I heard the sound of gun blasts, worried about what might be happening to my parents, Waed, and Abu Yazan. I had stayed home with Salam, who was only three and didn't quite understand what was going on. I glued myself to Tata Farha, who tried, with little success, to calm me down. When my family members returned home close to sunset, I was horrified to see that my mom had been shot by a rubber-coated steel bullet. I begged them all never to go out again and to give up the idea of the marches, but to no avail. The very next Friday, and each Friday after that, the people of Nabi Saleh, joined by university students, solidarity activists, and journalists, attempted to make it down to the spring. They wanted to send a message to the occupier that we didn't accept their presence in any way. They wanted to send an even bigger message to the world: that the Palestinian people wouldn't accept life under Israeli occupation. And finally, they wanted to send a message to the Palestinian people that the natural reaction to life under occupation was resistance and that it was their responsibility and their duty to stand up to our oppressors. The Israeli army's crackdown grew increasingly more violent in response. But a grassroots movement was born. We called it "the popular struggle," because it was led by the people, from the ground up.

My father and the people in the village didn't come up with the plan for this resistance movement overnight. Instead, it was the outcome of years of activism and strategizing, trial and error. They had read Martin Luther King Jr. and Gandhi. They had critically examined Palestine's history and determined that there were two distinct moments when the people were able to mobilize everyone to work toward a common goal and unite in a grassroots national movement. The first was in 1936, during the Arab general strike under the British Mandate, which had been ruling Palestine for well over a decade by then. Palestinians launched a nationwide strike to protest many British policies—most notably, the policy of allowing unrestricted Jewish immigration from Europe into Palestine. Britain, after all, had famously promised to establish a Jewish home in Palestine. Palestinians feared they would be displaced by this growing immigrant community, which made no secret of its aim to claim Palestine as a Jewish state. The strike lasted three years, but it failed in the face of the British Empire's overwhelming military and political power. British forces ultimately killed hundreds of Palestinians during the protests.

The second incidence of proper mobilization took place during the first uprising against Israel, or the First Intifada, which broke out in 1987 after an Israeli military truck killed four Palestinian laborers in a refugee camp in Gaza. That was the spark that led to Palestinians everywhere exploding in protest against decades of Israel's brutal occupation and ongoing colonization of Palestinian land. The uprising was spontaneous, featuring boycotts, organized strikes, a refusal to pay taxes to the Israelis, marches, and stone throwing. Israeli forces responded by beating and killing protesters, closing schools and universities for a year, and imposing curfews that lasted weeks. Undeterred, Palestinian communities banded together to protect themselves from the soldiers, feed one another during the curfews, and educate their children in underground schools when the regular schools were shut down. The Israelis had all the military power but were still unable to quell the rebellion.

The First Intifada officially ended with the signing of the Oslo Accords in 1993, a peace agreement between the Israeli and Palestinian leadership (the Palestine Liberation Organization, or PLO) that was brokered by the United States. Oslo, as the agreement is called for short, saw Israel officially recognize the PLO as the representative of the Palestinian people in exchange for the PLO recognizing Israel's right to exist. It was intended to lay the groundwork for a two-state solution. Instead, what resulted was Palestinians giving up more of their land and their rights and Israel conceding nothing.

Oslo also created the Palestinian Authority, or PA, which was meant to serve as an interim governing body until a final status agreement could be reached—something that never happened. And so, the PA has instead functioned as a subcontractor for Israel, carrying out security coordination and taking on the responsibilities of administering the occupation, a heavy and expensive burden that international law says Israel should shoulder. My father has always called Oslo "a conscientious Nakba," even though he, like many Palestinians, is employed by the PA.

A Second Intifada erupted in September 2000, a few months before I was born. But unlike the first uprising, this one ultimately took an armed approach. The Second Intifada was sparked when Ariel Sharon, who would soon become Israel's prime minister, stormed the Al-Aqsa Mosque compound in occupied East Jerusalem with a thousand heavily armed police officers. Al-Aqsa is the third-holiest site in Islam, and Sharon's deliberately provocative move was meant to cement Israeli claims over all of Jerusalem at a moment when negotiations had been proposed to make part of Jerusalem the Palestinian capital.

Prior to this major provocation, Palestinians, Muslim and Christian alike, had already been inching closer to a breaking point after years of successive Israeli governments refusing to abide by the Oslo Accords and end the occupation. Oslo had gotten them no closer to achieving a Palestinian state. Economic prosperity hadn't materialized. On top of that, the number of Israeli settlers had doubled between 1993 and 2000. The occupation was more entrenched than ever.

The demonstrations during the first days of the uprising were largely unarmed. But the Israeli military was determined to quash them with excessive force: rubber bullets, live ammunition, and eventually full military incursions into densely populated Palestinian areas, with tanks and helicopters. What started out as peaceful protests morphed into an armed rebellion, characterized by suicide bombings targeting Israeli civilians and soldiers. Many Palestinians, including my parents, criticized this form of resistance.

But there was also an unarmed component to the resistance during the Second Intifada, one that ended up influencing how we mobilized in Nabi Saleh years later. In 2002, Israel began constructing a massive separation wall under the pretext of security. Palestinians call it the apartheid wall because it's meant to separate Palestinians in the occupied West Bank from Israel "proper," but also from occupied East Jerusalem and from the Israeli settlements built inside the West Bank. The wall is several hundred miles long and, in some areas, made of imposing concrete slabs that stand over fifteen feet tall. If that's not egregious enough, the majority of the wall was not built along Israel's internationally recognized pre-1967 boundary, but rather on Palestinian land inside the occupied West Bank. This means its path was deliberately planned to swallow up more of our land and cut right through our villages.

This was the case for several small villages like Budrus, which risked being cut off from the rest of the West Bank by the wall's planned route. The residents there decided to organize against the construction of the wall and used their bodies to stop Israel's bulldozers from uprooting their precious olive trees to clear the way. They were joined by Israeli and other international solidarity activists in weekly nonviolent demonstrations to block the wall from being built. The villagers adopted a strategy of nonviolence, but the Israeli army's response was anything but. Soldiers regularly shot at the demonstrators with rubber bullets, tear gas, and even live ammunition. Many protesters were injured, beaten, and arrested. Eventually, though, the people of Budrus succeeded in forcing the Israeli government to reroute the wall away from their village. They managed to save their olive trees and almost all the land Israel had intended to annex. It was a significant victory. Other villages followed suit and also won.

My father and relatives of ours in Nabi Saleh had joined

the protests in solidarity and were inspired by what they witnessed. The grassroots efforts had proven yet again the success of civil as opposed to armed resistance. They also presented the right image of the Palestinian people and their struggle. This image contradicted the widespread stereotypical and inaccurate portrayals of our people, particularly in the West, as violent terrorists.

And so, they sought to build upon that model of civil resistance and apply it to Nabi Saleh. But they wanted to make a few modifications, to improve upon what they saw. The first was to expand the role of women in a way that more accurately reflected women's traditional prominence in Palestinian society. In the villages' demonstrations against the wall, women weren't always as involved or as visible as they should have been—there was certainly nowhere near the robust levels of female participation seen during the First Intifada. Luckily, Nabi Saleh has always been exceptionally egalitarian gender-wise. Starting from when we're children, boys and girls play together equally, with no discrimination between the sexes. We all learn the importance of cooperation at a young age. This certainly helped our cause, as women (including my mother and Amto Manal, my aunt) took on key organizing roles in the movement.

The other critique my parents and others had of the villages' protest movement against the wall was that the tactic of blocking the wall became more important than the greater strategy needed to be pursued by all Palestinians: dismantling the occupation. The problem has never been just the wall, or the uprooted olive trees, or the settlements, or even the confiscation of Ayn Al Qaws spring. These are all manifestations of the root problem, but not the root problem itself. The root problem is Israel's colonial settler project, which seeks to control us, steal our land, and ethnically cleanse us from it. The problem is the occupation itself. And so, exposing the injustices of the occupation for the world to see was one of the most important goals of our movement.

We wanted to pursue this approach and ground it in the principles of human equality, justice, and inclusivity. To do that, my dad and the other leaders of our resistance movement knew they would need to foster a type of awareness in everyone in the village and in those who wished to join our cause. Revolution, they believed, required first and foremost a level of consciousness, not just strategies for fighting or protesting. They raised people's consciousness through holding teach-ins and putting on cultural events. We planted olive trees on Israeli-confiscated land—such as the area around the spring—and we advocated boycotting Israeli products. We also discouraged Palestinians from working in Israeli settlements, where they often take jobs as laborers due to the lack of other employment opportunities. We were proud to boast that, ultimately, no one from Nabi Saleh worked in a settlement.

It was equally imperative for everyone to be on the same page in terms of the rules of our demonstrations. The main rule was that our grassroots resistance movement had to be unarmed. The aim was to struggle and resist without hurting or killing anyone. Detractors have pointed to our youth throwing stones as a contradiction of this principle, accusing us of being violent. Our response has always been that a stone is not a weapon. It has long been a symbol of defense in Palestinian consciousness and mythology. If a Palestinian walking around his land encounters a wild boar or a snake, he instinctually reaches for a stone to defend himself against the creature, but not to preemptively attack it.

The other point to consider is the armed and violent nature of the Israeli soldier who is intruding upon our land.

Given the bulletproof uniform he's wearing and the armored vehicle he's riding in, a stone is highly unlikely to cause him any serious bodily harm. A stone, for us, is a symbol. It represents our rejection of the enemy who has come to attack *us*. To practice nonviolence doesn't mean we'll lie down and surrender to our fate submissively. We still have an active role to play in defending our land. Stones help us act as if we're not victims but freedom fighters. This mindset helps motivate us in the fight to reclaim our rights, dignity, and land.

And so, with those principles and ground rules, Nabi Saleh's grassroots resistance movement took off. My father hoped that we could model a form of resistance that would spread to other West Bank villages and towns. And if there was to be a Third Intifada, Nabi Saleh would be its birthplace.

THE MARCHES BEGIN

THAT SAID, I HATED FRIDAYS. All week, I dreaded the day's approaching, and once it finally arrived, my anxiety would be in full force. Friday was the day everyone I loved went out to march, risking their safety, while I stayed home. As a terrified eight-year-old, I strategically sought refuge in the room in the house with the fewest windows and spent all day crouched in its farthest corner. I figured this was the safest place to protect myself from getting struck by anything the Israeli soldiers might fire through the window. I usually hid there until the early evening, when everyone returned home.

When they got home, my family members, with their adrenaline still rushing, would brief me on the battle that had raged right outside our house: who got shot, who was arrested, how the settlers had attacked them, and how the soldiers had cracked down. With each passing week, I began to better grasp the scope of the struggle and what was at stake. I understood the asymmetry of it all; despite the fact that our flags, chants, and stones were no match for their rubber-coated steel bullets, tear gas, and sound grenades, the Israeli forces had no moral qualms about unleashing brute violence upon us.

This realization filled me with even more fear, because I knew I could lose someone I loved at any moment. But I also knew that our cause was righteous. Even as a child, the moral stakes were obvious to me. Daring to defend what was ours was not a crime. If anything, it was a duty. After three months of hiding indoors, I finally mustered the courage to say, "Okay. I'm ready to join." And of course, I took my best friend, Marah, with me.

In the beginning, even as we joined the marches, Marah and I stood as far as possible from all the action, watching it unfold from a safe distance. We flinched each time we heard the booms and pops of the sound grenades and the rubber-coated steel bullets being fired. As soon as we saw the streaks of tear gas smoke line the sky, we ran as far as we could to avoid inhaling it. We didn't dare get close to the main street or the spring, for fear of being attacked by soldiers or settlers. Instead, we became merely apprehensive spectators, often having to jump into action to help one of our parents or siblings or cousins when they came hobbling up the hill bruised or bleeding because they had just been shot. It didn't take long for violence to become a completely normalized aspect of our lives.

Some of the hardest moments for me during those early days of our demonstrations were when my mother got arrested—something that would happen six times during the course of our resistance movement. On one of the first occasions, I was standing with Marah outside her house when I heard someone yell, "Nariman's been arrested!" My heart dropped to my stomach, and I began to scream. Along with what felt like every resident of Nabi Saleh, I ran down to the main street at the entrance to the village.

"Mama!" I cried in a frantic, high-pitched shriek as I searched for her, afraid I'd lose her forever. "*Maaaaa-maaaaaa!*"

I couldn't see her, as she was being detained in an army jeep. Everyone was shouting at the soldiers to release her, their anger bubbling. Each time I tried to run closer to the jeeps, a soldier would block me or push me back. I was hysterical. Nothing could be more devastating to a young girl than seeing her mother stripped from her, let alone by the foreign army terrorizing her village.

I don't know how long I spent wailing in the street. All I remember is that, at some point, it occurred to me that Salam, who was only three, was home alone with Tata Farha. From the day he was born, I had prided myself on being a second mother to him, always helping to feed him, dress him, and play with him when our own mother was too busy. He was just as attached to me as he was to our mom. So, when I finally returned home to find him crying, I instantly switched from being a child in distress who just wanted her mom to a substitute adult figure who had to soothe her toddler brother.

After six hours of being detained by the Israeli army, my mother finally returned home at sunset, bruised and battered. She explained that the soldiers had arrested her when she was protesting down by the spring simply because, as a Palestinian (as opposed to an Israeli settler), she was not supposed to be there. They pinned her to the ground and handcuffed her. And then, as she lay there helpless, five of the soldiers, all men, kicked and punched her.

"That beating almost killed me!" she exclaimed while applying ice to what appeared to be every inch of her body. Surprisingly, she was somehow in good spirits. But I wasn't. Hearing about my mother being brutalized like that introduced a new layer of fear and trauma in me, a scab that would be repeatedly picked at and reopened.

The next time she was arrested was no easier. An Israeli soldier had to hold me back to restrain me from running to her and trying to free her while members of his unit handcuffed her and led her to a jeep. I punched the soldier and kicked him with all my might, but it made no difference.

"Mama!" I howled desperately, trying to propel my body forward to free myself from the soldier and run to my mother.

"Don't cry!" she called out to me. "Don't cry, and don't be scared!"

To set an example for her children, my mother's philosophy has always been to display strength and fearlessness. And in that moment, she was putting on a brave face so I wouldn't crumble.

Once the jeep drove off, whisking her away, the soldier let me go, and I sprinted after it as fast as I could, hopeful that I could somehow catch up to it and free my mom. Marah ran after me. But alas, I was quickly outpaced, left in the middle of the road to catch my breath and wipe the tears from my face.

This time, Mama and my Amto Manal were taken to prison, where we later learned they were repeatedly beaten and strip-searched. But at the time of my mother's arrest, I had no idea how long she'd be imprisoned, and the uncertainty left me and my brothers in a perpetual state of distress. Her absence in the house created a huge void that nothing and no one could fill. By then, we had learned to survive without our father's regular presence, but not having our mom around was a new kind of pain.

Tata Farha was also unsettled; Israeli forces had jailed her beloved daughter-in-law. She prayed for my mother's release every chance she got. One night, I woke up to her praying aloud in our shared bedroom. "Oh, my dear Bassema, may God protect you! My beloved Bassema, may God set you free!" she beseeched. Old trauma compounded by new shock had left my poor grandmother confused, and she mistakenly prayed on behalf of her long-deceased daughter, Bassema, instead of my imprisoned, yet still alive, mother, Nariman. That night, I got a glimpse into the depths of my grandmother's sorrow. It has never stopped haunting me.

A couple of days after her arrest, my mom appeared before a judge in an Israeli military court. My dad attended the hearing, shouting out words of support to her from the back of the courtroom. "Be strong!" he said. "You're strong, and we want you to remain that way! We love you, and we're all very proud of you!" Comforted by his encouragement, my mother smiled back at him and nodded reassuringly to let him know she'd be okay. I wasn't there, but my father reported back the details of the day, and I was relieved to hear that she was doing well. His words boosted not just her morale but ours as well. This was the first of many instances where I learned that courage can be contagious. It is both observed and transferred. I never saw my parents cower or crumble in the face of the Israeli military's intimidation and abuse, and this taught me that I, too, could withstand anything.

Ten days after their arrest, we got word that Amto Manal was being released. Israeli forces customarily drop off Palestinian prisoners at a checkpoint, where their relatives pick them up and bring them home. Everyone in Nabi Saleh gathered in front of the house Amto Manal shared with her husband, my Ammo Bilal, in anticipation of her imminent arrival. The village erupted in cheers as the car carrying her drove up and she descended from it. Everyone took turns hugging her and welcoming her home.

My eyes remained glued to the car. I was waiting for my mom to emerge from it at any moment. I plotted how, once she did, I'd be the first one to run up and embrace her. But several minutes passed with no sign of my mother. Eventually, someone told me she wouldn't be coming home today. I tried to fight back the tears because I didn't want to kill the joyous atmosphere that my Amto Manal deserved. But once I got home, I lost it, collapsing to my knees and sobbing uncontrollably. I couldn't rid my mind of the prospect that my mother would be in prison forever. I'd never see her again, except in brief visits like the ones we paid my dad when I was younger. Once again, I cursed our resistance movement.

The next night, the Israelis plucked my mother from her cold, dingy jail cell and threw her into a jeep. They dumped her on the side of a road, leaving her completely clueless as to where she was or how she'd be able to get home. She had to rely on the mercy of strangers, who let her borrow a phone to call my father. When she finally arrived home, I could see that she was visibly shaken. Who wouldn't be? But the experience by no means deterred her from protesting. After completing her month-long house arrest, she went right back to joining the demonstrations and even forced herself to get more comfortable speaking with reporters.

I was happy to have Mama back and somewhat relieved by the guarantee her house arrest provided: She wouldn't be going anywhere for at least a month. With her home, I was able to go back to being a kid again instead of acting as her proxy, taking on the responsibilities of ensuring that my younger brothers were fed and clothed and did their homework. Life felt stable once again—at least temporarily.

OVER TIME, THE SHOOTINGS and arrests of my loved ones became routine. The smell of tear gas grew familiar, and the loud bangs fired from the soldiers' weapons were no longer as startling. The popularity of our movement meant that more people from outside Nabi Saleh—including foreign activists, Palestinians from other towns, and even Israelis—would increasingly join us in solidarity. Every Friday afternoon, in an attempt to suppress us and stop our demonstrations from even happening, the Israeli army would declare our village and the area by the spring a closed military zone. This meant they effectively laid siege to the entire village, shutting down the road, sealing off all entrances, and forbidding anyone from outside to enter Nabi Saleh. To subvert this, dozens of determined activists would arrive early on Friday morning, before the army closed the village, and join us for breakfast to fuel up for the day. Then, we'd all wait for the march to begin.

Hospitality is an intrinsic part of Palestinian culture, but for my father, welcoming guests with open arms was also an enshrined principle of our movement. This was shaped by something he had witnessed years prior, in a protest against the apartheid wall in the village of Ni'lin that affected him greatly. On that particular day, once the demonstration ended, my dad had walked over to the home of one of his friends from the village to enjoy some afternoon coffee. From the veranda of that house, he could see all the foreign activists who had come to take part in the protest milling about the street, left on their own to try to find cabs to take them back to Ramallah. Many didn't even speak Arabic. No one had waited around with them to offer help. The scene ate away at him. "It made me feel that we aren't respectful," he'd recount many times after the incident, always shaking his head in deep remorse. "I felt I wasn't decent."

The activists, he reasoned, had traveled all that way, inhaled tear gas, and risked their safety to stand in solidarity with the Palestinians, some of whom (like my dad) had then thoughtlessly gone off and had coffee afterward. Baba felt he had betrayed our values and customs as Palestinian people, which saddened him deeply. So, when our popular resistance movement began in Nabi Saleh, he made it his mission to go above and beyond to welcome any and all foreign activists to

our home. Sometimes, they'd come as early as the night before and sleep on spare mats we'd furnish for them all over
the house. Typically, though, they'd arrive at around 8 A.M. on
Fridays, just in time to devour a huge breakfast my parents
prepared for everyone. At times, there were more than fifty
people over at once.

By the time everyone was properly fed and had gulped
down enough cups of coffee and tea to power them through
the day, the afternoon prayer was over, and it was time to
congregate outside the mosque and begin the demonstration.
This was always my favorite part. I loved waving the Palestinian flag, chanting revolutionary slogans, and clapping in unison with everyone. Often, the other children and I marched
at the very front of the procession, proudly carrying the signs
and banners. We wore shirts that read FREE PALESTINE and,
depending on the theme of that week's protest, sometimes
dressed up in costumes. One week, for example, we took up
a soccer theme in solidarity with the campaign to expel Israel
from FIFA, with some of us dressing as soccer players. For
added drama, I ran up to one of the soldiers and flashed a red
card in his face. Each week, we took a different path. Sometimes, we tried to march to the spring. Other times, we
headed to the main gate at the entrance of the village. Clashes
would invariably break out shortly after we began to descend
the hill or street, kicking off an hours-long battle in which
youth attempted to repel the Israeli soldiers with thrown
stones, even though they knew they were far outmatched by
the soldiers' military might.

The collective nature of the movement inspired everyone
and made us feel we were in the midst of a revolution. Every
home in Nabi Saleh was open to the activists, regardless of
whether they needed shelter from tear gas, a bathroom break,
or a labneh and pita bread sandwich. One Israeli activist told

my parents that despite his having joined countless demonstrations at several other villages over the years, this was the first time he didn't feel like an outsider; from day one, he had felt accepted. I know that hearing those words meant the world to my parents.

When the march and subsequent clashes ended hours later, nobody was ever again left stranded in the street to fend for themselves. They came back to our homes, joining us for dinner and even the occasional evening hookah with tea over endless conversations about politics, history, and resistance. Even though I typically busied myself playing with the other children, I was exposed to enough of these conversations to eventually understand politics in a way most kids my age didn't. As night drew near, our parents helped the activists find rides back home. A social bond had been forged among the villagers and our new foreign friends who sacrificed their time and their safety to join our cause.

Seeing so many people stand with us who didn't have a direct stake in our fight affirmed for me the righteousness of our cause. The presence of the Israeli activists taught me another valuable lesson: For the first time in my life, I saw that our struggle was not as black-and-white as I had understood it to be. Like most other Palestinians who had grown up under occupation, I had little experience with Israelis other than the armed uniformed soldiers who raided our villages and stopped us at checkpoints and the illegal settlers who stole our land and then attacked us for trying to defend it. I knew that, historically, Jews, Muslims, and Christians coexisted prior to Israel's establishment, living side-by-side as neighbors and friends. But today's apartheid system has all but ensured that we have no civil interaction with Jews. And so, it blew my mind to be meeting, for the first time ever, Jewish Israelis who had traveled to our village, in defiance of their own government's policies, to stand in solidarity with us. They condemned the occupation with their words and their actions, and they fervently advocated in support of Palestinian rights.

They weren't simply allies in our struggle. Many of them, like Jonathan, Sarit, and Yifat, grew so close to us that my parents considered them some of their best friends. Jonathan Pollak, for example, is a well-known Israeli activist who became one of the pillars of our movement and a rock for our family. He also bore such a striking resemblance to my mom that the long-running joke has always been that he's her long-lost brother. And just like a brother, he has always come through for her and the family. There has never been a time when someone was in trouble that Jonathan wasn't there by our side. Anytime someone was arrested, for example, he'd put his fluent Hebrew and his knowledge of the Israeli legal system to work to arrange a lawyer for them and explain what was happening to the rest of us in his fluent Arabic. He also helped get our story out to the media. And during the demonstrations, regardless of the level of danger, he was always out there alongside everyone, confronting the soldiers who belonged to the army in which he had refused to serve. Jonathan was arrested and injured dozens of times while defending our village.

Getting to know Jonathan and the other Israeli activists gave me tremendous hope, perhaps for the first time in my life. I began to think that if they could stand in solidarity with Palestinians and criticize their own state for the injustices inflicted upon us, perhaps, in time, other Israelis would as well. Through them, I learned that our problem was not with the Jewish people but, rather, with Zionism. It's not a religious problem, but a political one. Zionism is the ideology that says that historic Palestine must be a country for Jews only. Zion-

ism is what led to the dispossession of our land, which continues to be seized and occupied. But more dangerous than that
is how Zionism has occupied the minds and the humanity of
far too many Israelis. *That* occupation is truly more frightening and intractable.

I see that occupation in the thirteen-year-old armed settler who carries a rifle slung over his shoulder everywhere he
goes. I see it in the twenty-year-old Israeli soldier who aims
his weapon right at us and shoots, undeterred by the presence
of children or by basic morality. But our Israeli activist friends
showed me that there are good people on the other side, people with whom we can build together. They showed me that
there's hope.

BY THE FALL OF 2010, the weekly marches had significantly
swelled in size. What began as a group of fed-up villagers inspired to take nonviolent direct action had grown into a more
sophisticated international protest movement whose momentum seemed to be gaining strength week by week. By this
point, the villagers and activists had become more accustomed to evading the tear gas and rubber bullets. And so, the
Israeli army brought in a new method of crowd control: skunk
water. It's hard to describe the putrid stench of skunk water
in words—because it's unlike anything I've smelled before or
since. But I'll try anyway. Imagine the odor of a pair of socks
pulled from the feet of a rotting corpse and drenched in sewage for days. That's skunk water.

No one had any idea what it was when it made its debut
in the village. We were marching that day when I noticed
everyone staring in awe at the sight of an armored tanker
truck equipped with a revolving cannon. It was spewing powerful jets of water all around the village. One of the many

horrible consequences of the Oslo Accords is that it gave Israel full control of the water supply in the West Bank. At best, we get only about twelve hours of running water a week, compared to the twenty-four-hours-a-day supply of water (plus swimming pools) enjoyed by the settlers of Halamish, across the road. It's one of the reasons the loss of our spring was so devastating for us. And so, seeing the surplus of free-flowing water gush out of that vehicle was naturally enticing.

Incredulous, the husband of one of my aunts raced over to the truck and stood directly under the water to enjoy an impromptu shower. "Hot water! Hot water!" he exclaimed, flailing his arms to summon the other men to join him. But by the time he got a whiff of what he was bathing in, it was too late—he was fully drenched.

The sadistic nature of skunk water is that its stench lingers for days, not just on your body and hair, but also in the street—a stench that seemed to be activated further by the morning dew. We'd often walk to school in the mornings struggling not to retch as our stomachs did somersaults from the lingering smell of skunk water in the street. By the time we made it to class, we were all queasy, unable to focus on anything besides fighting the urge to vomit up our intestines.

Skunk water was invented by an Israeli company called Ordotec, which hails itself as a "green" company and calls its product "100% safe for people, animals and plants" in addition to being "the most effective, cost-efficient and safest riot control solution available." The Israeli military has praised skunk water's efficacy as a nonlethal riot-dispersal method, and the Israeli police have called it a "humane option." But there's nothing humane about how the military deliberately targets our homes with the skunk truck, shattering windows and punishing even those who seek refuge indoors; nor how it can injure anyone in its path. One time, my mother was participating in a march when the skunk truck accelerated in her direction and began spraying skunk water right at her. She lowered herself to the ground and sat on her knees with her back turned to the truck. The water sprayed her from behind with such great force, it propelled her forward onto the cement. When she came home, her knees and shins were cut up and bloody, and she reeked. Even after showering, the odor was so offensive that my dad joked that he was on the brink of divorcing her.

MOST OF THE TIME, though, it was hard to find humor in the hell we suffered at the hands of the Israeli military. And the hell only got worse as the protest marches increased in size and notoriety. The nighttime military raids were a particularly cruel and terrifying method of punishing us, and they took place hundreds of times. It would typically be past 1 A.M., with everyone fast asleep, when a unit of fully armed and sometimes masked soldiers banged on our doors and barged in without a warrant. They'd rummage through all our belongings as if they owned the place, turning the house upside down and breaking things in the process. Sometimes they even brought dogs with them.

It was scary enough to be children witnessing everything we did in the daylight hours. But to then have our slumber interrupted by an invading army pointing their weapons at us while we were still half asleep was beyond traumatizing. One night, I woke up to a couple of soldiers standing right above me. Abu Yazan had fallen asleep in my room, and the soldiers had come to arrest him for his participation in a march. On another summer night, I was fast asleep alone in my room when I heard a noise nearby. I turned on my bedside lamp only to see a rifle aimed a few inches away from my face as I lay in bed. A soldier had poked it through my bedroom window, which I had kept open to try to circulate some air in the sweltering summer heat. I stared at him blankly, too paralyzed even to scream. As soon as he pulled his rifle back, I ran to my parents' bedroom to tell them what I'd seen, but by the time I got there, the soldier was already banging on our front door.

Despite the fact that they occurred in the middle of the night, the raids were never peaceful or quiet. The invading soldiers often demanded to see our identification cards, an outrageous display of brazenness, considering we were in our own homes. They frequently filmed the raids as part of their continuous effort to collect data on us and map out all the households and relationships in the village. Such intelligence came in handy for the Israelis as they plotted whom to arrest or how to question those who had already been arrested and were undergoing interrogation.

But we filmed the night raids, too. It was important to document them to show the world the gross violations and overwhelming aggression we routinely faced. I recall one raid when the army invaded our house to arrest my dad—a punishment for his role in organizing the grassroots resistance movement. My mother was filming the raid in the kitchen when a few male soldiers started pushing her around and hitting her, ordering her to stop filming. Tata Farha tried to jump to her rescue, but a soldier aimed a rifle at her, forcing her to freeze in her tracks. So my mom turned to where I was standing, several feet away, and tossed the camera over to me.

"Here, take this and keep filming," she instructed.

There was no way she was going to let them confiscate the camera along with everything stored on its memory card. I managed to catch the camera and took advantage of my notably short height to weave myself through the crowd of soldiers, eventually making my way to the entrance of the house, where I had a better vantage point to film the whole scene. I tried my best to capture the soldiers hitting my mom and grandma and arresting my dad, but the sight of it all left me trembling in fear, and my hands couldn't manage to get a steady shot. The second I saw Waed standing on the other side of the room, I sprinted over to him to hand him the camera and told him to keep filming. Then I ran over to my mom to try to save her from the soldiers' abuse. While I was clutching on to her, a soldier slammed my shoulder with the butt of his rifle, nearly knocking me to the ground.

We chased after the soldiers as they abducted my father and took him to prison yet again. My brothers and I hurled rocks at their jeeps as they drove off with him. Later, Amnesty International would declare my father a "prisoner of conscience" because he was once again being held for "peacefully exercising his rights to freedom of expression and assembly." But such labels didn't mean much to us at the time. We wanted nothing more in the world than to have our dad at home with us.

On other occasions, when they weren't raiding our house to arrest a member of our family, they confiscated our belongings. One such raid took place when my father was in prison. The Israeli soldiers took a laptop from one bedroom and a computer tower from Abu Yazan and Salam's room as they lay in their beds, petrified, peeking their heads out from under the covers occasionally to see what was happening.

Tata Farha implored the soldiers to leave, reminding them that there were young children in the house. "Have mercy on us!" she begged. "The children are sleeping!"

The soldiers then made their way to my bedroom and went through all my papers: homework assignments, report cards, and artwork I had drawn.

"You thieves!" my mother shouted at them in Arabic. "Leave our stuff alone and get out of here!"

"Shut up," a soldier barked at her in Hebrew.

"I don't want to shut up! You're in my house. You shut up."

"Go away," another soldier said.

"*You* go away. This is my house! Go to your own house!"

At this point, I was now fully awake and had joined my mother as backup. Witnessing how strong and defiant she always was in the face of armed soldiers had always instilled courage in me. If she didn't cower before the Israeli military, neither would I.

"Why did you come here?" I demanded, trying my best to sound older than ten. "Leave!"

Instead, the soldiers stormed into my parents' bedroom and started opening the closets.

"Yeah. Go ahead. Take some lingerie," Mama mocked them. "Maybe you need it. Go fix yourself up and take a shower while you're at it."

They proceeded to open all the drawers in the kitchen and living room and asked us questions in Hebrew that none of us understood. By the time the raid was over, they had stolen our computers, various papers, some cassette tapes, and a gas mask. We were livid as we watched them march out with our belongings, knowing we'd never see them again. My mom tried to block them from leaving by standing in front of the door and saying she wouldn't move until they gave us back our possessions. But they just bulldozed right past her.

"You thieves!" I cried. "You stole our stuff!"

Our complaints were useless. In the end, they got away with it.

But losing our belongings was one thing. Losing a life was another, and one that we'd soon suffer.

———

THE MARCH ON FRIDAY, December 9, 2011, started out like any other. By then, our resistance movement was exactly two years old. Journalists from around the West Bank and even around the world regularly flocked to Nabi Saleh to document the increasingly popular story of the heroic little Palestinian village whose residents dared to stand up to the powerful military ruling over them and protecting the illegal settlement built on their land. I was almost eleven years old and had been reluctantly joining the demonstrations for some time, always striving to strike a balance between being close enough to feel like I was participating and being far enough away to avoid any danger. It was easier said than done.

What started out as an ordinary march that day, though, ended in a tragedy that none of us was prepared to handle. Mustafa Tamimi, my distant cousin, who was twenty-eight at the time, was shot in the face with a tear gas canister by a soldier who was no more than ten feet away from him. I was standing farther back on the same street when it happened. I had begun retreating to avoid inhaling tear gas when I heard people shouting that someone had gotten shot and to call an ambulance. From a distance, I could see Mustafa lying on his back in the middle of the street in his crisp white shirt and jeans, his face completely covered in blood. A friend of his rushed over to him to try to stop the flow by pressing a checkered black-and-white kuffiyeh scarf, a symbol of Palestinian identity and resistance, to his face. Photojournalists snapped pictures of the nightmare from all angles. Mustafa's sister screamed his name hysterically.

Within seconds, a taxi pulled up to where Mustafa lay bleeding, and a medic joined a few guys from the village to carry Mustafa's nearly lifeless body and place it inside the vehicle. That's when I summoned the courage to get closer to see what had happened. Nervously, I took a few steps forward and peered into the car. The gory details of Mustafa's bleeding face are forever seared in my memory. His right eyeball was completely removed from its socket, and the right side of his face looked like it was ripped open. The second I caught a glimpse of him, I backed away, horrified.

As Mustafa was taken to the hospital, the eyewitnesses to his murder—corroborated by photographs from the journalists who captured the moment—revealed what exactly had happened. Mustafa and his friend had been following a couple of armored jeeps, demanding that they leave the village. He was poised to hurl a rock at the jeep right in front of him when a soldier inside it opened its rear door; aimed his high-force, long-range tear gas canister gun directly at Mustafa; and shot him point-blank in the face. The soldier then closed the door, and the jeep drove off as Mustafa fell to the ground.

The Israeli army's own regulations forbid soldiers from firing tear gas directly at people. It must be fired from a distance of roughly one hundred feet and pointed upward, so that the canister lands at the feet of demonstrators. Such rules never stopped the army from aiming directly at people, though, as many demonstrators in Nabi Saleh got hit in the legs. But the head? This was an egregious first.

Mustafa's wounds were so severe that he died in the hospital the next morning. Initially, I couldn't absorb the fact that I had seen someone killed before my very eyes. Everyone knew Mustafa. He was a member of our family. And he had been part of the protest movement from the start.

Our grassroots resistance movement had officially gained its first martyr, a price that no one had been prepared to pay. We knew our freedom wouldn't come cheaply, but that knowledge didn't make the pain any easier to handle.

The news of Mustafa's death sent shockwaves through the village and across Palestine. In accordance with Islamic customs, we buried him the next day. Hundreds of mourners joined in his funeral procession in Ramallah—Mustafa's final march. From a distance, I watched as he was carried on a stretcher atop the shoulders of several men, his body cloaked in a Palestinian flag and his head wrapped in a kuffiyeh not unlike the one his friend had pressed down on his face to stop the flow of blood just a day earlier—only, this time, part of it was draped over the right side of his face, to conceal his fatal wound. Everyone chanted nationalistic and religious slogans to honor his life and condemn his murder, a partial release for their anger and sorrow.

"The blood of a martyr isn't cheap!" they proclaimed in unison.

"There is no god but Allah, and Mustafa is beloved by him!" they went on.

Many held up posters of Mustafa looking young and vibrant, accompanied by an image of his mangled, bloody face photographed the instant he was shot—a gruesome reminder of the barbarity of the Israeli military.

From Ramallah, we drove to Nabi Saleh in an endless caravan of cars. As we approached the village, we saw soldiers and armored jeeps stationed along the route. Killing Mustafa wasn't enough; now they were taunting us in our grief, it seemed.

Hundreds more mourners from neighboring villages poured into Nabi Saleh to pay their respects to our slain martyr. There were so many people that the mosque where the Islamic funeral prayer was held completely overflowed.

The deluge of tears and prayers that poured out of everyone as Mustafa was brought to his grave and lowered down into the earth were not enough to convey our collective devastation. For the first time in my life, I saw grown adults completely fall apart. One of Mustafa's friends collapsed to the ground as he sobbed. Many women wailed, their shrieks piercing, agonizing. Until that moment, I hadn't known the human body was capable of making such sounds. Tears flowed endlessly from the eyes of grown men. Then there was Mustafa's mother, my aunt Ekhlas, who was so devastated, it was as if one of her limbs had been ripped from her. I thought about my father and Ammo Naji, both languishing in cold prison cells instead of being there with us. Who was consoling them in their grief?

I would later watch a video of Mustafa's aunt, to whom he was very close, speaking to reporters about her last moment with him. "I swear I saw his eye open when I went to kiss him goodbye. It made me feel his soul is still alive," she said. "Like the Quran says, martyrs are not dead. They're alive with God. Mustafa will always be alive because he lives on in all of our hearts and in the hearts of everyone here who loves him."

After the last shovelfuls of dirt were smoothed over his grave, I watched as, for some, sorrow gave way to anger and defiance.

"Mustafa sacrificed his blood! The occupation has to end!" many in the crowd fervently chanted.

With emotions high and anger boiling, a number of youth rushed down to the Israeli military outpost near the settlement to express their rage over his murder. Skirmishes broke out as the Israeli forces responded to the stones being hurled in their direction with a heavy barrage of tear gas. As more people joined the demonstration, the army unleashed the skunk truck to try to repel them. Things quickly turned violent. A funeral turned into yet another asymmetrical battle. The soldiers arrested six people that day, all of them activists, and injured several more. The latter included Jonathan, who lost consciousness after a soldier placed him in a stranglehold, and he had to be taken to a hospital.

It took me months to recover from Mustafa's murder. No matter how desperately I tried, I couldn't sleep. Each time I closed my eyes, I saw his bloody, disfigured face all over again and was forced to relive the moment I had witnessed him dying. Not even an invitation to play soccer or a game of *Jaysh o 'Arab* could entice me to go outside. I comforted myself by trying to come to terms with his senseless murder in a way that didn't feel so tragic. "What's more noble than dying for your country?" I reasoned with myself. "He died defending our land, and he's lucky to be a martyr. May God have mercy on his soul."

This positive outlook helped relieve some of the shock and trauma I felt trapped inside, but it got me only so far. We eventually learned that no one would be held accountable for Mustafa's death. An investigation by the Israeli Military Advocate General (MAG) determined that the soldier who had fatally shot Mustafa did not break any rules. Despite photographic evidence and eyewitness accounts proving the opposite, the MAG believed the soldier's bogus claims that he hadn't seen Mustafa when he fired the tear gas canister directly at him from close range.

There would be no justice for Mustafa, but he was by no means the only Palestinian victim to suffer this fate. In 2009, Bassem Abu Rahma, an activist from the village of Bil'in, was killed when an Israeli soldier fired a tear gas canister directly at his chest. Even though three separate video cameras captured footage of the atrocity, the MAG failed to hold anyone accountable for that death, either, and closed the case, citing lack of evidence. In fact, out of 739 complaints filed by the Israeli nonprofit human rights organization B'Tselem regarding the death, injury, or beating of Palestinians, only 25 resulted in the implicated soldier being charged. Expecting our oppressors somehow to deliver us justice was a fool's errand. The outcome would always be consistent with what the Palestinian people had experienced for decades: Israel can murder us, displace us, ethnically cleanse us, and usurp our land and resources—all with impunity.

I decided that, from that point on, I'd be staying indoors, where it was safer.

At least, that's what I thought.

FORBIDDEN LANDS

ONE OF THE MOST memorable days of my childhood was when my family took a trip to Akka (also known as Acre), a picturesque coastal Palestinian city that was taken by Israel in 1948. It was my first and only time seeing Akka, but I was so enamored of what I saw that the details are forever etched in my memory.

It was the holy month of Ramadan, which meant that on Fridays, Israeli authorities granted some Palestinians from the West Bank rare permits to go to Jerusalem and pray at Al-Aqsa. Only women and girls, boys under seventeen, and men over forty were eligible. Luckily for my family, we all met the age qualifications. On this particular Friday, though, my parents decided to take advantage of the access to the 1948 lands that we're normally forbidden to visit and venture out to Akka. And this meant that for the first time in my life, I'd get to see the Mediterranean Sea up close.

When speaking of the villages and cities stolen from us in 1948, most Palestinians will hardly ever refer to them as "Israel." Instead they use *ad-daakhil*, which means "inside"; "the 1948 lands"; or, more simply, "1948" or just "'48." It's an affirmation of our continued claim to the land and a constant reminder of the tremendous losses we suffered just decades ago—a still-fresh wound.

One of the greatest pains to our existence as Palestinians is that despite living in such a geographically small area—

historic Palestine is roughly the size of New Jersey—we're cut off and isolated from one another. Palestinians from the West Bank, like my family, must remain only in the West Bank. The 2.2 million Palestinians in the Gaza Strip, a tiny enclave that Israel has blockaded by air, land, and sea since 2007, are literally trapped there, in what's called the world's largest open-air prison. Those of us in the West Bank and Gaza are disconnected from one another and from our Palestinian brethren who live in occupied East Jerusalem and in the cities within '48. The Palestinians of '48, the ones who managed to stay in their villages despite the Nakba, now make up 20 percent of Israel's population. But, thanks to Israel's systemic discrimination and the institutionalized racism that defines Palestinians' existence there, they live as second-class citizens. Most of us in these disparate territories cannot visit one another. This form of divide and conquer is imposed by Israel as yet another method to control us. As a result, we're fragmented as a Palestinian nation and lack the social cohesion and unity needed to achieve self-determination and, ultimately, liberation.

I grew up hearing romanticized depictions of the cities and villages of 1948 and imagined them as forbidden lands, fabled places of beauty and splendor. "The Israelis took our most beautiful cities" is a common refrain I've heard since childhood.

From the hilltop near our home in Nabi Saleh, I could stare out at Tel Aviv and catch glimpses of the distant sea. I fantasized about how life there used to be and what it might be like currently. Tel Aviv should only be a forty-five-minute drive from Nabi Saleh, but given the checkpoints we'd have to cross and the nearly impossible permit we'd have to get from Israel, it might as well be in another country.

Imagine having parts of your ancestral homeland totally off-limits to you. They're within sight, but completely out of reach. Such deprivation tears at your soul. It gnaws away at you. At times, you want to break down and cry. Other times, you want to destroy the apartheid wall and dismantle the checkpoints with your bare hands. Even more infuriating is knowing that practically any Jewish person in the world can immigrate to Israel and get citizenship, even if they had never previously stepped foot in the country. And that so many tourists from around the world can easily see more of your country than you'll ever be able to, despite the fact that *you're* indigenous to it. While they can breeze right through Ben Gurion Airport in Tel Aviv, you need permission from the state that stole your land. And you're very lucky if you get it.

This is why our day trip to Akka was monumental.

On the drive there, my brothers and I could hardly contain our excitement. Abu Yazan had his nose pressed to the window practically the entire time, eager to be the first one to spot the sea. As soon as we arrived in Akka's Old City, we bolted out of the car and began exploring our surroundings. My jaw dropped in awe as I took in the scene of the historic port city around me. Akka was more magnificent than I could've imagined. It contained hundreds of years of history, including relics of the Crusaders. The ancient, well-preserved walls that surrounded the Old City teleported us back centuries to when the Ottoman Empire ruled our land. My father explained how those walls helped determine Napoléon's defeat in Akka, which ultimately crushed the world-renowned conqueror's dreams of carving out an empire in the East. It made me love the city even more.

Unlike many other cities within '48, Akka still has a significant Palestinian population. I heard Arabic spoken everywhere we went and instantly felt right at home. I loved walking down the bustling old harbor with its fishermen, vendors, and children running around playing. With each inhalation of the salty, fishy scent filling the air, I felt more alive.

My brothers and I raced over to the ancient seawall encircling the Old City and watched in amazement as local boys jumped off it and plunged right into the blue Mediterranean Sea. It didn't matter that I couldn't swim well. I was inspired to dive right in after them, but just as I tried to hoist my body over the wall, my dad grabbed the back of my shirt. My brothers' attempts to imitate the boys' jumps were similarly intercepted. Still, that seawall stood out as my favorite part of the city.

There, in Akka's Old City, I felt transported to the past, but also to an alternative present, a realm of what was and what could have been had Israel not conquered our land and exiled us from it. I also caught a glimpse of a possible future when we could return to this land. I felt a sense of nostalgia, loss, and hope all at once.

So this *is what I've been missing out on*, I thought.

A charming old Palestinian house built of stone that sat by the water captured my imagination. To enter it, you had to walk through a tiny turquoise door that was rounded at the top. I wondered who the inhabitants of this enchanting little dwelling were and if they knew that they were the luckiest people in the world.

"I wish it were mine!" I told my family longingly. In that moment, a new dream took root inside me: to move to Akka one day and live right by the shining sea.

My parents honored their promise to us and saved the best for last, letting us end the day at the beach. I ran into the water and stayed there for hours. My brothers and I excitedly splashed around and squealed with joy—thrilled to finally experience the privilege of swimming in the sea, which we had long imagined and fantasized about. Something in its vastness, and in the fact that there was only water as far as your vision could stretch, made me feel free for the first time in my life. No settlements, no wall, and no checkpoints to mar the landscape. Just sea. It was the most beautiful feeling of my life, a literal dream come true, and I never wanted it to end.

We swam until the sun set and a chorus of *adhan*, signaling the hour for the Maghrib prayer and the end of the day's fast, rang out from the colorful minarets of the old mosques around us. That's when our parents called for us to get out of the water and begin drying off so we could begin the two-hour journey back home.

But I wasn't ready to leave.

I remained in the water, trying to soak up as much as I could, not knowing if I'd ever be able to come back. Baba eventually had to wade in and drag me out, scolding me while doing so. I threw a small tantrum and tearfully insisted to my parents that I wanted to stay. I wasn't done smelling the soil of Palestine there. I hadn't yet had my fill.

On the car ride home to Nabi Saleh, I felt increasingly suffocated with each checkpoint we crossed. The world was closing in on me once again, and I'd soon be returning to my life of constant army raids and arrests, clashes, and closed military zones—a life of endless limitations and dreams denied. I love my village with all my soul, but I felt a strong sense of belonging in Akka. And I left a part of myself there. Akka was a part of my homeland that was foreign to me, and I deserved to get to know it. I now understood with every fiber of my being that it was the birthright of every Palestinian to do so.

MY AFFECTION FOR AKKA is rivaled only by my deep love for Jerusalem, our cherished holy city of Al-Quds, which is unlike any other place in the world. Walking through the Old City of Jerusalem is best described as an exhilarating assault on the senses. The air is thick with the aromas of freshly baked *ka'ak* bread, spices, incense, Arabic coffee, and falafel all blended together. If Palestine could be bottled as a scent, it would smell like this. A maze of narrow alleys with cobbled streets ensures you can walk around for hours and never walk down the same alley twice. Along the way, you pass countless shops with their colorful displays of Holy Land souvenirs, spices, candy, fresh juice, jewelry, clothes, and shoes.

Jerusalem teems with religious, historic, and political significance and is as coveted as it is contested. Sadly, I've been there only a little more than a handful of times, but each trip further deepened my attachment to the city. In the Old City of Jerusalem, the Muslim, Christian, and Jewish quarters are home to some of the holiest sites of the three major Abrahamic faiths. There's the Western Wall, sacred to the Jewish people; the Church of the Holy Sepulchre, which Christians believe to be the site of the crucifixion and burial of Jesus; and the sacred Al-Aqsa Mosque and the Dome of the Rock, where the Prophet Muhammad prayed with the souls of all the other prophets and ascended to heaven. Jerusalem is the third-holiest city in Islam and preceded Mecca as the first *qibla*, the direction toward which the Prophet Muhammad and the early Muslim community faced to pray. Beyond that, the city is central to the Palestinian struggle and integral to the soul of every Palestinian, Muslim and Christian alike. It's our eternal capital.

I sneaked into the city for the majority of my visits, and I chose to do so out of principle. I refused to seek the permission of my oppressors to visit a city they're illegally occupying. Instead, I rode with family friends whose car bore a yellow license plate, hoping not to get stopped and searched at any checkpoints, banking on my ability to pass as a foreigner with my blond hair and blue eyes, to quell any suspicion the soldiers might have. The privilege of being unrecognizable is one that I continue to mourn intensely now that I'm well-known in Israel and easily identifiable.

Each time I arrived in the Old City and began to walk down the old steps at the Damascus Gate, I felt the same magnetic pull. There was always the same special energy buzzing in the air, energy that drew me in and made me feel as though I were traveling back in time through the various eras in which the city was conquered, destroyed, and rebuilt time and again. Standing there within the ancient walls that had hosted so many civilizations, religions, and empires made me proud to be a daughter of that land.

Each time I approached the Damascus Gate, I was captivated by the sight of the *hajjehs*, the elderly Palestinian women, sitting on the ground with okra, mint, grape leaves, or whatever other produce they were selling splayed out on newspapers in front of them. The *hajjehs* managed to command my respect and adoration at the same time. I've always fantasized about spending days on end with them, sitting right beside them on the ground and getting to know each of them one by one. I see them as living, breathing Palestinian history books and priceless national treasures. I imagine asking them all the burning questions that float in my mind:

Were you around in 1948, during the Nakba?
What was your experience like?
What was life like when you were my age?
Are there any martyrs or prisoners in your family?
What did you do during the First Intifada?
How did you confront the occupation?

From the moment I first saw those *hajjehs*, they've never left my mind. To this day, I still dream of hanging out with them.

It's the small details that define Jerusalem and make me love it: the vendors pushing their carts stacked with goods as they try to squeeze their way through the crowded alleys; the resonant sound of the church bells ringing; the shimmering golden glow of the majestic Dome of the Rock, which never fails to take my breath away; the beauty of the ancient stones in the walls; the various worshippers embarking on their unique spiritual journeys; the rich diversity found in the historic quarters inhabited by Palestinians of African, Moroccan, and Armenian descent, a reminder of how many people traveled from afar to make the magnificent capital their home. These are just some of the tangible things that tie the Palestinian people so intimately to Jerusalem.

There are also the intangible.

Even more than Akka, Jerusalem's Old City feels like a portal to the past and, at the same time, an elusive glimpse at a possible future. It's one in which Palestinian Muslims and Christians can once again peacefully coexist with our Jewish brothers and sisters in a single state. But through its calculated efforts to erase the Palestinian presence in the city, Israel has crushed all hope of that vision being realized anytime soon.

In my romanticized memories of Jerusalem, I didn't always account for the ugliness that also defines the city—to which it's impossible to turn a blind eye. You see it in the armed Israeli soldiers patrolling the Old City, bumping into you with assault rifles flung across their chests. You see it in the young Palestinian men who are routinely stopped by soldiers and forced to endure humiliating body searches simply because they're Palestinian. You see it in the giant Israeli flags that hang from the balconies of homes that once belonged to Palestinians.

As part of the Zionist state's long-standing plan to claim the whole city as its undivided capital, Israel is undertaking a steady ethnic cleansing of Jerusalem's Palestinians. This systematic attempt to demographically alter the makeup of Jerusalem by increasing its Jewish population plays out through the impossible set of conditions it imposes on Palestinians, which force many to leave or punish them if they stay. This includes revoking Palestinians' residency permits, forcibly displacing them, banning the construction and expansion of homes to accommodate growing families, and demolishing homes to clear the way to build more illegal Jewish settlements. Israeli courts have even recently ruled that Jewish settlers can move into Palestinian homes in the East Jerusalem neighborhoods of Sheikh Jarrah and Silwan and forcibly expel the Palestinian families that have been residing in them for generations. There's even a campaign being carried out by right-wing Israeli activists to cover or scratch off Arabic names from street signs around the city, leaving only the Hebrew and English names displayed.

But under international law—and like the West Bank—East Jerusalem, which includes the Old City, is considered occupied Palestinian territory. It has been so ever since it fell under Israeli military rule in 1967. Additionally, since 1948, the United Nations and most of the international community have refused to recognize any country's sovereignty over any part of the city until a permanent peace agreement is reached. This was also the United States' position until 2017, when the Trump administration recognized Jerusalem as Israel's capital, an inflammatory move that had far-reaching repercussions for the Palestinian people, the region, and for me personally. For it was during the aftermath of this announcement amid heightened tensions that I was arrested.

Jerusalem is and always will be the most important city for the Palestinian people. If we give it up, it means giving up the Palestinian cause. And that's something we'll never do.

BREAKING THE BARRIER

MARAH HAS ALWAYS BEEN more than a cousin and best friend to me. From the moment I opened my eyes in this world, she's been by my side. She's a year older than me, but this has never stopped us from being inseparable. Every detail of my life has been shared with her. We went to school together, we'd eat together, we'd have regular slumber parties—everything. When we were young girls, our big dream was somehow to find a way to live together. It wasn't enough that we lived on the same street and that it took all of one minute to walk from one of our houses to the other. No—we had to live under the same roof. And that's why when, in 2010, Israel issued a demolition order for my family's home, just months after our weekly protests began, I was over the moon.

Home demolitions are a regular occurrence under Israel's military occupation, and because my home is located in Area C, I truly believed it would happen. Once again thanks to the ill-fated Oslo Accords, the West Bank is divided into three noncontiguous areas: A, B, and C. Area A, which today constitutes 18 percent of the West Bank, falls under the control of the Palestinian Authority. That means the PA is in charge of education, health, the economy, and policing there. In Area B, which constitutes 22 percent of the West Bank, the PA is similarly in charge of civil affairs, but its police presence exists only in coordination with the Israeli army. In both Areas

A and B, the Israeli army can enter whenever it wants to carry out raids and arrests, and it does so frequently.

Finally, there's Area C, which makes up an overwhelming 60 percent of the West Bank and is fully under Israel's civil and security control. This includes all matters related to land allocation, planning and construction, and infrastructure. Area C is where all of Israel's illegal settlements are located, in addition to the accompanying bypass roads built exclusively for the settlers to use. Area C is also richly endowed with natural resources, like the main water aquifer for the entire country, which Israel controls.

The division of Areas A, B, and C was intended to be temporary, and the PA was supposed to gain incremental control of all these areas. But more than two decades later, the arrangement persists. And despite the PA's having some administrative and internal security control over parts of the West Bank, Israel ultimately has full military control over the entire area.

The majority of Nabi Saleh, including our home, falls under Area C, even though our house was built with permission in 1964—decades before the Oslo Accords sliced up the West Bank. Any construction in Area C, whether by Palestinians or Jewish settlers, requires an application process with the Israeli Civil Administration, but virtually all Palestinian applications for building permits are rejected. This means that Palestinian families aren't allowed to legally expand the homes they've been living in for decades to make room for their growing families. And any sort of construction that occurs without a proper government-issued permit gives Israel the pretext for issuing a demolition order—which is precisely what happened to us.

In 2010, our house was one of thirteen in the village that the Israeli military ordered to be demolished. We knew it was retaliation for our burgeoning protest movement, a form of collective punishment for our daring to resist the occupation and fight for our rights. By then, our home had already been raided by the military more than 150 times. But as a nine-year-old who wanted nothing more than to be with her best friend at all times, I rejoiced at the prospect of being forcibly displaced. Marah's house was spared a demolition order, and so, she and I figured that once the bulldozers came in and destroyed our house, my family would migrate down the street to take refuge in hers. It's embarrassing to admit now, but every night before bed, I prayed to God for the military to come demolish our house. Marah prayed, too. We even had all the details figured out, like where I'd sleep and hang my clothes. Our lives would be so much better once we were living together. We just knew it.

Months and eventually years went by, but our house remained standing. Then, one night in 2015, I woke up at 4 A.M. to the loud roar of a nearby bulldozer. It was razing an uninhabited home in the village, one of the thirteen facing pending demolition. The owner of the home lived in the United States. The military hadn't even given anyone a heads-up.

In the morning, I ran over to see what had happened. Only piles of large stones and rubble remained of the home that predated Israel's 1967 occupation of the West Bank. Sure, no one was living in it at the time, but it was still a Palestinian home, owned by one of our relatives, and it was part of Nabi Saleh. I stared at the destruction in disbelief. Our village had paid the price of our blood, our loved one's lives, and now our homes. At that moment, it hit me that the demolition order wasn't just a hypothetical scenario that would allow me and Marah to be roommates; it was a real and terrifying possibility that would ruin our lives. I couldn't shake the fear that, at any second, the Israeli army might reduce my own house to rubble. How foolish I was for ever having wished it. There was no place in our lives for such childish fantasies. Dreaming could wait. I now understood that I needed to do whatever was in my power to defend my home.

The experience made me realize that, as Palestinians, simply by residing in our homes, we practice a form of resistance. That's because the Israeli government is continually seeking to secure maximal land for Israel and its Jewish settlers with a minimal Palestinian population on it. This strategy plays out differently in the various territories. The fact that our West Bank home falls within Area C means we can lose it at any time. It also means that when Waed is married one day, he won't be able to build a home for his new family next to ours. He'll have to find somewhere in Areas A or B to live. These densely populated areas weren't very big to start out with, and over time they've only gotten smaller. That's why many Palestinians in predicaments like Waed's resort to moving to another country: They simply can't find anywhere in Palestine to live. The same goes for Jerusalem's Palestinian residents, who are being systematically pushed out of their city. Having their homes demolished, being forcibly expelled from them, or seeing their residency permits revoked means that they, too, must search for another place to live, often in another country.

Bethlehem, which is in the West Bank, is a prime example of how Israel has taken more Palestinian land while ridding it of its native Palestinian population. Israel built its illegal apartheid wall to encircle Bethlehem, surrounding it on three sides. Each time I see the monstrous structure there, I cry. It breaks my heart to witness how the city believed to be Jesus's birthplace has been strangled, cut off from its historical sister-city Jerusalem and isolated from the rest of the West Bank. And it enrages me to know that twenty-two illegal Israeli settlements have been built on the occupied Palestinian land belonging to Bethlehem. Now, only 13 percent of Bethlehem is available for Palestinian use.

Divide and conquer. Usurp and expel.

The endless limitations Israel imposes on us are not just about controlling the present, but about robbing us of dreaming and planning our futures. Confined to the segmented and constantly threatened patch of Palestinian land where we were born, we're denied the right to choose where to live, work, or study. Social media has allowed young people like me to connect with fellow Palestinians in Gaza, '48, and Jerusalem, people with whom I'd ordinarily never cross paths. But even if I were to one day fall in love with a young man outside the West Bank, there'd be virtually no way for us to get married and live together—or even to meet face-to-face, for that matter.

Like many Palestinians my age, I cannot simply accept this status quo. It's no way to live. And in my heart, I know it's only a matter of time before we won't have to anymore.

THE ADULTS OF NABI Saleh are often asked why they allow their children to partake in the protests, willingly putting them in harm's way. They're accused of not loving us enough to protect us. "Aren't you scared for them?" is a question that inevitably gets asked by journalists and even well-meaning foreign visitors—as if any parent would be okay knowing that fully armed soldiers in their backyard might shoot or kill their child at any moment. But the answer is that our parents had no choice. Or, to be more accurate, the Israeli military robbed all of us, young and old, of a choice. At a very young age, most of us learned the hard way that we weren't any safer inside our homes than we were out on the marches.

I learned this lesson when I was eleven. It was 2012. By then, Mustafa had been killed before my eyes and the Israeli military had been routinely firing at us before we even reached the bottom of the hill. The prior courage I had reluctantly mustered to join the marches was gone. Home was where you could find me on Fridays.

On this particular Friday, as the clashes raged outside, I was hiding in the veranda of our home with Salam and one of our cousins. We were startled by the sound of our window shattering as something crashed through it. Before we knew it, the room filled with smoke, and we began coughing, crying, and screaming. The military had fired a tear gas grenade directly into our home. Disoriented, we frantically wiped away the tears and snot from our faces. We gasped for breath, unable to see clearly what was in front of us or how we'd escape. In that terrifying moment, I realized that those who remained home faced as much danger as those who joined the protests.

Thankfully, some young men from the village rushed in to rescue us and took us outside to safety. At least, we thought it would be safer. We fled to an area behind my house that was clear of tear gas. It took us around fifteen minutes to recover from the chemical's effects and begin breathing properly again. Once I had regained my composure, I made my way down the street toward Marah's house and watched the soldiers and protesters face off in the distance. Suddenly, an Israeli soldier began running toward me. He stopped ten feet in front of me, aimed his weapon in my direction, and fired several rubber-coated steel bullets. One hit my hand directly.

At first, I was too stunned to realize what had happened. But the pain quickly became so intense, I nearly threw up.

"I'm shot! I'm shot!" I cried out.

An older male relative who was standing behind me, but much farther back, got hit in the leg, although his injury was less severe than mine. My hand eventually turned blue and swelled up like a balloon. When my parents took me to the hospital, we found out the hand was broken. I went home in a cast and in shock over the day's events.

At eleven years old, in the span of minutes, I was tear-gassed in my own home and shot in my hand. But despite this terrible misfortune, I'm considered lucky that my house was only one story, and I was able to evade the fog of tear gas relatively quickly. Others weren't so lucky.

Everyone in Nabi Saleh knew the recent horror story. It started when the army fired a tear gas canister into my cousin Janna's home. She was only four years old at the time and, just like me when I was younger, deathly afraid of the marches. Every Friday, you could find her hiding under a table or alone in the bathroom crying. So, naturally, when a tear gas canister was fired directly into her house, she was terror-stricken.

Her mother, Nawal, pulled her out of the house, and they ran to the home next door for safety. They were joined there by several adults, including some photojournalists eager to escape the tear gas and thirteen other children. It was a two-story house, so they figured the second floor offered them the most protection. But once they got there, the soldiers targeted them with even more tear gas. One canister went off in the stairwell of the house, making any sort of escape attempt downstairs impossible. Another broke through the veranda window and ignited the curtains on fire. A cloud of tear gas quickly began to fill the room. In a frenzied panic, everyone shuffled into a bedroom and shut the door.

The children, most of whom were no older than six, wailed in terror as the tear gas slowly began to seep in under the door and permeate the room. Now they were absolutely trapped. A young boy named Hesham, who was barely six at the time, almost stopped breathing altogether.

Janna's aunt opened the window and desperately called out to some men below, saying, "For God's sake, help us! The house is full of tear gas! We have no way to escape!"

Acting quickly, the men climbed atop one another, forming a human ladder. The adults in the gas-filled room carried one crying child after another to the window and handed them to the young man at the top of the human ladder. The poor children who had yet to be taken to the window watched this all unfold in horror, thinking they were about to be tossed down two stories.

Janna sobbed hysterically as her mother carried her to the window.

"Please, Mama. I love you!" she pleaded. "I beg you. Please don't throw me out the window!" But to save her daughter's life, my aunt Nawal had no choice but to hand Janna over.

Everyone eventually managed to escape the tear gas–filled house. Ambulances rushed to treat the children who were still gasping for air and coughing up streams of mucus. Many of them cried in utter disbelief at what they had just gone through. But that was just the physical harm inflicted on them. The psychological trauma they suffered was deeper and far more enduring. One little girl refused to go near her mother for weeks, unable to reconcile how she could throw her own daughter out the window. If her own mother couldn't protect her, who could?

Yet, when the trauma subsided, a transformation occurred. The children now understood that being indoors was just as dangerous as, if not more dangerous than, being outdoors. At least outside they could see where the tear gas was being fired and run the other way. After that, Janna and many of the other children began joining the marches. But it wasn't just a question of relative safety: Being attacked in your own home ignites a strong determination in you to want to defend yourself. You summon a type of courage you didn't know you had, and as you grow, that feeling of courage grows, too. With time, we all stopped letting our fear control us. Our self-confidence increased, and, for better or worse, so did our irreverence toward authority. This was a great character trait in the face of the occupying soldiers, though it didn't go over so well when we used it to undermine our parents or teachers.

For her part, Janna didn't just join the marches. She emerged as one of the most prominent children in our resistance movement, if not in all of Palestine, even earning the unofficial title of "the world's youngest journalist." Like me, once she overcame her fear of the marches, she started looking forward to them and partaking in them enthusiastically. One Friday, Janna noticed that there wasn't the typical media presence we had grown accustomed to by then. Other than our uncle Bilal, who dutifully filmed every single demonstration, there were no outside journalists to document the march or the ensuing confrontations with the Israeli military. So Janna took matters into her own hands. She grabbed her mother's cellphone, opened the camera, and hit Record. She filmed everything, and at the end of her report, she even signed off like a correspondent, saying, "Janna Jihad, Nabi Saleh, Occupied Palestine."

Her mother uploaded the video to Facebook, and it saw instant likes and shares. Week after week, Janna filmed the marches, reporting what was unfolding in real time. At first, she was nervous, stuttering and having to do multiple takes to get out what she wanted to say. But not long after, she was broadcasting like a professional and filing reports in both Arabic and English, which she worked hard to master. Often, I held the camera and filmed her while she did her stand-ups. Because she was only seven when she started, her mother managed her Facebook page.

Janna didn't limit her reporting to Nabi Saleh. She traveled to other Palestinian cities, including Hebron, Nablus, and Jerusalem, filming everything from protests to people being detained at checkpoints. It didn't take long for her page to accumulate a quarter of a million followers from all around the world. The sight of an innocent little Palestinian girl reporting on the suffering of other children and adults under occupation moved people. It compelled them to open their eyes to the countless injustices perpetrated by Israel. Janna always says that her camera is her gun. And truly, what she's able to shoot with it is far more powerful than any weapon.

But the fact remains that Janna, just like the rest of us, should have been busy playing, not resisting. No seven-year-old should ever feel she has to shoulder the burden of documenting the human rights abuses taking place in her own backyard. We shouldn't have to grow up seeing our parents arrested and fearing they could be shot or killed at any moment. Nor should we children be able to know instinctively whether the blasts outside our doors are from tear gas, sound grenades, rubber bullets, or live ammunition. And yet, we all acquired this skill even before we hit puberty. For example, it didn't take me long to stop flinching when soldiers fired something in close proximity to me. That's how normalized the violence in our lives has become.

So, to return to the question our parents are always asked, about why they allow their children to protest: It is the occupation that forces the children to go out into the streets. Of course our parents worry about us, but they raised us to be strong and not to cower in the face of oppression. They also taught us that while it's important to resist, we must never hate, because hatred will eat us up from inside. We resist to live because, ultimately, we truly love life. The occupation seeks to defeat our spirits and rob us of any semblance of a normal or safe childhood, but we refuse to let it. Just as we refuse to let ourselves be controlled by fear.

Still, I grew up dreaming about what a normal childhood might be like, of how it would feel to be free. I imagined being able to move from city to city without being stopped at checkpoints. I imagined playing outside, maybe even on a real playground or an actual soccer field with grass, without armed soldiers interrupting my game. Instead, I played in streets and on hills and in front and back yards littered with the remnants of bullets and explosives fired at us by Israeli forces, much of this ordnance marked "Made in the United States." It's impossible to play without accidentally kicking or stepping on these artifacts.

But, rather than feeling like defeated victims, we began collecting and repurposing these relics of war. We'd plant flowers in empty tear gas canisters. I've transformed bullets fired at us into necklace pendants, some of which I've gifted to close friends. The fence in front of Janna and my uncle Bilal's home is decorated with dozens of empty tear gas canisters, an unusual display that sends a message to the Israeli army that despite its attempts to literally choke and suppress us, we're still standing. We strive to create life out of death, and we'll continue to find beauty even in the ugliest parts of our lives.

IT WAS A SEQUENCE of traumatic events that no child should have to endure that ultimately rid me of any remaining ounce of fear I had left in me. After I was shot in the hand, all bets were off. Nothing could keep me indoors and away from the marches. This was the beginning of a certain numbness that overcame me and only intensified in the years that followed, one informed by a feeling of complete lack of safety and by the knowledge that, at any moment, anything and anyone I held dear could be taken away.

The week after I was shot, another tragedy took place that marked a turning point in my life. At the time, Israel was pummeling the besieged Gaza Strip yet again with air strikes, in what it called Operation Pillar of Defense. Anytime Gaza was attacked, protests in the West Bank flared and were often more intense and violent than usual. This time was no different, and there were daily clashes in Nabi Saleh that week.

My mother's youngest brother and close confidant, Khalo (meaning "maternal uncle") Rushdie, had come over to our house that Saturday afternoon. By far my favorite uncle, he had a four-year-old daughter named Ghazal, but he still always carved out time to play with me and my brothers. Khalo Rushdie knew all about my big dreams to become a soccer player for Barcelona and would practice with me outside in the street. At times like these, he acted as a proxy for my father, who was still in prison. My uncle knew how difficult our father's imprisonment was for us—we were banned from visiting him—and he tried to lessen our pain by checking in on us often. Khalo Rushdie was a policeman with the Palestinian Authority and typically worked on Fridays, which meant he was never able to join our weekly marches. Because his shifts ran late, he'd usually come home early Saturday and sleep the entire day. This day, though, he stayed awake and came over to visit us.

We were chatting in the living room when one of the young men in the village ran in to tell us that someone outside had been hit by a rubber bullet. While the rest of us stayed inside, Khalo Rushdie hurried out to see what was happening. Moments later, we heard successive pops of gunshots coming from the hillside behind our home. Live rounds. We raced outside to see what was going on.

Halfway down the hill behind my house, right by the carob tree, I saw a man splayed out on the ground. Soldiers hovered around him, firing at anyone who tried to get close to help him.

"They shot Rushdie!" one of the guys yelled.

My Khalo Rushdie. I felt my heart drop to the pit of my stomach.

My mother, who had been documenting the violence in our village for the Israeli human rights organization B'Tselem to use as evidence in cases against the army, grabbed a video camera out of someone's hands and ran down the hill. I began to follow her as bullets zipped past us, narrowly missing our bodies.

"I'm press with B'Tselem, and I want to film!" Mama yelled to the soldiers as she approached them.

I tried to reach the spot where they were standing, but each time I took a few steps forward, the soldiers fired more live rounds in my direction. I felt the bullets whiz past the sides of my head and between my legs. They narrowly missed me, instead hitting the rocks around my feet, which exploded and sent fragments flying into the air that hit my and others' faces. This was the moment I completely broke the fear barrier. I thought if I could survive being this close to death, I could survive anything. Or, maybe I simply stopped caring.

I couldn't make it down to my uncle, but I'm haunted by what happened next, because my mom captured it all on video. She pointed the camera at her brother, who was bleeding from the side of his head, barely able to move.

"What happened, my brother? Where did it hit you?"

"In my leg," Khalo Rushdie groaned.

Two older men from the village tried to come over to carry my uncle away, but they were stopped by the soldiers.

"He's been shot! He needs an ambulance! He needs help!"

my mother screamed at the soldiers at the top of her lungs. They argued back in Hebrew, shoving the men who were trying to rescue my uncle and firing more live rounds, which mercifully didn't hit anyone.

My poor Khalo Rushdie lay there in excruciating pain, bleeding on the rocks and soil as the soldiers yelled at us, stalling us from getting him medical aid. Amid the chaos and hysteria, I could see my uncle slipping in and out of consciousness. Eventually, a few of the men from our village managed to pick him up, despite the soldiers' relentless shoving, and carry him to the top of the hill. They laid him on the ground for a few minutes and inspected his body to see where exactly the bullet had entered.

That's when I saw him up close.

Khalo Rushdie's eyes met mine, and he smiled. I knew he was trying to put on a brave face for me, but there was no masking the agony he was suffering.

For a second, time froze. My mind flashed back to my favorite memory with my uncle. I was four years old, and we were on a family day trip to the West Bank city of Nablus, where there was a public pool. It was probably my first time seeing a swimming pool, and I certainly didn't know how to swim.

That day, Khalo Rushdie suddenly lifted me in his arms and asked, "Are you ready?"

"No!" I howled in fear as he poised, ready to toss me into the water.

"Okay, then drown!" he joked as I plunged into the pool. "Drown!"

I frantically splashed around in a panic, but before I knew it, I had managed to strike a rhythm that had me smoothly treading water. I gazed up and saw my uncle standing at the edge of the pool, smiling proudly down at me, his grin stretching from ear to ear.

I never could have imagined then that I'd one day watch him smile for the last time ever, as he lay barely conscious and bleeding.

I looked on in shock as someone from the village drove up in their car and my mother and some men helped pull Khalo Rushdie into the back seat. Mama held his head in her lap as they sped off for the hospital in Ramallah, twenty-five minutes away. Everyone followed. At the hospital, they kissed Khalo Rushdie and told him to be strong as he was wheeled away on a gurney to an operating room. Though weak, he was still conscious. We all assumed that he'd make a full recovery in no time.

Before the surgery, the doctors had informed everyone that a live bullet fired at him from close range had entered his buttock, continued up his body, and torn his intestines. Still, as we all left the hospital that evening, we had hopes that he'd emerge just fine. But two days later, we got word that his internal bleeding had been too severe. He didn't make it. At thirty-one years old, my Khalo Rushdie was dead. He had had his whole life ahead of him. His four-year-old daughter, Ghazal, would grow up without her father.

I didn't cry when I heard the news. I felt numb the entire drive to the hospital to retrieve his body. And even as we walked in his funeral procession, I shed no tears. It wasn't until we returned to Nabi Saleh to bury him at sunset that I lost it. I looked at his dead body, dressed in his police uniform, and broke down in tears. The pain of his loss pierced my soul and filled me with rage. I ripped the cast off my broken hand and threw it to the ground. I tried running down to the military watchtower by the entrance to the village, to yell at the soldiers, but my cousin Mahmoud caught up with me and brought me back. I don't remember how long I screamed and cried after that. Like many traumatic memories I have, it's all a hazy blur.

Once her youngest brother was officially buried, my mother fainted at his grave and had to be rushed to the hospital. It was a panic attack, and she'd be just fine, the doctors said. But in the days, weeks, and years that followed, she never forgave herself for holding a camera instead of holding on to her brother when she first reached him on the hill. In that sense, she'd never go back to being fully fine.

Months later, an Israeli army probe found that the soldiers fired eighty live bullets that day, including the one that killed my uncle. It's a miracle the death toll wasn't higher. The investigation even conceded that there was no reason to use live ammunition and that the commander who gave the order hadn't even indicated the target or the reason for opening fire. The soldiers didn't even know why they were spraying live bullets at us. Despite this, once again, none of the soldiers or their commanders would ever be held accountable.

Palestinian lives are cheap. Israel couldn't make that any clearer.

When my Khalo Rushdie died, a part of me died, too. But so did my fear. Death, at this point, had become normalized and expected. I'd seen Mustafa get killed by the Israeli army. And now I had seen my favorite uncle murdered by them, too. That's on top of the countless young men I had already witnessed getting shot during the marches. In addition to my parents getting shot. And my brothers getting shot. And even me.

I had had enough.

Any remaining fear I had was erased. From that point on, even if the soldiers fired live rounds at us, I stood unflinching, sometimes throwing stones back at them. The fight for Palestine never felt more high-stakes or urgent. And this fight was no place for mere spectators. Knowing that in order to win back our rightful land, we would be bound to incur losses and forced to make sacrifices, I joined all the subsequent demonstrations. I was prepared to make sacrifices, too. I changed my lifelong dream of becoming a professional soccer player to becoming a lawyer, so I could fight for the justice we were so regularly being denied. I wanted justice for Khalo Rushdie, for Mustafa, for my father in his many arrests, and for us in being banned from visiting him. Soccer was great and all, but it wouldn't benefit us the way the law would. In this one life I was given, I knew I had to do something to help my people. If I didn't, I'd have to answer to God for it.

THE SPOTLIGHT

TWO WEEKS BEFORE MY final confrontation with fear, I had inadvertently made my debut in the international spotlight. It was a Friday, and as always, the usual demonstration was underway. I was still too scared to fully join, so I stood at the top of the hill with my mother, who was capturing it all for B'Tselem. She held her camcorder and diligently filmed the clashes down below between the Israeli soldiers and the youth from our village throwing stones.

"It looks like they caught someone," my mother said and zoomed her camera lens in as far as she could, to decipher whom. A familiar face came into focus.

"It's Waed!" she exclaimed. "They're arresting Waed!"

Without thinking, I took off down the hill, sprinting toward my older brother. It took me less than two minutes to run from the top of the hill down to the main street. I ran so fast that when I got to where the soldiers were standing, I was completely out of breath. Panting, I scanned the area around me, searching for Waed. I didn't see him.

It was hard enough that my dad was already in prison. Now they wanted to take away my big brother, too? Not if I could stop it. A wave of rage came over me. I approached one of the soldiers and raised my clenched fist up at him.

"Where did you take him?" I demanded, barely reaching his chest.

He peered down, past the rifle slung across his body, at the undersize girl screaming up at him.

"Where did you take him?" I shouted at the top of my lungs while shaking my fist at him.

He looked amused. A moment later, he turned from me and walked to the rest of the soldiers. I followed him, yelling at them to tell me where my brother was. Marah and some of the other kids had arrived by then and stood around me, backing me up. We were dwarfed by the armed soldiers towering above us. Still, we cursed them and stomped on their boots with our little feet. They looked down at us and laughed, which only riled me up more.

"You're laughing now, but we're the ones who will be laughing when Palestine is free!" I shrieked. "I'm not scared of you!" I went on. "You think just because you're in body armor and you're holding a gun you scare the Palestinians? You don't! And if you uproot an olive tree, we'll plant one hundred instead!"

I pushed and hit them, unleashing my fury at them for having abducted my big brother. When I got home later that day, I had completely lost my voice from yelling so much. Still, I felt utterly helpless. I had no idea what they were doing to Waed or when I'd see him again.

It turned out that upon arresting Waed, the soldiers severely beat him up in the jeep. He went to jail for five days. The judge in the military court ultimately sent him home after seeing that he was covered in bruises, his face swollen. The experience was traumatic for Waed. Perhaps the only silver lining was that he was briefly able to see our father in prison.

Meanwhile, my confrontation with the soldiers, which had been filmed, went viral on the internet. People all over the world were captivated by the image of a small, blond

Palestinian girl defiantly brandishing her tiny fists at fully armed Israeli soldiers at least two feet taller than her. Some viewers commented that I exemplified the bravery of Palestinian children and the spirit of our people's resistance to the occupation. I honestly didn't care what people thought. I just wanted Waed to be free.

The image of me standing up to the army earned me an invitation to Turkey, which I thought was to attend a conference. My mother and I crossed the border into Jordan, the only way a Palestinian from the West Bank can travel out of the country, and made our way to the Queen Alia International Airport, outside Amman. It was the first time I'd seen an airplane up close, much less flown anywhere. We boarded a Royal Jordanian flight from Amman to Istanbul, and as we took off, I gazed out the window, mesmerized as Jordan and Palestine disappeared into a tiny speck below and we ascended into the clouds.

When we arrived at Istanbul's airport, we were met by dozens of excited Turkish children. They were waving Palestinian flags and wearing white T-shirts bearing the image of me holding my fist up at a soldier. I was perplexed. What was going on? Then a girl my age took a few steps forward and handed me a big bouquet of flowers.

I soon learned that the real reason I was flown out to Turkey was because I was being honored with the Handala Courage Award by the Başakşehir Municipality. Handala is an iconic Palestinian cartoon character created by renowned Palestinian cartoonist Naji al-Ali. He is a ten-year-old boy with spiky hair and bare feet who stands with his back turned and his arms clasped behind him—his posture meant to signify the Palestinian people's rejection of the status quo. Handala symbolizes the Palestinian people's identity and defiance. Naji al-Ali drew him as a ten-year-old because that's how old he himself was in 1948, when his family was forced to flee Palestine due to the establishment of Israel. The famous cartoonist once explained, "Handala was born 10 years old and he will always be 10 years old. It was at that age that I left my homeland. When Handala returns, he will still be 10 years old, and then he will start growing up."

On the night of the ceremony, I accepted my award dressed in a red-and-black embroidered *thobe*, a traditional Palestinian dress, with a kuffiyeh wrapped around my neck. As I stood onstage, the master of ceremonies, a Turkish man, asked me which hand I had held up in a fist at the soldiers, right or left?

"Right," I answered, and he took my right hand in his and kissed it.

He asked how I felt to be receiving an award named after Handala.

I told him it made me feel proud and stronger.

I was indeed proud to be receiving such an award, but at eleven years old, I couldn't fully absorb the magnitude of the moment. It was the first time in my life that I had to give a speech or stand before so many cameras, and it was nerve-racking. I did more media interviews during the two weeks I spent in Turkey than I can remember, but I would much rather have been back in Nabi Saleh playing *Jaysh o 'Arab* outside with the rest of the kids.

For the longest time, I couldn't bring myself to watch any of the interviews I gave. In my memory, I had fumbled and stuttered my way through them all. Waed even made fun of me in his bullying, big brother kind of way. But I recently watched some of them and was pleasantly surprised: I was much more articulate than I gave myself credit for. On one television program, filmed in front of a live studio audience, the host asked me why our village continued to carry out its resistance movement. I replied, saying, "Are we just going to wait for Saladin to come liberate us again, just as he liberated Jerusalem from the Crusaders? Why not create a Saladin among ourselves, as a Palestinian society?" The audience applauded. The host was speechless.

The absolute highlight of my trip to Turkey was once again seeing the sea. Even though it was winter at the time and much too cold to swim, simply being seaside without having to apply for permits from Israel or cross checkpoints was enough to fill me with joy. The freedom to be able to walk to the shore at any time was liberating. *If only I were allowed to live in Akka*, I thought, *I'd be able to do this every day.*

I realized what a splash I had made in Turkey when President Recep Tayyip Erdoğan flew us to his hotel in the southeastern province of Şanlıurfa. There, he invited me and my mother to breakfast one morning and lavished us with several gifts for the family. He told me how much he loved Palestine and that Turkey would always support the Palestinian people.

In response, I asked, "How can you say you love us when we have to enter your country with a visa, but Israelis can travel here with no visa?"

He was quiet. What could he possibly say?

At one point, he picked up a date stuffed with a walnut and tried to hand-feed it to me.

"Ew!" I said as I swatted his hand away. "I don't like dates."

What was true about me as a child remains true now: I've never been scared of anyone or put anyone on a pedestal—not even a head of state. For better or worse, no matter the circumstances or the person in front of me, it's always been impossible for me to silence what's on my mind.

THE DEATH OF MY uncle was the straw that broke the camel's back. After that, it wasn't just a case of my willingly joining all the marches; now they became the highlight of my week. Despite the inherent risks posed just by going out and protesting, I ultimately felt I was doing something productive, if not cathartic. Because I refused to remain quiet or feel defeated, my conscience was at ease. Going out and expressing myself by telling the soldiers they were not welcome on my land somehow filled me with optimism and hope. It made me love life even more. Aside from fulfilling my patriotic duty and serving the Palestinian cause, I felt I was defying the entire occupation by staring down a soldier who wore the same uniform as the one who had killed my uncle.

Often, the mood of our marches was triumphant and fun. If someone threw a stone and it hit a soldier, it was a huge accomplishment. If a soldier tripped and fell to the ground in front of us, we were elated. We did anything we could to antagonize them, including cheering, singing, dancing *dabkeh*, and playing soccer in the streets. Everyone played their part. I'd help make sandwiches and pass them out to the young men tirelessly carrying out the demonstration until the sun went down. The resistance was still growing.

Even though I was a child, I understood that my life had to be devoted to a cause greater than myself. My parents instilled the notion in me and my brothers that if we didn't do anything to benefit our homeland, then we didn't do anything to benefit ourselves. If I was successful in life but my success didn't help Palestine, then it wasn't truly a success. They planted this seed in us while we were very young, but even if they hadn't, everything I had witnessed from a young age would have been enough to make the liberation of Palestine the main goal of my life.

Still, as our popular struggle continued, so did the sacrifices we were compelled to make. The arrests, night raids, shootings, and injuries never subsided. If anything, they only intensified. I knew I was putting myself at risk by going out, and it often crossed my mind that a soldier might shoot me. I could get seriously wounded, I thought. I could become paralyzed. Or perhaps I'd get shot in the eye and lose my vision. Or in the neck and lose my life. I never let myself get too bogged down by these scenarios, though; I was focused on a larger goal. My biggest fear, in any case, was that one of my family members would get shot and killed, or injured so badly they'd be disabled.

It was during this period of heightened violence that another incident took my life in a new direction and one of my biggest nightmares came true: My mother was shot in the leg with a live bullet. It happened amid clashes on a Friday in late November 2014, when we were marking the two-year anniversary of Khalo Rushdie's death. My mother and I had joined a group of women who were throwing stones. Israeli soldiers raided the village with their jeeps, forcing us to escape to the street below the hillside. Mama was about to hurl a stone at an armored jeep when a soldier inside opened the rear door—just as another soldier had done when he killed Mustafa—and shot her with a .22-caliber rifle. The bullet struck her in the leg, and she instantly fell to the ground, in nearly the identical spot where Mustafa had fallen. Watching this, I saw the scene of his murder unfold all over again. Fearing my mother would suffer his fate, I burst into tears and raced over to help her, along with everyone else. But seeing her in excruciating pain, with her leg bleeding, only caused me to panic further.

We rushed her to the hospital, where doctors operated on her leg. She survived, but once she was released and came back home, nothing was the same. My mother couldn't walk for more than a year and a half. Her ability to do most things was severely limited, so at barely fourteen years old, I found most of the responsibilities of the house falling on my shoulders. When guests came to visit us, I served them. I was responsible for keeping the house clean. With the limited culinary skills I had, I helped cook for the family. I helped my younger brothers with their homework. I also assisted my mother in cleaning her wound and replacing the bandages. The sight of her ghastly injury soon became normal, and I no longer cringed while cleaning it.

All this caused my grades at school to suffer. I couldn't concentrate on my studies for the life of me. The toll everything had taken on me was so high, I simply lacked the time or energy to care. I had been a good student up until then. I didn't get straight As, but I certainly never failed anything. Now, though, my scores were slipping below fifty. And once that happened, I started hating school and dreading studying. I took these failures as a sign that I was incapable. Even when I did open the books and push myself to study, I was simply unable to pull off good grades. With my confidence decimated, I sunk into a deep depression. Nothing mattered anymore—certainly not studying. My grades suffered for years as a result. It wasn't until my *tawjihi* (or "senior") year in high school that I cleaned up my act and began to take school seriously again.

After what felt like forever, Mama began walking with the help of a walker, and life felt a bit more bearable. Still, it wasn't easy seeing my typically energetic mother so limited in what she could do and where she could go. Sometimes, as she moved about on the walker, her uninjured leg would suddenly tire from the pressure she was placing on it and give out, causing her to fall to the ground. It was agonizing for me to see the strongest woman I knew so helpless.

Meanwhile, the Israeli army had become even more brutal in their repression of us. By 2015, the level of danger on our streets had reached an alarming new height. Sometimes, within just minutes of our demonstration starting, the soldiers would open fire on us without any warning. They also began deploying snipers, who fired live .22-caliber ammunition at protesters, aiming for their legs. We all knew they were aiming for a particular nerve in the lower leg that can leave a victim paralyzed. This wasn't just happening in Nabi Saleh, but across other cities in Palestine, too.

In the densely populated Dheisheh refugee camp, near Bethlehem, for example, Israeli forces regularly carried out raids in the middle of the night. Hidden snipers positioned themselves on the rooftops of residents' homes and shot at youth who dared defend their camp from the invading army. It was reported that in 2015 and 2016, at least eighty-one youth in Dheisheh were injured by bullets in the limbs and about sixty of them suffered permanent disabilities. Most were shot in the legs and knees. In this way, the soldiers could ensure that their young victims would never be able to walk again, let alone throw stones in protest. The tactic was barbaric and cruel. Dheisheh's residents were already struggling with high rates of poverty and unemployment. To have to deal with the costs of medical care to treat the injured was an unfair burden that only added to their hardships.

But that's not the extent of the army's inhumanity. Many youth in the camp reported that an Arabic-speaking intelligence officer who went by the alias "Captain Nidal" had been deliberately provoking them during clashes and threatening to hurt them. Some testified that Nidal had told them, "I will have all of you walking with crutches and in wheelchairs" and "I will make all of the youth of the camp disabled." They claimed that he was the one to direct snipers to shoot protesters during the raids.

I was so outraged by the presence of snipers that I began trying to block them from shooting the young men throwing stones by standing directly in front of the young men, literally putting my body on the line. I know I risked getting killed by doing this, but I wasn't scared. I told myself that you had to be willing to die for your convictions and for the message you wanted to send. There was also a feeling inside me, a comforting voice, that assured me that if I stood in front of the snipers to protect the men from my village, I'd be safe.

It was during one of these protests that another memorable incident took place: I waged a fight with soldiers to stop them from arresting Miko Peled, an Israeli American human rights activist and dear family friend. Miko is the son of the famous Israeli general Mattityahu Peled, who fought in the 1967 war and was a celebrated hero in his country. But soon after the war, the military hawk retired from the army and became a tireless peace activist, advocating for dialogue with the PLO and for Israel's withdrawal from the occupied territories. His son, Miko, grew up as a Zionist but eventually underwent a transformation that led him to embrace an honest view of his country's occupation of Palestinian land. Miko supports the Palestinian call for Boycott, Divestment and Sanctions (BDS) targeting Israel. He calls for the creation of a single democratic state in historic Palestine with equal rights for all. During his visits to our village, Miko often spent Thursday nights at our house, to be able to join us for the following day's march. Over time, he became a close and trusted family friend.

That day's march began as usual. Once the afternoon prayer finished, we walked down the hill toward the spring, all chanting and carrying Palestinian flags. Miko wore a black T-shirt that read BOYCOTT ISRAEL, FREE PALESTINE. Moments after the march began, we were met by Israeli soldiers who were already positioned to confront us. They ordered us to disperse, which we refused to do. Why should we? We were in our own village. The soldiers pushed and shoved us, fired tear gas and stun grenades, and positioned their snipers to fire live rounds at the guys on the hill throwing stones.

Miko heard one of the officers order the snipers in Hebrew to "shoot them in the legs." This command wasn't something we took lightly. Just two weeks earlier, Israeli forces had killed Saba Abu Ubeid, a twenty-three-year-old man from the nearby village of Salfit who had joined our march in solidarity, by shooting him in the chest with a live bullet. He was the third martyr since our resistance movement began, after Mustafa and Khalo Rushdie. The last thing we wanted that day was a fourth.

The confrontation went on for a while, with the Israeli forces relentless in their crackdown. Miko saw that my aunt was being pushed around by soldiers, and he ran up to help her. A soldier thwarted his attempt to reach her, and before he knew it, several of them had closed in on him. I was standing at the bottom of the hill when I saw the soldiers grabbing Miko's arms and trying to drag him down to the street to arrest him. As soon as he stepped down from the hill on to the street level, where I was, I wrapped my arms around his torso and hugged him as tightly as I could. He had already been arrested, during one of our previous marches, and I wanted to protect him from meeting that fate again.

My mother and aunt also rushed over to try to help, but more soldiers surrounded us. A giant brawl erupted.

"Get rid of the girl!" a soldier barked at Miko in Hebrew.

"If you touch the girl, I will find you and kill you!" Miko shouted back.

As the soldiers shoved us around and tried to pry me away from Miko, I clung on to him with all my might. I felt my hair getting pulled and my body shoved. One soldier flung me back a few feet and shot pepper spray directly into my eyes and into my mother's and aunt's faces. I took a few seconds to recover and then ran back over to try to free Miko, but I was repelled by the same soldier, who sprayed me in the face yet again.

At that point, I became dizzy and couldn't open my eyes, so I went to sit down on the side of the street. Someone handed me an antidote to pepper spray with which to wipe my eyes, but I still could barely see anything. I eventually managed to get up and walk toward the ongoing clashes with one eye open and one shut. I could see that the skunk truck had crept up behind me, so I moved to the side to avoid standing directly in the path of where it was aimed to spray. But because I hadn't yet fully regained my vision, I didn't notice that the cannon had begun to revolve and spray in my direction. Suddenly, the entire right side of my body, including my face and hair, was soaked in skunk water.

The soldiers eventually succeeded in arresting Miko. I felt bad that I wasn't able to save him and had gotten a proper beating by them instead. On top of that, I reeked. Still, I know Miko was touched by my attempt at helping him—he says it was one of the most moving moments of his life.

It might strike some as odd for a young Palestinian girl to put her body on the line to defend an Israeli, but that's not how I see it. Miko is on the right side of history. Even though it means going against his society and the army in which he once served, he puts *his* body and privilege on the line to support us and fight for justice. His allegiance is not to a particular country or flag, but rather to those who share his values. Miko puts humanity over nationality, and that fact alone makes him one of us.

I CONTINUED TO BE alarmed by the new levels of ruthlessness Israel's army exercised against us. In the late summer of 2015,

I had another confrontation with a soldier that was captured on camera and went viral. This time, it was Abu Yazan I was desperate to rescue. His arm had been broken the previous week when he tripped and fell while running from the tear gas the soldiers had fired. On this day, though, he was standing on the hill watching some guys throw stones at the soldiers down below. Suddenly, out of nowhere, a bunch of masked soldiers charged toward everyone on the hill. They had strategically hidden themselves to create a trap and ambush us before anyone could spot them. Most of the soldiers ran toward the group of stone throwers, but one veered off and captured Abu Yazan, who was standing all by himself, a cast on his broken arm.

I had run toward the larger group under attack by the soldiers, to try to help whomever I could, when I heard someone yelling, "Abu Yazan! Help Abu Yazan!"

That's when I saw a masked soldier pinning my younger brother down on some boulders, attempting to arrest him. He locked Abu Yazan in a chokehold and forcefully held him down, showing no regard for the fact that this young boy's arm was clearly broken. Abu Yazan screamed for help. I was the first to arrive and immediately tried to pull my brother from the soldier's grip. Our mother, who still couldn't walk properly, hobbled over to us on her crutches as fast as she could.

"He's a young boy!" she cried as she dropped the crutches and grabbed the soldier from behind, trying to pry him off her son.

My father and aunt and a few others also ran over and joined the effort, hitting and pulling the soldier to try to rescue Abu Yazan. At one point, the soldier extended his hand and clasped it around my neck to push me back, effectively choking me. I instinctively grabbed his hand and sank my teeth into it, biting him with all my might.

We eventually managed to free Abu Yazan, but when the soldier who had captured him stood up, he attacked us. He kicked me and my mom and aunt and hit my father with the butt of his rifle before throwing a stun grenade at the group of us. I felt tremendous pain in my side where I was kicked. A few other soldiers, who had come over to aid their comrade, pushed us around even more. Incredulous at what I had just witnessed, I stood facing the soldier trying to arrest Abu Yazan and, in English, shouted, "You are a terrorist! He's just a child!"

My parents thought it prudent to rush Abu Yazan and me to the hospital, to make sure his broken arm hadn't been further damaged and so I could be checked out after the beating I had just gotten. But as we made our way down to the main street to find a ride, the soldiers fired rubber-coated steel bullets at us. We heard a scream and saw that my brother Salam, who was only nine at the time, had been shot. My dad carried him, Jonathan, our Israeli activist friend, carried Abu Yazan, and Marah's dad (Ammo Naji) carried me; the pain in my side at that point made it difficult for me to walk. At the hospital, we discovered that Salam had suffered the worst injury of the day. The rubber-coated steel bullet struck my baby brother in the foot and broke his toe.

I was surprised to see how photos of the incident, taken by Reuters and Agence France-Presse, spread across the world. People were horrified at the sight of an armed Israeli soldier pinning down and strangling a twelve-year-old Palestinian boy with a broken arm, and of that boy's fourteen-year-old sister (wearing a pink Tweety Bird T-shirt) using her teeth in a desperate attempt to free him. The asymmetric nature of Zionist brutality, something we had long grown accustomed to, was now laid bare for all to see. I was mainly happy that the masked bully was being shamed on an international scale.

But visibility and fame had a downside. The more recogniz-

able I became, the more harassment I was subjected to by Israelis in all segments of society—soldiers, settlers, and ordinary
citizens who attacked me online. My family was accused of
staging such confrontations and faking it all to garner sympathy. Some of our Zionist critics even alleged that we were paid
actors in a make-believe industry they dubbed "Pallywood."
They ignorantly pointed to my blond hair and fair features as
proof that I couldn't possibly be a real Palestinian. They called
me "Shirley Temper," a name originally given to me by an Israeli right-wing blogger. On social media, some Israelis called
me a terrorist and incited others to find and kill me.

I wish I could say the harassment was just verbal, but it
wasn't. Anytime a soldier recognized me, they purposely did
something to make me suffer. After that viral confrontation,
Waed was arrested and jailed for ten months. Toward the beginning of his incarceration, my mom got a permit to visit
him in prison. Because I was a minor, I tagged along, assuming
I'd be allowed to see him, too. But as soon as we got to a
checkpoint near Jerusalem, Israeli soldiers boarded the bus
we were on and pointed me out. They pulled me off the bus
and told me I wasn't allowed to enter Israel. I was left by the
side of the road and had to find my way back home all by
myself. Other times, during the demonstrations in Nabi Saleh,
the soldiers would shout my name and say, "Look! It's Ahed
Tamimi! Shoot her!"

I was afraid, of course, but glad that all of our protests
were filmed. The camera was our weapon and our shield—
the most powerful way we could educate the world about the
barbarity of Israel's occupation. So long as their immoral
army continued firing its weapons at us, we'd continue aiming
ours right back at them.

———

ACTS OF TERRIBLE VIOLENCE by Israeli settlers in July 2015 awakened a new level of fear in my heart. Settlers firebombing Palestinian homes and murdering the children inside made global headlines, but those headlines could not capture how such incidents made each of us feel—the shiver of terror that ran down the spine of every Palestinian child the day they learned what had happened to the Dawabsheh family.

It happened in the middle of the night, while the young family of four was fast asleep in their home in the West Bank village of Duma. Two Israeli settlers threw a firebomb into their house, setting it ablaze. Flames engulfed the home and baby Ali, just eighteen months old, was killed. His father, Sa'ad, was so badly burned that he died a week later. That left the mother, Reham Dawabsheh, and her four-year-old son, Ahmed, as the only surviving members of the family. Reham, who was a teacher in an elementary school, suffered third-degree burns on 90 percent of her body—and after nearly five weeks on life support, she also died. And so, four-year-old Ahmed became the sole surviving member of his immediate household. Second- and third-degree burns covered 60 percent of his body. And this little boy was now motherless, fatherless, and brotherless.

I was haunted by the news of the Dawabsheh family. The level of cruelty needed to commit such a heinous crime against an innocent, sleeping family was beyond comprehension. The family was targeted simply because they were Palestinian. I couldn't fathom the level of hatred the attackers must harbor for us. But beyond that, I couldn't stop thinking about poor little Ahmed. How would he ever overcome this trauma? How could he grow up without his mother, father, and only sibling? Ahmed Dawabsheh could have been my brother Salam, I thought. Or Abu Yazan. The Dawabshehs could easily have been my own family. That could have been my home.

The Dawabshehs were not the first. Just one year earlier, we were shaken by a horror story of a settler attack against a sixteen-year-old Palestinian boy named Mohammed Abu Khdeir. Mohammed was walking to a mosque near his home in the East Jerusalem neighborhood of Shu'fat one night during Ramadan when he was suddenly grabbed and forced into a car. The three Israeli settlers who abducted him drove him to a forest in Jerusalem, where they beat him with a crowbar. They then forced him to drink gasoline, poured the remaining gasoline over him, and lit him on fire. When his mutilated body was found dumped in the forest hours later, it was burned beyond recognition. An autopsy later discovered soot in the lungs, suggesting that Mohammed was still alive and breathing when he was set on fire. He suffered beyond belief. It was later reported that his attackers were seeking revenge for the kidnapping and murder of three Israeli settler teens whose bodies had been found the day before. Still, nothing could justify the grisly torture and murder of Mohammed Abu Khdeir, who looked even smaller and younger than his age.

News of the Dawabsheh family and Mohammed Abu Khdeir attacks made me even more fearful of the Halamish settlers across the road from us. By then, they had already directly threatened me. After my confrontation with the soldiers went viral, some settlers published my address online, the name of my school, and the path I took to walk there every day. I had overcome my fear of physical violence from the army, but this new, unpredictable harassment by settlers like the ones across the road left me paralyzed with fear. For a long period, I was too scared even to leave my home. On my walks to school, I could feel my heart beating in my mouth. I constantly looked over my shoulder, scanning the area around me to see if I was being followed.

I know I wasn't alone in feeling no sense of safety—all the young people of my generation did, too. We were already under enough threat by the army, and now we weren't even safe on our streets or in our homes. Seeing other kids so heinously murdered left a deep and enduring imprint on our psyches.

Disenchanted with the leadership of the Palestinian Authority, which had failed to deliver anything meaningful or substantive throughout our lives, some chose to take matters into their own hands. They wanted to retaliate against the Israeli state that had caged them in, denied them freedom, and robbed them of their dreams and potential; the state that had built the illegal settlements on their stolen land and that enabled and protected the violence of settlers like the ones who had left Ahmed Dawabsheh a burned orphan and Mohammed Abu Khdeir a charred corpse.

By late 2015, some young Palestinians launched a spate of knife attacks and car rammings targeting Israeli soldiers and settlers in the West Bank and East Jerusalem. It wasn't an organized operation with any sort of central command but, rather, a series of individual attacks by Palestinian youth who felt they had nothing to lose and couldn't bottle up their anger any longer. Long-simmering tensions were boiling over.

I, too, was outraged by the murders of Mohammed Abu Khdeir and the Dawabsheh family. I wanted their killers to pay for what they'd done. But despite how compelled I felt to get justice for my fellow Palestinians, I knew that attacking a soldier or a settler with a knife wasn't the way to achieve it. Israeli soldiers would likely shoot and kill me on the spot, as they had so many others. On top of that, the army would demolish my family's home as punishment, a policy they carry out against Palestinians who attack Israelis, but never apply to the settlers who kill Palestinians in the same territory. In any case, I knew that seeking revenge with violence wouldn't help Mohammed Abu Khdeir or Ahmed Dawabsheh. While I believe that it's the right of all colonized, occupied, and oppressed people to stand up to their oppressors, I've always been convinced that staying alive and conveying our message through unarmed resistance is more powerful and strategic than our dying. I can't serve the Palestinian cause if I'm dead.

WHEN AHMED DAWABSHEH WAS in the hospital recovering from his severe burns, he drew a picture of himself standing outdoors, wearing a hat and holding an umbrella to protect his sensitive skin. But above him, he drew not one but two big, yellow suns, because he said he wanted the world to be extra sunny and bright. Ahmed explained this to Nadia Meer, a South African NGO worker who traveled to Palestine to work with children using art intervention techniques to help them cope with their trauma.

That's how Nadia arrived at Shamsaan, Arabic for "Two Suns," as the name for the initiative she created. She wanted to use art as a platform for dialogue and social change, while also highlighting the trauma children suffered as a result of growing up amid violent conflict. The name paid tribute to Ahmed and to so many other Palestinian children who dreamed of a brighter future despite their difficult circumstances.

Ahmed's drawing had a big impact on me. When I first saw it, I was touched by the innocence that remained within him even after witnessing the ugliest side of humanity. Despite the violence that had destroyed his family and childhood, he still seemed to want happiness for everyone. He wanted the world to have double the sunshine.

I got involved with Shamsaan when I, along with my cousin Janna, the budding reporter, was invited to travel to South Africa as part of a small delegation of Palestinian youth selected to take part in the Shamsaan Pals4Peace Tour. The tour would take us to various schools, universities, mosques, and community groups around South Africa, where we'd speak about our experiences growing up under occupation while learning about our hosts' lives and the history of their country. Part of our mission was also to launch and distribute the inaugural Shamsaan calendar to the audiences we addressed. The calendar profiled thirteen Palestinian children between the ages of five and sixteen, including Ahmed Dawabsheh, Janna, and me. Each child featured in the calendar had showcased triumph over adversity through artwork. Our drawings were accompanied by our portraits and life stories set against the articles of the UN Convention on the Rights of the Child.

I couldn't wait to visit South Africa. I knew a bit about the interconnectedness between the Palestinian and South African struggles, such as how Palestinians had stood in solidarity with their South African comrades in the anti-apartheid movement while Israel had closely aligned itself with the apartheid regime, even supplying them with weapons in defiance of a UN arms embargo. I admired the role Nelson Mandela had played in freeing his people from white-minority rule. He was a true revolutionary and a leader of great moral conviction who showed the world that his cause was just—words I could never use about Mahmoud Abbas, the president of the Palestinian Authority. Setting aside the fact that Abbas's democratic mandate as the president of the PA expired in 2009, I've never been a fan of his leadership. Abbas has devoted his career to pursuing fruitless negotiations with Israel that the majority of the Palestinian people reject. Rather than executing the will of his people, he has catered to Israel by effectively using his security forces as sub-contractors of the occupation. They coordinate with Israel to ensure that their occupation runs as efficiently and as afford-ably as possible. Under Abbas's rule, while many Palestinians don't have enough money to make ends meet, PA officials have gotten rich, their children boastfully showing off their flashy Mercedes and BMWs on joyrides around Ramallah. If that wasn't bad enough, Abbas truly lost all legitimacy in my eyes in 2012, when he gave an interview to an Israeli news channel. When asked if he wanted to live in Safed, the village of his birth, which was taken over by Israel in 1948, he re-plied, "It's my right to see it, but not to live there . . . Palestine now for me is the 1967 borders, with East Jerusalem as its capital." With that answer, Abbas betrayed every Palestinian, especially the refugees who hold sacred their right of return. For me, this offense was unforgivable.

Mandela, by contrast, was a legendary leader. In 1997, he even affirmed his people's support for Palestine in a famous speech, saying, "We know too well that our freedom is incom-plete without the freedom of the Palestinians." It spoke vol-umes that Mandela tied his people's freedom to ours. It showed the world that just as they ultimately opposed South African apartheid, they should also take action against Isra-el's.

Over the decades, Israel has imposed its own brand of apartheid on Palestinians. Whereas South African apartheid was based on white supremacy and the colonial subjugation of other ethnic groups, with the Black African majority at the very bottom, Israeli apartheid is characterized by Jew-ish Israeli supremacy over the native Palestinian population. There's even a similar hierarchy in our oppression. The '48 Palestinians, for example, who are second-class citizens in

Israel, have more rights and privileges than those of us living under military occupation and rule in the West Bank and Gaza, like my family. We have absolutely no political rights over the government that controls us, which is Israel's. And just as Black people under South African apartheid weren't allowed to vote for the government that controlled their lives, we don't get to vote in Israel's elections. Palestinian citizens of Israel do have voting rights, but they are subject to more than fifty discriminatory laws affecting everything from immigration and family reunification to land ownership rights, simply because they're not Jewish.

I discovered other parallels with South African apartheid. I learned that to control the movement of Black people, the apartheid regime had imposed a "pass" system forcing every Black person to carry an identity document indicating whether they had permission to be in a given area—and permission to be in any city was granted only to those employed by white farms, mines, or businesses. Black people who lacked a pass to be in a city could be summarily deported to a rural economic wasteland known as a Bantustan. Similarly, to control our movement as Palestinians in the occupied territories, Israel imposes color-coded identification cards and license plates, has installed an elaborate permit and checkpoint system, and has designated specific roads we're allowed to drive on—not to mention that Israel erected an apartheid wall. Israel's continuous annexation and expropriation of our land has divided and fragmented the little that remains of Palestinian territory. What's left resembles South Africa's Bantustans, the pockets of land onto which Black farmers were forced as their own property was taken from them—land dispossession that coerced them into serving as cheap labor for white-owned mines, farms, and factories. The South African regime later gave these territories fake "independence," claiming that all Black people were "citizens" of these fake "countries," as a way of justifying denying democratic rights to the Black majority.

Our delegation spent over a month in South Africa, and with each stop along our tour, I learned more about the country's painful past. What struck me most was how, despite apartheid's officially ending in 1994, its legacy endured. The system of white-minority rule had clearly left the country's Black majority poor and powerless. Even when apartheid ended, the country's wealth did not return to its original residents. My heart broke as I witnessed Black South Africans' living conditions—overcrowded slums called townships, warrens of dilapidated tin-roof shacks with sewage running in the streets and one shared bathroom per every seven homes. I saw people lying in the streets looking like they were dying of hunger. The level of abject poverty shocked me. These were sights I'd never seen before, not even in the most impoverished Palestinian refugee camps.

Right next to some of the townships were affluent white suburbs overflowing with greenery and dotted with huge, newly built homes. Some resembled the splendid palaces I'd seen only in Disney movies. This jarring contrast reminded me of our humble Palestinian villages, like Nabi Saleh, against the modern, immaculate-looking Israeli settlements sitting neatly on hilltops adjacent to them. I realized then that just as the work didn't end when apartheid was over in South Africa, the inevitable end of Israel's occupation would not solve all our problems as a Palestinian society.

One of the most memorable moments of the trip was our visit to the Hector Pieterson Memorial and Museum in Soweto. Soweto, a well-known township in Johannesburg, was the site of a famous student-led uprising that played a pivotal role in the anti-apartheid struggle. On June 16, 1976, the students there organized a huge demonstration against an apartheid government decree that mandated they learn Afrikaans, the language of their oppressors, in school. Thousands of students set out to march peacefully in protest of the directive, but along the way, they were confronted by a brutal police crackdown. Heavily armed officers fired at them with tear gas and, later, live ammunition.

Hector Pieterson, a thirteen-year-old Black boy, was the first child to be killed by police on that fateful day. A photographer captured what would quickly become an iconic image: Hector being carried in the arms of another young man, his body hanging limp as he bleeds to death, his older sister running alongside them. The violence seen that day marked a turning point, one that made clear that apartheid was intolerable and that the Black population would never accept life on their knees. It ignited a widespread revolt that began in Soweto and later spread across the entire country. The haunting photograph of Hector became a symbol of the Soweto Uprising.

Learning about what had happened in Soweto moved me profoundly. I was inspired by the pivotal role the students had played in one of the most important chapters in the country's history. The violence they encountered in the process of claiming their rights was all too familiar to me. Still, it gave me hope. Janna was likewise affected. Knowing that the photograph of Hector Pieterson helped to harden international opinion against the apartheid regime reaffirmed her belief in the power of journalism as a weapon against oppression. I also believed this, but it saddened me to think of the multitude of images of Palestinian children injured or murdered at the hands of Israeli forces and settlers that already existed.

As we toured the country and spoke to different community groups, schools, and local organizations about our experiences as Palestinian children living under occupation, one thing really surprised me: Everywhere we went, the South Africans we met, from whatever background, saw us as victims. They kept offering to give us money to take to our people back home. Many wept as we spoke. This bothered me. Yes, our lives were exceptionally challenging, but I've never wanted to be seen through the lens of pity, and I certainly hadn't traveled there to solicit it. Plus, why would they be offering us money when some of their fellow countrymen, like the ones in the townships, were clearly in dire need of aid?

Eventually, I couldn't contain my frustration any longer. The next stop on our tour was the screening of a documentary on Nabi Saleh's struggle against Israeli occupation. As the film ended and the lights came back on, I noticed that many members of the audience once again had tears in their eyes. That's when I stood up and decided to address the situation head-on.

"Thank you for your tears," I began. "But I don't want your sadness. Nor do I want your money. Please save that for the people in your own country who need it. My people have dignity and don't want your pity. We're not the victims. The brainwashed Israeli soldier who carries his rifle and shoots with no humanity—he's the real victim. We want you to see us as the freedom fighters we are, so that you can support us the right way." I went on to explain how important it was for them to show their solidarity by boycotting Israel politically, economically, and culturally. After all, they knew more than anyone the critical role global boycotts had played in ultimately ending apartheid in their own country.

Before our trip ended, we rode a cableway to the top of Cape Town's iconic Table Mountain. The view from the summit overlooking the sprawling city and the vast Atlantic

Ocean was breathtaking. As I gazed down, I reflected on everything I knew the country had gone through and all the losses it had incurred to achieve freedom from apartheid. My visit there—all the people I had met and the things I had learned—renewed my hope that Palestine, too, would one day be free.

That day, we planted an olive tree at the top of the mountain, as a symbol of hope and peace and a gesture of our solidarity with the people of South Africa. I found it beautiful to leave part of our heritage and identity in another land in such a meaningful and enduring way. We'd soon be returning home, but future visitors might inquire how a random olive tree ended up at the top of Table Mountain, and they could now be told that it was planted by Palestinian children who had traveled from afar to be there. It solidified our connection to each other.

Just a few months earlier, in Ramallah, a twenty-foot-tall bronze statue of Nelson Mandela raising his right fist had been erected in a square named after the titan, a donation from the city of Johannesburg. Each time I pass by it, I'm reminded of our shared humanity and common principles. If he were alive today, Mandela would reaffirm that our struggles are indeed incomplete. As I brushed the soil from my hands after planting the olive tree atop Table Mountain, I vowed to play whatever part I could to advance them.

BY 2017, THE PRICE we paid for our resistance movement in blood, tears, arrests, and lives became too high to justify our continuing to hold our regular march. At that point, twenty-three young men from the village were locked up in Israeli prisons. Eighteen others had been shot by live bullets, mostly in the legs, rendering them unable to walk. Three people had been killed, and considering the Israeli military's escalation of the violence, it was inevitable that we'd see an additional martyr soon. The army had already started using a new kind of tear gas, one that could reach very far distances. As soon as the march began, they'd target us with it. Even though we weren't yet close to them, they'd fire directly at us from afar, including right into our homes. Getting down to the entrance of the village or main road became impossible. And so, with this new impediment, and with a considerable portion of the movement either arrested, immobile, or dead, we stopped the weekly march.

But we didn't stop demonstrating altogether. We still went out and protested in the village on major occasions, like when Israel attacked Gaza in yet another brutal air bombardment, or when Palestinian prisoners were carrying out a hunger strike. We never stopped resisting the occupation. Often, we traveled to other Palestinian villages and cities in the West Bank, like Nil'in, Kafr Qaddum, and Bethlehem, and joined the protests there.

Even though our demonstrations were less frequent, the soldiers didn't pull back on their constant antagonism. At some point every day, they'd arbitrarily erect a checkpoint at the entrance to the village, holding up for hours any car trying to enter or leave. They also still carried out raids and arrests at their whims. Like other Palestinians, we continued to be humiliated, subjugated, and terrorized on our own land.

THE SLAP

THE ELECTION OF Donald Trump as president of the United States was one of the worst things to happen to the Palestinian people in recent years. The United States had long tried to sell itself as an honest broker of peace between the Israelis and the Palestinians, though anyone even remotely paying attention knew this was a farce. We had decades of proof that the United States would always favor Israel's interests over ours. This much was evident in how America has repeatedly used its veto power at the United Nations to protect Israel from having to comply with various UN and human rights resolutions; in how it has turned a blind eye to Israel's continued illegal settlement construction despite such construction's being in violation of long-standing U.S. policy; and, perhaps most notably, in how it has demonstrated its unwavering support for Israel by consistently giving the country more military aid than it has ever provided to anyone else—a trend that shows no sign of ending anytime soon. Before leaving office, President Barack Obama signed a Memorandum of Understanding with Israel that included a record $38 billion to provide the country with military assistance over a ten-year period. It guaranteed a steady flow of American-funded and -manufactured weapons—which Israel uses, among other applications, to kill us.

But whereas previous U.S. administrations at least pretended to possess some degree of neutrality, Trump burst onto the scene fully embracing Israel's right-wing policies and appointing Zionists to key positions. He tapped his bankruptcy lawyer, David Friedman, as his ambassador to Israel. Friedman threatened the International Criminal Court over a war crimes investigation into Israel and declared that the illegal settlements did not violate international law. Trump's own son-in-law and senior adviser, Jared Kushner, was a personal friend of then–Prime Minister Benjamin Netanyahu and even had financial ties to the illegal settlements. And this was the man Trump had tasked with leading the "peace process."

With people like Friedman and Kushner guiding Trump, instead of getting an inch closer to peace, we were dealt repeated blows. For example, the Trump administration cruelly cut virtually all humanitarian aid to Palestinians, including funding for Palestinian hospitals and for the UN Relief and Works Agency for Palestine Refugees in the Near East, to which the United States was the largest donor. UNRWA was set up after Israel's creation in 1948 to help Palestinian refugees and had served as a lifeline to millions of Palestinians ever since.

But the true moment of reckoning came on December 6, 2017, when Trump announced plans to move the U.S. embassy from Tel Aviv to Jerusalem, thus recognizing the holy city as Israel's capital. This was a profound betrayal of Palestinians and a significant break from previous U.S. administrations, which had considered, yet put off, making such a bold move.

In the heart of every Palestinian, Jerusalem has always been the eternal capital of Palestine. Palestinian officials have repeatedly sat at the negotiating table with the goal of making East Jerusalem, currently illegally occupied by Israel, the capital of a future Palestinian state. Most countries, including the United States, had declined to recognize the city's status and borders until a final peace deal could be reached. So, when Trump claimed that moving the embassy was "a long-overdue step to advance the peace process and to work towards a lasting agreement," it wasn't just a slap in the face to us; it was an outright lie.

With this seismic policy shift, Trump handed Netanyahu and Israel's right wing the biggest gift ever—and sparked a wave of protests all over Palestine and in various other Arab and Muslim countries. Day after day, protesters in the West Bank and Gaza unleashed their rage in the streets, burning Israeli and American flags and stomping on posters of Trump's face.

I was in the first semester of my *tawjihi* year in high school. I had finally gotten back on track as a diligent student; I knew my future rested on the scores I'd receive on my matriculation exams at the end of the school year. They determined what university, what major, and ultimately what career trajectory I'd be able to pursue. *Tawjihi* is one of the most stressful years in the life of a Palestinian student, as the stakes are extremely high. I set a goal to study harder than I ever had in my life. Each time I felt overwhelmed, I'd picture myself dressed in the graduation cap and gown at the end of the year, a kuffiyeh draped around my shoulders, smiling proudly with my diploma in hand. But even with my nose constantly in the books, I still felt a sense of duty to take part in the demonstrations. So, every day after school, while they were still taking place, I did just that.

By then, I was attending an all-girls school in Ramallah, the administrative and economic hub of the West Bank, because the only school we had in Nabi Saleh stopped at the tenth grade. Logistically, it was a pain to get to my new school: I never knew when the army would arbitrarily close the village or erect a checkpoint, holding everyone up for hours.

Some mornings, I was forced to sit in a shared commuter minibus for hours, held up in gridlocked traffic, the easing of which depended solely on the soldiers' whims. The mood inside the minibus was always tense and angry.

"Goddamn this army!" a passenger would curse. "How am I supposed to make money when I can't even get to my store on time to open it?"

"I'm sure I'm going to get fired this time," another fretted.

I'd glance constantly at my phone to check the time, wondering how much of the lesson I was already missing and how far behind I'd fall as a result. Some days, we were held up so long that I didn't make it to school at all. Occasionally, I'd sleep at one of my aunts' houses in Ramallah just to ensure I wouldn't miss another day.

My school was within walking distance of Beit El, a popular flashpoint for protests and clashes with the army. Beit El has both strategic and symbolic importance. It is the site of an Israeli settlement and a military base, and headquarters for the Israeli Civil Administration—a name that sounds innocuous, but is held by the governing body administering the occupation. The Civil Administration is responsible for issuing travel permits to Palestinians in the West Bank and Gaza who want to go to Israel, work permits for Palestinians who obtain jobs inside Israel, and construction or demolition permits in Israeli settlements and on Palestinian land that falls in Area C. Beit El is surrounded by several schools and isn't too far from Birzeit University, which often means that once classes get out, students flock there to protest.

Trump's embassy announcement came during our winter semester final exams. The minute we finished our last exam of the day, we'd head out to the schoolyard and wait for everyone to gather. After greeting one another, we'd talk about the exam and recap the questions that had most stumped us.

Some of the girls would then go home, but the rest of us would set out for the protests in Beit El.

We had a mission.

Our first stop was at a nearby mechanic's shop, to pick up the old car tires the mechanic planned to throw out. The tires were heavy, so we'd take turns rolling them to the site of the protest, where we'd hand them off to our male peers and then turn around to make a second trip for the rest. Our hands and clothes would turn black in the process, but it was worth it. Tires served several important functions in the demonstrations. Young Palestinian men would arrange them strategically in the middle of the street to form a physical barrier and prevent the army jeeps from crossing over to our side. Then they'd light them on fire to create a thick, dark cloud of smoke that would block the soldiers from being able to see us well. The columns of smoke rising from the tires also absorbed some of the tear gas the soldiers would inevitably fire at us, mitigating its suffocating effects.

Even though most of us didn't know one another, we felt a sense of urgency and unity in partaking in this rebellion. We kept our faces wrapped in kuffiyehs as a safety precaution, to avoid being identifiable to the Israeli army and, in many cases, to our parents. But our anonymity to one another didn't matter. We each had a part to play in our generation's uprising against the apartheid and injustice that had deprived us of even a single day of freedom in our lives. We hadn't inherited any victories in the fight against Israel, only the defeats our parents and their parents had suffered. Our role was to challenge those defeats, like the ones incurred trying to pursue a two-state solution. We wouldn't accept settling for a mere fraction of our own land, and we refused to keep our anger bottled up.

It didn't matter that my girlfriends and I couldn't throw

stones very far. If one of us had a slingshot, we used it. Otherwise, our significant contribution to these demonstrations was delivering the tires, because once they were ignited, the army came and the confrontation officially started.

Everyone tried to advance as far as they could, to get as close to the soldiers as possible to be able to hit them with stones, but once they opened fire or started to chase us, we would all have to retreat. One of the strategic benefits of Beit El is that it's spread out over a large open area, making it easier for us to escape if the soldiers moved in to surround us.

An unspoken rule at these clashes was that the Palestinian guys weren't allowed to wear long shirts, and whatever shirts they wore had to be tucked into their pants. They did this to distinguish themselves from the undercover Israeli agents, or *mista'rabeen*, who dressed in plainclothes to disguise themselves as Palestinians in order to ambush and arrest us. They'd even wear kuffiyehs to try to fully assimilate with us. What often gave them away, though, was that they pulled their shirts down over their waistbands, to conceal the guns they'd hidden there. Anytime we saw men walking together with untucked shirts, we became extra wary—we knew they were likely undercover soldiers. So, by tucking their shirts in, the Palestinian youth signaled to everyone else that they were indeed among us.

Often, in between throwing stones, the guys would do things just to get a rise out of the soldiers, like sing and clap and dance the *dabkeh*. They had mastered such antics to spite the soldiers, all while unintentionally entertaining the rest of us. When a soldier fired a tear gas canister, one of the guys might wait for it to land on the ground and then run over and place a bucket over it to contain the smoke. He'd then take a seat on the bucket, cross one leg over the other, and stare at the soldiers with a big smile on his face. Once he stood and picked up the bucket, the tear gas would be fully extinguished. It was a brilliantly hilarious little victory.

But it wasn't all fun and games. At points, it felt like a full-on war zone. The bangs and blasts from soldiers' weapons made me shudder. Ambulance sirens blared regularly. Things got scarier and even more violent when the army began firing live rounds at everyone. But even as that was happening, we were overcome with an unnatural brand of courage. Everyone was brave, worrying more about the people surrounding them than about themselves. If I saw a guy without a face covering, I'd run over and give him my kuffiyeh, to help keep him anonymous. I always kept a spare one in my backpack for moments like these. The last thing any of us wanted was for someone to get arrested, which did happen, though we carried on regardless. We had a goal to achieve and a message to convey. The goal was to defend our land, and the message was that we rejected the occupation and we rejected the United States' role in advancing only Israel's interests.

Growing up, I'd heard that Israel's founders said of the Palestinians they forced from their homes to create their state, "The old will die and the young will forget." But my generation is living proof of the contrary. The resistance of our grandparents lives on through us, and in truth, we perhaps have even more patriotism and energy than our elders. Even during a stressful period of school exams, we still felt compelled to go out and protest. I thought of the schoolchildren in Soweto and the instrumental role they played in advancing the anti-apartheid movement. Their example fueled the fire within me to keep fighting. It filled me with hope that my generation would be the one to finally end the occupation and hand freedom over to the generation after us.

One thing consistently got under my skin, though. As we shut down the streets in the Beit El area with our acts of civil disobedience, we were often rebuked by fellow Palestinians. Frustrated by the inconvenience of getting unexpectedly stuck in traffic, they'd curse at us and tell us that if we wanted to protest, we should do it somewhere farther away, where we wouldn't interfere with people's everyday lives. It was a depressing reminder that my generation wasn't suffering only from the occupation, but also from our own countrymen, many of whom seemed resigned to the status quo. Rather than supporting the youth who were choking on tear gas and getting shot at for defending their homeland, they'd cuss us out, not wanting to be delayed even the slightest bit. My message to those people is that if you don't love Palestine and aren't willing to fight for her, rather than sabotaging our struggle for freedom, you should leave.

THE BACKLASH TO TRUMP'S embassy announcement showed no signs of dying down, and the collective anger spilled over into the weekend. On Friday, December 15, as my relatives in Nabi Saleh carried on the demonstrations against Israel's army, a series of events transpired that would forever alter the course of my life. It was my day off from school, and I had sequestered myself in my bedroom to try to cram in as much studying as possible ahead of my upcoming English exam. I tried as hard as I could to drown out the sounds of the army firing their weapons at the youth throwing stones outside, but once I heard soldiers right outside my bedroom window, I was too provoked and distracted to get anything done. Just being a *tawjihi* student is enough to keep anyone constantly on edge. But to have soldiers right outside your room, potentially firing at your brothers or cousins on top of that, was enough to set anyone off, and it ruled out any possibility of my being productive that day. I tossed my books aside and went out to see what was happening.

The soldiers were shooting at some of the children on my street. They then moved inside the nearby home of one of our elders, a woman who had suffered a stroke years before. I ran over to the house with a few adults and other children and began pushing the soldiers away. What justification did they have, first, to fire at children and, then, to invade the home of a sick and helpless old woman?

We successfully fought off the soldiers, and they repositioned themselves at the top of the hill, near my house. A handful of them stood behind the wall that encircled our house and began firing tear gas at the youth in the street. One young man picked up a canister that had landed near his feet and hurled it back in the direction of the soldiers. A soldier then picked it up and threw it back. This time it landed near my house, close to where I was standing. I was outraged that the soldiers would endanger us all, and with so many young children around. So, I ran over, picked up the canister, and tossed it right back at them. By the time I picked it up, it had already exploded and was emitting gas; it was also extremely hot, and I burned my palm. I raced inside to treat my burned hand and put a glove over it to protect it.

While I was at home tending to my burned hand, I didn't realize what was happening outside, but what I would soon learn would devastate me. A soldier had just shot my fifteen-year-old cousin Mohammad in the head at close range with a rubber-coated steel bullet. Mohammad had gone into an empty villa not far from our house to see if the soldiers who had earlier positioned themselves there were gone. He climbed the stone wall surrounding the villa and, as soon as he got up to the top, looked down below. A soldier was aiming his rifle up at him. That was the last thing Mohammad saw before being shot and falling ten feet to the ground. He was unconscious and unlikely to survive the critical wound.

After she received a phone call from one of my uncles, my mom relayed the news to me: Mohammad was being rushed to the hospital, but we should prepare for the worst. I broke down in tears when she told me what had happened—and then I panicked about how I'd break the news to Abu Yazan. He and Mohammad were beyond best friends—they were practically twins, two peas in a pod, inseparable from the time they learned to crawl. Abu Yazan and Mohammad spent their every waking hour together, so much so that Mohammad practically lived at our house. He'd enter without knocking and casually plop himself on the sofa to watch television as if he were in his own home. When he and Abu Yazan weren't watching TV, the duo was guaranteed to be out in the village's hills exploring nature, a passion they both shared. They loved birds and insects and snakes and would even wake up at 6 A.M. on their days off to set out on their expeditions. There wasn't an inch of the hills that had gone unexplored— literally no stone left unturned. The two boys relished picking up rocks and discovering what creatures lived beneath them, and they found climbing trees in search of bird's nests thrilling. Each evening, they'd return home and excitedly report back to me the details of their discoveries, sometimes even bringing back one of them and sticking it in my face.

How was I now supposed to tell Abu Yazan that his favorite person in the world might die? I began praying to God to somehow miraculously allow my younger cousin to survive.

I was still processing the news that Mohammad was on the brink of death when I heard soldiers moving around the exterior of my house again. Through the window, I saw two of them hop over the wall surrounding our home. I immediately ran outside, to chase after them and yell for them to get off our property. My mother, who was still too traumatized by her brother's death to use a camcorder again, grabbed her cellphone and began using Facebook Live to stream it all from the front door of the house. She didn't have very many followers on Facebook, but that didn't matter to her. She still felt an obligation to document what was happening in our village in whatever small way she could.

The two soldiers took a position behind the wall in our front yard, right by the driveway. Enraged by what had just happened to Mohammad, and furious at the sight of them on my property, I approached them and started shouting at them to leave.

"Get out of here!" I yelled. "Just leave! Leave! Leave!"

They didn't budge.

I pushed one of them with my gloved burned hand. My cousin Nour joined me and took out her own cellphone to film. I continued to yell at the soldiers to leave and tried pushing them away. The soldier closest to me flung his arm out to swat me away, which angered me even more.

"Don't touch me!" I screamed, and I began to kick and hit him.

He was fully armed, and I came up only to his shoulders, but I didn't care. My aunt, who is even shorter than I am, inserted herself in between us to try to push him away and de-escalate the situation.

"Just get out of here," she said, trying to reason with the two soldiers as she pushed them toward the street. "Just leave."

They wouldn't budge, so I continued to hit them both.

Unless you've experienced a foreign army occupying your land, imprisoning your parents, killing your loved ones, and shooting you and virtually everyone you're related to, you'll have a hard time understanding the rage with which I was overcome—seeing the entitlement of these soldiers as they walked around our property like they owned it.

As soon as the soldiers finally took a few steps toward the street, my aunt, Nour, Salam, Abu Yazan, and I linked arms to form a human chain and keep them off our property. We remained positioned like this until we'd ensured they were off our turf.

I didn't think anything of the confrontation at the time. It was merely the latest in a series of countless occasions on which I had fought Israeli soldiers to repel them from our village. Scenes like this had played out weekly for years, after all.

After sunset, as soon as the clashes died down and the soldiers finally left Nabi Saleh, we all drove to the hospital in Ramallah, where Mohammad was being treated. The anxiety over the likelihood of having another martyr—and the youngest one at that—kept everyone silent on the car ride there.

Mohammad was still undergoing surgery when we arrived. Dozens of my relatives packed into the waiting room, crying, praying, and cursing his fate. Mohammad's mother wailed loudly, knowing full well that a bullet in his head meant she'd likely be burying her son soon. His sisters were likewise distraught. Abu Yazan wept in a way I had never seen. Everyone was on edge.

After a six-hour operation, one of the doctors notified us that Mohammad had miraculously survived. The bullet was lodged a mere centimeter away from his brain. Any closer, and he would surely have died. The doctor said that he had suffered intracranial bleeding. They had had to remove part of his shattered skull, and his face was badly disfigured. He now had only half a skull. But he was alive, despite all the odds.

Everyone breathed a collective sigh of relief, but we were

still nervous, knowing he wasn't out of the woods yet. We stayed at the hospital until shortly after 3 A.M. and then went home to try to sleep a bit before returning shortly after sunrise. Abu Yazan refused to go home with us, insisting on remaining close to his best friend. By midafternoon, a full twenty-four hours after he arrived at the hospital, Mohammad began to regain consciousness while still in the intensive care unit. A path toward recovery was looking more likely. Many of us cried out of gratitude and sheer relief.

All the time I spent in the hospital took away from my ability to study for my English exam. I fumbled my way through the first of two days of the exam, disappointed that I hadn't prepared as well as I had hoped to. Once again, the occupation had found a way to interrupt my studies and derail my life goals. After the exam was over, my classmates and I headed to the mechanic's shop again, to get more tires to take to the protests in Beit El. I was wearing a beige coat over my school uniform, and it turned progressively blacker each time I rolled one of the tires forward.

The clashes were full of energy, and it seemed that more people had shown up than on previous days. Many defiantly waved the Palestinian flag and sang nationalist songs. The tires were ablaze, and thick, dark smoke filled the sky. The soldiers aimed their weapons from the other side of the smoke and fired tear gas and rubber-coated steel bullets at us. The young men ran up to the tires and hurled stones above the smoke barrier at the soldiers, who responded by advancing toward us and firing from an even closer distance. I felt that the situation was getting too dangerous, and I told my cousin Lana, who was standing beside me, that we should move back. She turned around to start running away from the soldiers, but then, suddenly, she stopped and warned, "Ahed, your dad! Your dad is here!"

Unbeknownst to me, my dad was also at the protest, standing just ten feet away from us. I never told my parents that I had been going to the protests at Beit El. In fact, before the Beit El protests, I had never gone to a demonstration without them. I panicked, thinking of how my father might react at seeing me there unsupervised.

"Let's get out of here!" I told Lana, grabbing her hand. We ran a few feet forward, away from my dad and in the direction of the soldiers firing right at us, before I realized the stupidity of what I was doing. But it was my knee-jerk reaction. In that chaotic atmosphere, I was simultaneously scared of the soldiers shooting at us *and* scared of my dad, who believed I should be spending all my time studying. I stopped in my tracks, figuring I might as well face the music.

I walked up to my father. "Hi, Baba!" I sang cheerfully.

"What are you doing here?" he asked, genuinely surprised to see me.

"Oh, you know, we were going home from school and saw this was happening, so we just walked over to watch," I lied. Meanwhile, my once-beige coat was entirely black from the tires, as were my hands and my kuffiyeh. I knew I wasn't fooling him by saying I was there only as a spectator.

"Do you want to go home now?" he asked.

"I'd like to stay just a bit longer," I said. With no parents around, Lana, Marah, and I were typically the last girls to leave. We liked staying until the very end.

"Okay. But don't get too close," he warned. "Stay as far back as you can." He knew I tended to get as close to the action as possible.

I returned to where Lana, Marah, and some of my school friends were standing observing the clashes. We had our eye on three men standing nearby who looked suspicious and out of place. They were wearing long shirts and long jackets and we suspected they were undercover soldiers. Once the uniformed soldiers moved in closer to us, there was no trace of these men anymore.

Then, suddenly, a jeep drove through the crowd and the same three men we had been watching jumped out and began chasing us. I sprinted as fast as I could, but at one point, I dropped my cellphone and quickly ran back to get it. That's when I saw a boy my age trip and fall while trying to escape. The undercover soldiers managed to tackle him to the ground. They used their weapons to beat him relentlessly.

"They got Ahmed Daraghme!" I heard one of the boy's friends shout.

That's how I learned his name. I felt terrible watching him get pulverized, knowing there was nothing I could do to help him. All he was doing was throwing stones to resist the occupation oppressing him, and now he'd end up in jail for God knew how long. More stolen youth. Another life cut short.

Shortly after Ahmed's arrest, my dad called me over and said it was time to go home. He insisted we first stop by the house of one of his friends who lived nearby, so I could wash the black rubber stains from my hands and not look like such a disaster when my mom saw me.

AFTER SHOWERING AND CHANGING my clothes at home, I headed down the street to Marah's house, where my parents were spending the evening with Ammo Naji and Khalto Bushra. My mom and Khalto Bushra worked busily in the kitchen preparing dinner. This evening, they were making *karshaat*, which are cooked sheep stomachs stuffed with rice, diced meat, and pine nuts. It's an intricate meal that involves thoroughly cleaning out the stomachs before stuffing them. They're then sewn shut with a needle and thread and boiled.

While I appreciate the labor that goes into making *karshaat*, I've always stopped short of eating them. The reality is they made *my* stomach turn. Still, I might have reconsidered had I known this would be my last chance to have a home-cooked meal in a while.

I was stressed about the second part of my English exam, which I would take the next day, and knew I should be studying. I told myself I'd hang out in the living room for a bit with Waed, Bisan, and Anan. A recent favorite pastime of ours was to broadcast live on Instagram, which was a fairly new feature at that point. My page was public, with six thousand followers, making it our preferred account, the one that would get the most engagement.

Our broadcasts typically took the form of a lighthearted question-and-answer forum. Twenty people tuned in to our shenanigans on this particular night. We talked about school and studying and cracked jokes about one another. Our viewers replied by typing more questions and sending heart or laughter emojis—engagement that naturally egged us on. We were having a blast for about thirty minutes when my dad barged into the room. It took only one look at his face to know that he was angry.

"Ahed, what are you doing?" he chided. "Don't you have an exam tomorrow?"

"I do," I replied meekly, looking down.

"Well, then, why are you playing around instead of studying? Is this how *tawjihi* students who want to succeed spend their time?"

I froze and kept my eyes locked on the floor. My dad rarely scolded me, but when he did, it was serious.

He then directed his ire at Waed. "You're her older brother, and you're supposed to look out for her! You know how high the stakes are during *tawjihi*. How could you let her waste this precious time when she should be studying?"

Waed had no response, either. My dad stormed off and went home.

I stuck around for another hour, pretending to study with Marah, but really just trying to buy time for my father to cool off before I went home. When I finally mustered the courage to leave, I returned to my house and slowly opened the front door. Baba was sitting on the sofa, reading something on his phone with intense concentration. Hoping he wouldn't notice me, I tiptoed to my bedroom, avoiding making eye contact with him. I was almost in the clear when he called out my name.

"Ahed," he said, in a tone more serious than I was used to hearing from him.

Great, I thought. *I'm about to get an epic scolding or, worse, be grounded.*

"Come here," he said, still fixated on his phone's screen as he patted the sofa cushion next to him.

I reluctantly obliged, bracing myself for a continuation of his lecture.

"The Israeli press has been circulating the Facebook video of you hitting that soldier. It's really spreading. They're saying you insulted Israel's honor. Some are even inciting violence against you and saying you need to be punished for humiliating their army like this."

"Oh . . ." I replied.

"This has really caused an uproar," he continued. Then he paused and drew in a deep breath. "I think they might arrest you."

It feels silly to admit now, but in that instant, my initial reaction was one of sheer relief: I had dodged the potential bullet of my father grounding me. I mean, of course I didn't want to go to prison, but in that second, I was thanking God I wasn't in trouble with my father anymore.

Prior to that moment, I had no idea what a stir the video had caused. I had been too busy studying, spending time at the hospital, or protesting at Beit El to pay any close attention to the news. I had received a few messages about the video when I was at the hospital awaiting news of Mohammad's condition, and I understood that it had circulated a bit, but not in a significant way. It didn't feel like a big deal. After all, this was by no means the first video capturing me confronting Israeli soldiers. At that point, plenty of them from over the years had spread way more intensely than this one. I didn't think my latest altercation with Israeli soldiers was anything special or unique.

But my dad's warning left me uneasy. In my gut, I sensed something major was about to unfold. I headed to my bedroom to collect my thoughts. A few minutes later, I opened up Instagram and messaged Marah.

"I think I might get arrested tonight," I wrote.

"What?! Don't be silly," she insisted in a DM. "What would they want with you anyway?"

I wanted to believe her, but I knew I should play it safe and take every precaution in case they came to arrest me in the middle of the night. Instead of pajamas, I slept in jeans, socks, and a long-sleeve shirt. I placed my burgundy winter coat and kuffiyeh neatly beside my bed and laid out my sneakers, just in case I had to quickly mobilize. Knowing that the soldiers would confiscate my phone if they arrested me, I deleted all my messages—texts, Instagram, DMs, everything. It was the responsible thing to do, to protect my friends. I had plenty of texts from them, messages like "Ahed, there are protests today, and we're going" or "Make sure to bring a kuffiyeh with you. I lost mine." These messages incriminated them, and the last thing I wanted to do was put them at risk of getting arrested, too. After taking these precautions, I set my alarm to 3 A.M., so I could wake up and study for a few hours before school. After all, I still had an English exam to take. I placed my book on the bedside table and slid beneath the covers.

I dozed off, but not deeply. My mind was racing too fast with fears of an imminent arrest to allow me to slip into any sort of restful slumber. A few hours later, with the sky still dark, I woke to the sound of my mom hurriedly opening my bedroom door. Her voice was more panicked than usual.

"Ahed, wake up. The army is at the door. Maybe they're here for Waed."

In my groggy state of half-awakeness, this theory made sense. Waed had been wanted by the army for throwing stones and hadn't been sleeping at home for the past year, to evade arrest. And for good reason: Soldiers came to our house in the middle of the night nearly twice a week asking for him. That's why even though my father had warned me, and even though I had prepared myself for the worst, in that moment, I assumed they had come to arrest my brother. I was accustomed to waking up to army raids of our home in the middle of the night. I wasn't accustomed to their coming for me.

I hid my cellphone beneath my shirt and made my way to the living room—the usual night raid drill. I joined Abu Yazan and Salam, who were still half asleep, on the sofa. We watched as soldiers poured into our house. One by one, they confiscated my parents' and brothers' cellphones. This guaranteed that no one could film the raid. An officer who had threatened to arrest me on previous occasions when he saw me in the village was also there.

"What do you want? Why are you here?" my mom shouted at him.

"We're here to take Ahed," he said.

Me.

My heart stopped for a second. I had grown up internalizing the idea that it wasn't a matter of *if* I'd be arrested by the Israeli army, but *when*. And that when was now. But strangely, I wasn't afraid. It's hard to explain the sudden strength that overpowered me in that instant. Perhaps it was the years of anticipation of this moment that had eliminated any fear in me. Instead, this felt like a challenge—yet another standoff between me and this foreign occupying army. I wanted to laugh in the officer's face.

"Where's your arrest warrant? Show us your arrest warrant!" my mom demanded.

"There is none," the officer said.

This wasn't surprising. There's never an arrest warrant.

"She needs to go to her room and get properly dressed," my dad insisted.

He followed me as I started walking toward my bedroom, but the soldiers grabbed him by his shoulders and stopped him. They sent three female soldiers into my room with me instead. Baba clutched my bedroom door, still trying to force his way in, but the soldiers pulled him back. One of the female soldiers now inside my bedroom with me shut the door. I put on my sneakers and started to reach for my jacket when the other female soldier grabbed me by my arms from behind and slammed me against the closet door. She forced my hands behind my back and shoved my head against the wooden door. Then she began patting me down from head to toe.

Crap, I thought as she discovered my phone, which I had tucked underneath my shirt, against my chest. She immediately seized it. When the body search was over, she pulled me by my arm toward the door, but I stopped in my tracks.

"I'm not leaving until I put on my jacket," I insisted. She

loosened her grip on my arm, and I put on my jacket and then grabbed my kuffiyeh and wrapped it around my neck like a scarf.

She dragged me by my jacket, leading me outside my bedroom, through the living room, and toward the front door. At this point, the entire house was flooded with soldiers. All I could see in every direction were green helmets. You'd have thought this was the home of a terrorist with explosives who was planning a major attack, not that of a five-foot-tall sixteen-year-old girl who hit a soldier with her bare hands in her own front yard.

The soldier escorting me stopped me at the top of our front stairs and handcuffed my wrists tightly in front of me. The metal cuffs dug so deeply into my wrists that I couldn't move my hands.

As she pushed me outside, it hit me: It was the middle of the night, and I was in the custody of the Israeli army. I had no idea where they would take me or what they would do with me. Were they going to hurt me, kill me, or leave me stranded in some remote location in the dead of night? This military occupation had proven itself to be unpredictable and cruel, and various terrifying scenarios began flashing through my mind—including the prospect of never seeing my family again.

My parents stood at the front door looking helplessly on as their only daughter was whisked away by the foreign army that had brutalized us for the last decade. Salam and Abu Yazan stood in front of them, embracing each other as tears welled in their eyes. I could see how terrified they were. I wanted so badly to hug them and assure them that everything would be okay, that I'd be just fine. While they were growing up, I had always given them that comfort when one of our parents was arrested, but now I simply couldn't. My chest tightened, but I stopped myself from crying. I had to be strong for them.

"I want to say a proper goodbye to my family," I told the soldier who had handcuffed me. She ignored my plea and instead grabbed my right side while another female soldier grabbed my other arm. They pulled me quickly down the stairs, ushering me toward an army jeep that waited in the driveway of our home. They pushed me into the back seat.

This was my first time in an army jeep, but I was struck by its familiar smell. It reeked of the tear gas canisters and munitions I was so accustomed to fleeing. A soldier forced me into a seat and began wrapping the unusually long seat belt across my body. Her rifle, which was slung in front of her chest, hit me in the head as she secured the belt around me. I felt instantly dizzy. I lifted my head up to regain my hold on consciousness, but the soldier pulled me by my hair and lowered my head.

For the next half hour, the jeep remained parked there while soldiers continued to raid our home with my family trapped inside. The thought of my family in the house with all those soldiers turning everything upside down and confiscating whatever they wanted, while I sat handcuffed in the jeep, infuriated me. It didn't help that the soldiers inside the jeep with me and a few of them standing outside began hurling every curse word under the sun at me.

"*Kuss immik, ya bint el sharmoota!*" one exclaimed, using the dirtiest Arabic words he knew.

"Look how strong this daughter of a whore is now," another sneered, while the others laughed.

Up until this point, I had been relatively calm. But now something within me snapped. I was enraged. I yelled back at them, "Whatever, no big deal! Free Palestine! Free Jerusalem!"

As soon as I blurted out these words, one of the soldiers

grabbed a clump of my hair from the top of my scalp and yanked my head down, forcing me to stare at the handcuffs digging into my wrists. They continued taunting me, yelling the dirtiest profanities imaginable in Arabic, English, and Hebrew. My blood boiled, which only further fueled my defiance.

I lifted my head again, this time shouting at the top of my lungs, "Free Palestine and free Jerusalem!"

The soldier grabbed my hair even more forcefully and jerked my head down again. A few of them began taking selfies with me. Camera flashes lit up the jeep's dark interior as they took turns proudly posing next to me, their prize catch of the day. I kept shouting "Free Palestine!" and they continued forcing my head down and taunting me until, finally, one of them closed the door of the jeep and we began driving.

I had no way of telling where we were heading. We drove for a bit before stopping, and I was let out in the middle of the street and transferred to another jeep. About twenty minutes later, we arrived. But where? I had no idea. They took me out of the jeep and walked me in front of it. A male soldier stood to my left and a female to my right. They were posing for one last picture. They each pointed a finger at me and smiled triumphantly, as if they'd caught a fugitive—as if to say, *Look at this girl who has caused such an uproar. Well, we've got her now.*

IT WAS ABOUT 4 A.M. when we entered a building. I was still totally clueless as to where I was. They guided me into a room and sat me down on a chair. I scanned the room for clues and registered a refrigerator, a conference table, and a few cabinets. I suspected I was in Shaar Binyamin Police Station—not because I had ever been there, but because I recognized the details of the room from the many stories I'd heard from my cousins and older brother about the times they were arrested.

I had a flashback of my cousin Mahmoud excitedly recounting the experience of his arrest to me. "They threw me in the 'refrigerator room' at Binyamin," he said, "and I started looking at all the guys who were all sitting on chairs. And there were closets. We were all starving, and the soldiers would come in and open the refrigerator and show us the food inside but not feed us any."

Now it was my turn to be in the Shaar Binyamin Police Station. In addition to the handcuffs still clasped tightly around my wrists, I was now shackled at the ankles, too.

Two female soldiers and three males huddled around a laptop and laughed as they watched the video of me hitting the soldiers. They were joined by a few police officers. They instructed me to sit still and stare straight ahead. I wasn't allowed to lower my head or lean it back. I closed my eyes a few times, succumbing to my exhaustion, but each time I did, they'd shout at me and bang objects to startle me. "You're not allowed to sleep! Wake up!" If I moved my feet, the shackles around my ankles would clank, and they'd yell at me to stop moving. So I had to sit locked in a frozen position. They gave me no food or water the entire time. They didn't even allow me to use the bathroom. My stomach was growling, and I was parched. *I wish I hadn't skipped dinner*, I thought. *Even if it was* karshaat.

After a couple of hours, a police officer walked to my chair and stood towering over me. He gazed down at me contemptuously and said, "Here I am in front of you. Get up and hit me!"

I looked up at him for a couple of seconds and then lowered my head back down, refusing to give him the satisfaction of falling for his trap.

But he wasn't done trying to intimidate me. "You little slut," he sneered. "I'll show you. You're going to die, all of you. I'm going to make sure you and your entire family rot in jail."

I looked back up at him, tilted my head sideways, and smiled. "Go ahead and do whatever you can," I said calmly.

This wasn't the response he'd expected. He cursed at me in Hebrew and briskly walked off.

They left me in that chair for around eight hours. My back and neck were aching terribly, and I was slowly growing delirious from lack of sleep. But I forced myself not to sink into despair. Instead, I imagined that Mahmoud and Waed were sitting there with me. I remembered the stories they'd tell the cousins over late-night gatherings in our backyard. We'd sit on plastic chairs huddled around a hookah, smoking and sipping mint tea while eating up their tales of being arrested. Other families in other places might sit around and talk about vacations they took or movies they watched. We sat around and talked about spending time in Israel's prisons. The guys joked about the time they spent in this same room, laughing with one another and acting irreverently toward their Israeli captors. It was common for a group of guys to be arrested together, put in the same room, and thus be able to entertain one another. I realized then that I was alone and, furthermore, that I was a teenage girl alone. But being able to summon the presence of my laughing cousins and brothers was comforting. I didn't actually *feel* alone then.

Finally, at around noon, I was taken into an interrogation room—the first of several times I'd be forced to sit through hours of nonstop interrogation alone, as a minor, which I'd later learn was a violation of international law. It was just me and one male interrogator, who was seated behind a desk. A female officer was in the room briefly but soon walked out.

"I want to talk to a lawyer," I said.

Thankfully, my parents had already arranged for me to be represented by Gaby Lasky, a well-known Israeli human rights attorney with a history of taking on high-profile cases. She had represented other Palestinian civilians arrested by Israel's security forces. My interrogator led me outside the room and down the hallway to a phone hanging from the wall. He dialed a number and then handed me the receiver.

"Hello?" I said, turning away from him in an attempt to get some privacy.

"Ahed, it's Gaby Lasky. I'm your lawyer now. Listen, you have to retain your right to silence while you're being interrogated. Remain quiet and don't answer their questions no matter what."

"I understand," I replied. "Don't worry. Just tell my parents I'm okay." This was truly my main concern.

"They know that," she reassured me.

We hung up. The interrogator led me back down the hallway and into the room where I'd spend the next seven hours.

"What are your parents' phone numbers?" he began.

"You took their phones. How are you going to call them?" I fired back.

"Don't worry about that. Just give me their numbers."

"I'm sure you can manage to get them yourselves," I replied.

He picked up the phone on his desk and dialed a number. After briefly speaking to someone in Hebrew, which I didn't understand, he paused and then switched to Arabic.

"I'm letting you know that we have begun to interrogate your daughter," he said and hung up.

He was speaking to my mother. She had come to attend my interrogation, which was her legal right as the parent of a minor under arrest. But as is commonly the case, the Israeli authorities didn't allow her to do so. It's standard for them to prohibit parents from sitting in on an interrogation for "security reasons," which are never actually made clear. That phone call did, however, let me know that my mom was in the same building as me, which gave me some solace.

I braced myself for what was coming next. The interrogator stared at me for a few seconds and then banged his fist on the table. It startled me. Next, he began shuffling some of his papers and organizing them into neat stacks, which he placed on the corner of the desk. Once that was done, he sat upright, met my gaze, and began speaking. His voice was calm.

"Who put you up to this?" he asked.

I said nothing.

"Who is behind you?" he tried again.

Silence.

"Why did you do what you did?"

More silence.

"Who put you up to this?" he asked again, this time speaking louder.

"I retain my right to remain silent," I said.

"Do you want to see all your family members end up here in handcuffs like you?" he threatened.

"I retain my right to remain silent," I repeated.

This went on for hours—he'd ask me the same few questions over and over, and I'd respond with that same line. I refused to be outsmarted or tricked into talking. All the stories I had heard growing up, from my father, uncles, brother, and cousins, about what to do while being interrogated had primed me for this moment.

I thought specifically of my father's story of the interrogation that nearly killed him in 1993, years before I was born, when Israel falsely accused him of killing an Israeli settler. That interrogation was so brutal, and my father's injuries so severe, that Human Rights Watch documented what occurred. I'd heard my father retell the story many times throughout my childhood. He recalled being hooded before being taken into the interrogation room. The interrogator tied his hands to the back of his chair and left him to sit in that agonizing position all night. The next morning, the interrogator proceeded to beat him while questioning him. He repeatedly grabbed my father's chin and flipped his head back and forth with great force. He also shook Baba's head left and right and twisted his neck around. My father said all the shaking and jolting was so painful that it felt as if his brain were rolling around loose in his head. He was ultimately shaken and beaten so badly that he suffered a cerebral hemorrhage and fell into a coma for ten days. He woke up temporarily paralyzed, with thirty-six stitches in his head. And he was never charged.

I thought about how he was tortured, possibly in the exact same chair I was now sitting in, so that he'd confess to something he hadn't done—and yet still he didn't speak. I told myself that if he was able to survive that, then surely I could endure this. All I had to do was say nothing that would incriminate me or give them any justification for adding a new charge.

I thought about all the other interrogation stories I'd heard from my relatives over the years. The Israelis often used physical force and harsh psychological tactics to break down Palestinian prisoners in order to get a confession and collect as much intelligence as possible that might implicate others. But it usually didn't end there. Sometimes, once they see that the Palestinians' spirits are destroyed and they are finally willing to talk, the interrogators will apply even more pressure, to get them to become collaborators—spies for Israel. That wouldn't be me.

What helped me withstand my interrogation, and the

ones that followed, was dissociating from my body in the interrogation room, switching myself to autopilot. My body might be physically in the same room as my interrogator, but my mind would drift off to a faraway space inhabited only by me. Once I was there, I no longer had to see what was in front of me. Sure, I might have been looking right at my interrogator, but I wasn't actually seeing him. I was in a totally different world, one that my mind had created as an escape, and I made sure it was a world I loved. And in that world, as a survival strategy, my imagination would kick into overdrive.

Here's how it worked: I'd pick a patriotic song about Palestine, one we used to sing in the marches, and I'd sing it in my head. It might be a song about *sumood*, or "steadfastness," and our love for the land. Such songs always gave me the courage to march on and to face off with the soldiers, and now they were similarly giving me the strength to withstand this interrogation and defy my interrogator. One by one, I mentally sang all the songs I had memorized. Once each song ended, I'd make up a story related to it—a little drama with an elaborate plot and heroic characters inspired by the lyrics. Then I'd move on to another song. When I finished all the songs I knew by heart and created all the corresponding stories I could think of, I moved on to poems. I'd mentally recite every poem I ever had to memorize in school, analyzing each stanza with newfound curiosity. When the poems ran out, I reminisced about my favorite people.

There were, of course, moments when my senses returned to that room. In one such moment, I began staring at a bulletin board on the wall. Various business cards and papers were pinned to the board, and I read what was written in Arabic. I fixated on one card. It featured a belly dancer striking a seductive pose. Beside her were two phone numbers printed against the backdrop of a green leaf. I made it my mission to memorize those numbers. I had a plan. The minute I got out—which, at that point, I imagined would be soon—I'd give that belly dancer a call. I'd let her know that I had come across her number while being interrogated at Shaar Binyamin Police Station and that my interrogator was a major fan of hers. Unfortunately, he wasn't so kind to me. Then I'd make her an offer: I'd pay her to film their next rendezvous and send me the video. I'd then send the video to the interrogator's wife, to teach him a lesson for making me suffer through hours of interrogation with no parent or lawyer at my side. This fantasy was highly entertaining to me. And so, while my interrogator's questions droned on in the background, I concentrated on memorizing the belly dancer's phone numbers.

I was too immersed in my reverie to realize the interrogator was losing his temper at my now hours-long refusal to answer any of his questions. I was jolted back to the room again by his incessant banging and shouting. His anger—juxtaposed to my scheming to entrap him with my soon-to-be conspiring belly dancer—was, at this point, hilarious. I couldn't hold back my laughter. The delirium I felt from the lack of sleep or food probably didn't help the situation. Tears streamed down my face, and I could barely breathe.

"Why are you laughing?" my interrogator asked incredulously.

"Is it illegal?" I replied.

"You're not allowed to laugh, so stop!"

After several more hours of him asking the same few questions and of me repeatedly exercising my right to remain silent, the interrogation finally ended. My interrogator had failed to coerce any sort of confession out of me. He stood up, slid a paper across his desk toward me, and said, "Sign this."

"I'm not going to sign something written in Hebrew," I insisted.

"Okay. I'll translate it for you."

"And why am I supposed to trust that you're going to translate it honestly?"

"Excuse me," he scoffed, looking terribly offended. "We're the Israeli police here, not the Palestinian Authority, which you can guarantee would deal with you dishonestly."

"Excuse *me*," I replied. "So, I'm just supposed to trust you're being honest with me and sign this paper?"

"Exactly."

"Well, I'm not going to sign something I don't understand. What are you going to do about that?"

"Don't sign it, then! You think you're dealing with the Palestinian Authority? We have integrity here, and your people need another hundred years to get where we are!"

I laughed again.

"Stop laughing. There's nothing funny here," he chastised. And then he left the room.

He returned for me minutes later, to take me out of the interrogation room. As we were walking out the door, I saw my mom sitting on a metal chair in the hallway. I was flooded with emotions. I wanted to run into her arms and cry and tell her everything I'd endured since they seized me from our home. But before I had the chance to say anything, the interrogator pulled me away and whisked me into another room. There, I had my fingerprints, DNA, and mug shot taken. When all that was over, I was put back into the refrigerator room and ordered to sit.

I later learned that the interrogator soon went back to find my mother—but not to fill her in on the interrogation of her child, which she had the legal right to sit in on. He wanted to interrogate *her*.

"Come with me. I want to ask you some questions," he said to her.

"I'm not under arrest, so you have no right to ask me anything," she asserted. My mom knew her rights, even if they were seldom honored by the Israelis.

"Just a couple of questions, and then you can go," he tried again.

But my mom was no fool. She told him, "You have no legal right to."

"Okay," he replied. "Well, as of this moment, you're under arrest."

And just like that, he slapped handcuffs on her wrists and took her in for questioning.

Meanwhile, I resumed the same frozen position in the refrigerator room, locked in that chair, still shackled at my wrists and ankles. It's hard to say how much time went by. Every now and then, I'd sneak a glance at the door, to see the officers and soldiers walking up and down the hallway. But at one point, I looked up and saw my mom.

She held up her handcuffed wrists to show me she had been arrested, too.

I sprang out of my chair and onto my feet. "What are you doing to my mom?" I cried.

As soon as I did, two officers rushed over to me and forced me back into my seat while demanding that I shut up. I complied, but my heart was racing. I had been able to withstand my arrest and interrogation and every awful moment in between because they were the consequences of actions I had decided to take. But at no point had I intended to endanger my mother. And now she was under arrest—because of me. The guilt consumed me.

They brought her into the same room I was in and seated her in a chair. To ensure that we couldn't speak to or even look at each other, they turned my chair to face the wall and had three soldiers stand between us.

At one point, a police officer walked over to me and stood above me with a pitying look on his face. "You're still a young girl!" he cajoled. "And you have your whole life ahead of you."

I rolled my eyes. He was an Israeli of Arab Druze descent and was thus speaking to me in fluent Arabic.

"What do you want with all this trouble? Do you really want to throw away your life like this?" he continued.

"If you had even an ounce of patriotism in you, you'd understand why I'm doing what I'm doing. And that this experience isn't going to negatively affect me. But unfortunately, you don't stand for anything, and you chose to sell out to the Zionists and don their uniform, so of course you wouldn't understand."

"Ha!" he scoffed and walked away.

I sat quietly in my seat and refused to talk to any other officers after that. I tried to take comfort in the fact that my mom sat just feet away from me, but she may as well have been in another room. Periodically, officers opened the refrigerator in the room, revealing all the food inside, but never offered to feed us any.

Finally, at midnight, nearly twenty hours after I was seized from my home, I left the police station. Both my mother and I were thrown into a van that would take us nearly two hours north to Hasharon Prison, in Israel. And just like that, in the dead of night, my imprisonment began.

IT WAS STILL DARK when we pulled up to the prison, but I could see the imposing high walls with their barbed wire and watchtowers. As I'd later learn, international law prohibits an occupying power from transferring prisoners outside occupied territory. But Hasharon Prison is in Israel, and like other Palestinian prisoners, I felt as though I were being kidnapped.

First, they made me take off my sweatshirt, because hoods violated the prison dress code. They gave me another shirt to wear instead. Then they patted me down and took another mug shot. Afterward, I was taken into an office where a female social worker asked me a number of questions, including *Are there problems at home? Do you deal drugs? Do you smoke marijuana? Have you ever attempted suicide?* Apparently, they'd arrested a lot of girls who struggled with mental illness.

When the social worker finished screening me, a female guard led me inside a small bathroom and told me to take off all my clothes, including my underwear. My face flushed with shame as her hands moved up and down my bare skin. I had never been physically violated like this before.

Once I was dressed, the guard led me through the door and down a narrow hallway lined with cells on either side. She stopped in front of one, unlocked the blue metal door, and pushed me inside. The cell was a tiny rectangle, barely wider than my arm span, with four other girls already crammed in there. And now I was the fifth. My eyes scanned the narrow room and registered that there were two sets of bunk beds, two cabinets, an old television, and a small bathroom. My bedroom at home was bigger than this. The girls had been asleep but woke up to greet me, the newest addition to their cell.

"*Ahlan!*" one of them said warmly, welcoming me in Arabic as she climbed down from her top bunk. She was thin and a bit taller than me, although we appeared to be the same age. She had an innocent, childlike face that lit up when she spoke.

"Hi," I replied. "I'm Ahed Tamimi from Nabi Saleh."

"We know who you are," she said, smiling. "We saw your arrest on the news." She tilted her head in the direction of the small television set above the cabinet.

The other girls, now wide awake, huddled around me. Their excitement was palpable. One by one, they introduced themselves to me.

"I'm Malak Salman from Jerusalem, and I'm serving a ten-year sentence," the first girl said.

"I'm Hadiya Arinat from Jericho, and my sentence is three years."

"I'm Iman Ali from Qalqilya, and my sentence is a year and a half."

"We're neighbors!" the fourth girl exclaimed. "I'm Malaak Al-Ghalith, and I'm from the Jalazone refugee camp in Ramallah."

"Really? Well, it's very nice to meet you, all of you." After the hours I'd just spent being taunted by soldiers and interrogated nonstop, it really was a relief to see some friendly faces.

"Tell me," Hadiya said, leaning in, her eyes wide with curiosity. "What's Ramallah like lately?"

"Ugh. I'm pretty bored of Ramallah, to be honest. You basically just go to the same cafés and shops over and over again."

"You say that now," she said, laughing. "But once you spend enough time in here, you're really going to miss it. Including all those played-out shops and cafés!"

"That's impossible." I giggled, mainly because I truly had grown tired of hanging out in Ramallah, but also because, in my mind, I was certain I'd be going back home within the next few days.

"Ooh, I love your pants!" Malak said, pointing to the black jeans I was still wearing. Jeans were banned in prison, she told me. The only jeans allowed in were the ones you were wearing when they arrested you. Otherwise, only cotton pants in certain colors were permitted. The families of the incarcerated women and girls provided clothes for them.

"I'll take a shower, and you can wash them and have them," I offered.

"Wow. Thank you! This is the most fashionable thing I've seen in ages."

I quickly came to learn that Malak had a lighthearted optimism about her that she was able to maintain in any circumstance.

The girls gave me a cursory lay of the land and some background on the prison. The women's cell block we were in was designated for what Israel calls "security prisoners." Israel classifies all the Palestinians it detains in its custody as "security prisoners," regardless of their alleged offense or criminal activity. But Palestinians use "political prisoner" to describe those of us detained in relation to the occupation. In total, there were about thirty-two Palestinian women and girls in our section at that point. Our cell was for minors, meaning we were all under eighteen. Some of the girls who served time with me had been arrested in the uprisings of 2015, accused of possessing knives and trying to carry out attacks against soldiers. But the overwhelming number of children are detained for participating in demonstrations and clashes, for creating social media posts Israel deems as incitement, or for "insulting the honor of a soldier." Most of the time, they're accused of throwing stones.

Once a girl turned eighteen, she'd be transferred to another cell, one with adult women. Meanwhile, new girls would come and go, as some didn't have long sentences. The other sections of the prison housed Israeli civilians who had committed criminal offenses. Despite their being housed in different cell blocks, we could easily hear their shouts and cries at all hours of the day and night.

My cellmates asked me about life in Nabi Saleh and about the political climate around Palestine after Trump announced his plans to move the U.S. embassy to Jerusalem. They also asked about the latest fashion trends and what the new popular songs were. As I would come to learn myself, a newly arrived prisoner offered a rare window to the outside world, a world that carried on while you were frozen in time, stuck in the confines of a claustrophobic cell. Even though it was painful, you still desperately wanted to look out that window.

As we were talking, my eyes fixated on the wall, where a three-inch-long cockroach was scurrying up toward the ceiling. Iman turned around to see what I was staring at.

"Oh, that?" she asked, walking over to the wall with one of her slippers in hand. She gave the cockroach a good whack with the slipper, killing it. "You'll get used to those. You'll basically see at least one in here every day."

I shuddered.

The girls and I spoke for nearly two hours before I excused myself to take a shower in the cell's small bathroom. The shower was so narrow that I had to stand completely erect and still in order to fit. When I finished, my cellmates gave me new clothes to wear from their shared wardrobe. I had barely finished drying off, and still hadn't slept, when a guard opened the door and told me to get ready; it was time to leave. To go where? I once again had no idea. It was 2:30 A.M. now, almost exactly twenty-four hours since they raided my house and arrested me.

I WAS REMOVED FROM my cell and taken to a tiny room with three female guards, who made me strip down to my underwear and frisked my entire body. They even patted down my hair, stroked the back of my ears, and made me open my mouth to see if I was hiding anything in there. I'd never felt more vulnerable or exposed, but I bit my tongue and forced myself to hold my head high despite the profound shame I was feeling.

Next, they put me in an outdoor cage, where I had to wait in the cold dead of night for at least an hour. A fence separated my cage from an adjacent one holding Israeli civilian prisoners. They were serving time for crimes like murder, rape, and drug dealing. They knew who I was, which made me an easy target. Several of them taunted me, saying they'd kill me if they got their hands on me. Some banged on the fence between us, the only thing stopping them from actually being able to hit me. I was far outnumbered and genuinely feared that if there weren't a barrier between us, they'd kill me. I ran to the farthest corner of my cage and crouched, trembling in fear.

The cages, it turned out, constituted a holding area. Prisoners, both the security ones and the civilian ones, would have to wait there before boarding the *bosta*, the loathsome vehicle that transported prisoners from prison to court, making stops at other prisons in between. It takes hours to make all the stops, during which some prisoners get off and others get on. Any Palestinian prisoner will tell you that the *bosta* journey is one of the most difficult parts of their experience of being incarcerated. To call it hell on wheels is an understatement.

To help you picture it, imagine a bus divided into narrow cells. The interior is all metal, including the seats. Many of the cells, like the one I was in, are barely big enough to fit one person. My cell was essentially as wide as the seat I was in, making it impossible for me to move at all. Never mind the fact that I was also shackled at the wrists and ankles. The cell was so tight that my knees hit the metal door in front of me, and if the driver accelerated or swerved, my body would bang into the sides.

Other than forcing prisoners to sit in an extremely uncomfortable physical position for hours, the *bosta* was poorly ventilated, and its odors were revolting. It often reeked of vomit from passengers who had thrown up on themselves or of urine from inmates who had peed themselves, unable to hold it in any longer. The stench of the police dogs who patrolled the bus was also always in the air.

The temperature in the *bosta* was another major hardship. In the winter, which is when I was arrested, it was freezing. The cold metal chair made it feel like I was sitting on a giant block of ice—for hours. I later learned that layering two pairs of pants, three shirts, and a jacket would help me survive, and I began to dress accordingly. But despite all the layers, each time I returned to the prison, my hands would be swollen and blue and it would take hours for them to regain normal sensation.

As if not breathing properly, being in perpetual physical pain, and almost freezing weren't bad enough, the psychological toll of riding in the *bosta* was enough to break anyone. There was no chance of sleeping during the journey, thanks to a metal chain hanging from the door of the cells. Every time the vehicle moved, the chain would hit the metal, resulting in a nonstop clanking that made my head want to explode. The sound was sometimes so tormentingly loud and incessant that I'd cry from the headaches pounding inside my skull.

None of this, of course, addresses the trauma brought on by the other prisoners on the *bosta*. I was confined to one of nearly a dozen isolated cells sectioned off for individual prisoners. But the *bosta* also had a larger cell, holding roughly twenty inmates. Unfortunately, I could see them and they could see me, which led to an onslaught of verbal harassment from them. To make matters worse, some of these inmates were legitimately insane. On that first *bosta* ride, an Israeli man in that larger cell stood up and exposed his penis to me while staring at me with a crazy look in his eyes. Later, two other men took off their clothes and had sex with each other for all the riders to see. As a sixteen-year-old girl who hadn't witnessed anything beyond a kissing scene in a Hollywood movie, I was appalled. I closed my eyes and tried my hardest to fight back the tears.

It took hours to get from Hasharon Prison, where I was detained, to Ofer Military Court, where I was tried. My *bosta* departed Hasharon at around 3 A.M. The next stop, about an hour and a half away, was the Ramla Prison. We arrived there at around 5 A.M. and were met by other *bosta* vehicles from other prisons. We all disembarked and were transferred to different *bostas* depending on which court we were going to. Because I was a security detainee, I was loaded onto the *bosta* bound for Ofer, where I finally arrived at around 9 A.M.

Ofer is an Israeli military court located inside a military base, and despite the fact that I was a civilian, I was tried there. But I was by no means an exception. Palestinians in the West Bank who are arrested by the Israeli army and charged with "security violations" are regularly tried through the military court system, where the chances of their receiving anything resembling a fair trial are nonexistent. These courts aren't meant to deliver justice. They are an organ of the occupation and a tool for Palestinian subjugation. The judges are military officers, and the prosecutors are Israeli soldiers, some of whom aren't yet even certified as attorneys under the Israel Bar Association. And the Palestinians tried in these courts? Because most cases end with the defendant accepting a plea deal to avoid the harsher sentence that would result from going through the full trial, we experience a near–100 percent conviction rate.

But that's not where the unfairness ends. Let's say an Israeli settler, like one living in Halamish, across the road from my home, committed the same exact crime as I had, or any other Palestinian had. Despite the fact that he also lived in the West Bank (albeit illegally under international law), that settler would not be tried through this military court system. As an Israeli citizen, he would have full democratic rights and would thus be tried through Israel's civilian courts. This dual and discriminatory legal system has been denounced by many in the international community as a primary example of the apartheid regime currently occupying Palestine.

As soon as I arrived at Ofer, I was put in a tiny cell that was so oppressively cold, it made the unbearable *bosta* climate feel pleasant in comparison. I sat alone on a cold bench, my body shivering and my teeth chattering. On the wall in front of me, a previous Palestinian prisoner had engraved FREEZER OF DEATH, presumably with the sharp edges of their handcuffs. It was an apt description of the cell, and I empathized with the former prisoner's desperation. I wondered where that prisoner was now. I hoped wherever it was, they were warm. And free.

The hours I spent alone in the "freezer of death" cell remain a blur. During that time, I tried to keep my mind as busy as possible, to avoid going insane. I thought about my relatives, my friends, my classmates, and even the shopkeepers whose stores I'd pass in the streets of Ramallah. When would I see them again? I thought about every minute detail of my life: the places I had visited, the horrors I had witnessed, the dreams I had had to forgo. I remembered my favorite bedtime stories, the ones Tata Farha had told me when I was a young girl, when we used to share a room.

One night, before I was born, Israeli soldiers raided our house in search of my dad, Tata Farha once told me. They knocked over objects and flipped the house upside down, but it wasn't until one of the soldiers in the kitchen began dumping out a bottle of olive oil, oil Tata Farha had pressed herself, that she really lost her cool.

"Please, not the olive oil! Anything but the olive oil!" she pleaded.

She always laughed when she recounted that night, amused by how, for a brief moment, she forgot all about her son being apprehended and cared only for her precious olive oil disappearing down the drain.

At around 5 P.M., I was finally taken into the courtroom. To my surprise, there was a good amount of press there, but to my disappointment, none of my relatives had been able to come. Reporters called out questions to me as I sat in a barricaded defendant's box with two female officers at my sides. This was the first time I met Gaby Lasky in person. I was relieved and grateful to see her there, knowing that she was my best hope of going home soon. Gaby leaned over the wooden barricade to speak to me. Amid the buzz within the courtroom, and as reporters continued to call out questions to me, it was hard to concentrate on what she was saying. Gaby told me that I had to stand when the judge entered the courtroom and that she would be speaking on my behalf the entire time. I asked her how my family was doing and told her to let them know I was okay.

Still, I was disoriented, sleep-deprived, and pale. A Palestinian reporter from a major news outlet who was yelling out questions to me eventually caught my attention when she asked, "Ahed, are you okay?"

I nodded and smiled, saying, "Yes, I'm okay," knowing my family was likely watching.

The proceedings were conducted entirely in Hebrew, which means I understood nothing. My head spun, and I struggled to make sense of anything, especially given the whirlwind day I had just had. When the hearing ended, Gaby informed me that the court had denied her request that I be released on bail and, furthermore, had extended my detention by six days, in order for the police to continue their investigation. My heart sank. This meant six more days of interrogation, six more days of psychological torment and physical stress. Up until then, I believed I'd be going home soon. But now, the reality was sinking in: My case was more serious than I understood.

After court, I was thrown back in the "freezer of death" for another few hours, where I had to wait until it was time to take the *bosta* back to prison. I scanned the walls of the room and the ceiling to ensure that no cameras were filming me. Once I saw that the room was camera-free, I began to bawl. I cried thinking of the endless hours I'd be interrogated and berated again. I cried recalling the grotesque things I had just seen and smelled in that *bosta* and how, when I left this freezing room, that would be my next destination. I cried thinking of my cousin Mohammad, wondering if he was still suffering in the hospital. I wondered where Mama was and what they were doing to her.

At 9 P.M., a full twelve hours after I arrived at Ofer, I was loaded back onto the *bosta*. This time, it was the reverse route: Ofer to Ramla, an exchange of prisoners at Ramla, and then on to another *bosta*, which would return me to Hasharon Prison. By the time I got back to my shared cell, it was midnight.

The girls were asleep when I returned, but they all got up to greet me. It was apparent to them how shaken and deflated I felt. They took turns comforting me, assuring me that even though the *bosta* was guaranteed to be an unspeakably horrible experience every single time, I would manage to get through it. They advised me never to talk to the Israeli criminal prisoners and to keep my distance from them at all costs. They told me always to stay calm in court. When I told them that the judge had extended the length of my interrogation by six days, they looked at me empathetically. I knew they felt my pain; they were ahead of me in this process.

"You haven't slept in days," Malak said. "You're exhausted. You'll sleep in one of the beds tonight."

As soon as she said that, I remembered that we were five girls in a room with only four beds. The girls began to strip two of the beds of their blankets and laid them out on the ground, side by side, perpendicular to the bunk beds. The cell was so narrow that the only way to fully spread out a blanket was to slide one end of it under the lowest bunk.

"What are you doing?" I asked, confused.

"Two of us will sleep on the ground. We always do this when there are more girls than beds. We're not allowed to sleep two to a bed, and as you can see, the beds are pretty narrow anyway," Malak explained. "We never want the girl sleeping on the ground to feel all alone, so at least one other girl will always join her. It just means we have to tuck our feet under the bed and hope we don't accidentally slam into it while sleeping—which, by the way, happens a lot. And it hurts!"

I watched the girls methodically pile their blankets on the cold, dirty concrete floor and wondered how many nights they'd each had to sleep like that. I was moved see them voluntarily leave the beds they had just woken up in to make space for me. This was my introduction to the informal system created by my fellow prisoners to give their lives behind bars more structure and humanity. It was also my induction into the unique and priceless sisterhood forged within the confines of a cell, where you cannot escape one another and where you grow close in a way that no relationship outside prison can rival. It's a sisterhood that would leave an indelible imprint on my heart.

I climbed into one of the beds and, for the first time in days, laid my head down. I instantly passed out.

PRISON

IT TOOK ONLY ONE night of prison for me to realize that a full night of uninterrupted sleep is one of the many necessities you're denied behind bars. Every thirty minutes or so, a guard would point a flashlight into our cell to count us while we were sleeping. Then, at 5:30 A.M., I was startled out of my sleep when the lights abruptly turned on and a male guard yelled, "Girls, it's time for the head count!"

The four other girls in my cell got up groggily and threw on the first headscarves they could find in time to be covered and decent when the guard walked in. They gestured for me to get up and stand alongside them.

"Hadiya?" the guard called out.

"Yes," she replied.

"Malak?"

"Yes."

"Ahed?"

"Yes," I said.

He continued his roll call until all of us were accounted for. And then he moved on to the next cell. The girls told me it was safe to go back to sleep, but that we'd have to be up again before 8:30 A.M. That was when everyone in our cell block had to exit their cells so the guards could conduct a thorough inspection. They searched the entire cell and then banged on the walls and windows to make sure we hadn't tried to dig our way out or removed any metal bars.

During this time, all the prisoners had to flock outside to the small courtyard, the only outdoor space allotted to us in the prison. But to call it "outdoors" was a bit of a mischaracterization. It was just another cage. When I stepped into the courtyard that first morning, I looked up, hoping to see the sky. Instead, all I saw was more fencing and barbed wire. Many of the women and girls sat on the ground of the courtyard as our cells were being inspected. Still barely awake, some rested their heads on others' shoulders and dozed off until it was time to go back to the cells.

Once everyone had returned to their cells, some of the girls tried to catch a bit more sleep, while those who had cleaning duty that day got to work. I learned that the girls divided the cleaning tasks up among themselves and had created a schedule. On this day, it was Iman and Hadiya's turn to clean. I watched Iman use the one broom shared by the whole cell block to sweep the floor of our cell. Next, Hadiya poured water from a cup onto the floor and used a large squeegee to spread it over the entire surface. Iman helped her, using a dustpan to scoop up the water now flooding the floor and dumping it all into the cell's small metal sink, which itself was sinking—it wasn't securely screwed to the wall and was weighed down by all the dishes in it. This was the only sink in the cell, and we had to use it to wash our hands, do our dishes, and drink water. Hadiya washed the dishes in the sink, while Iman dried them and stored them in a small cabinet. After that, the girls wiped down the walls of the cell with a cloth dabbed with water and a splash of perfume to try to mask the moist stench of so many human bodies crammed into a confined space with poor ventilation.

AT 10:30 A.M., THE guards came back again for yet another count. Once they finished, our cell doors remained open, and we were free to walk around the cell block until 5 P.M. At this point whoever wanted to eat breakfast headed to the communal kitchen, which all thirty-two women in the cell block shared. I learned that the responsibility for meal preparation fell squarely on the prisoners. In fact, the cost of most of the food also fell on the prisoners. The prison administration provided the bare minimum: some chicken once a week, rice, some vegetables, and a box of fruit (either oranges or apples), which they'd distribute so that each of us got precisely one orange or one apple a week. None of the food they provided was ever enough, so we'd have to supplement it by purchasing more from the canteen with money our families deposited into our accounts.

Securing a spot in the kitchen to make your meal was a competitive ordeal, as the kitchen space was way too limited for everyone to try to cook at once. Plus, the prison administration allowed us only one knife, which everyone had to share, and only at certain times. The dearth of resources forces you to get crafty, and I eventually learned to use the lid of a tuna can as a knife, even though I'd inevitably slice up my hand while doing so. Those who didn't get to the kitchen in time had to try to prepare some food on the single-burner hot plate in their cell, probably the most inefficient way to cook anything; it took forever to heat anything up.

During this "free time," when we were allowed to be outside our cells, the women and girls visited one another. My cellmates encouraged me to introduce myself to Yasmeen Shaaban, the representative of our cell block in the prison. Yasmeen was in her thirties, but commanded so much respect and authority that the girls called her Khalto Yasmeen as a sign of their deference to her.

"Welcome, Ahed," Yasmeen said when I found her in her cell; she gestured for me to sit beside her on her bed. The thick black-rimmed glasses she wore made her look sharp and astute. She had big cheeks that were accentuated when she smiled, making me feel she was trustworthy and sincere. Khalto Yasmeen asked me a few questions about my arrest, interrogation, and first court dates. She explained to me that she was the representative for the female security prisoners, the sole point of contact between the women and the prison administration. Only she was authorized by her fellow prisoners to speak to the guards on behalf of the collective. This system had been put in place by Palestinian prisoners in part to ensure that if there was a spy among them, speaking to a guard out of turn, that person could be easily uncovered.

Khalto Yasmeen had a strong personality—a necessity in a role like hers. She had been groomed for the position by the previous representative of the section, and she had a deputy who stood in for her, if necessary. In this organized chain of command, each of the nine cells also designated a woman or girl to be their unofficial representative. As I soon witnessed, the members of each cell held regular meetings to voice their grievances and their discomfort around the conditions in the cell. Each cell representative would relay those grievances to Khalto Yasmeen, who would channel them up to the prison administration. When the prison did things to make our lives more stressful, she'd frequently have to strategize a response.

Let's say they threatened to deprive us of essential items in the canteen, like maxi pads. Khalto Yasmeen would speak to the senior official in the prison and inform him that if they didn't provide the women with maxi pads within two days, we'd all go on strike, meaning we'd refuse to leave our cells. Her role as our advocate required tremendous self-sacrifice, as she had to put her own safety on the line to try to pressure the prison administration into doing or giving us things to make our lives a little more bearable. She was often threatened with solitary confinement. I truly admired the bravery she summoned on behalf of our collective.

Khalto Yasmeen introduced me to Khalida Jarrar, one of her cellmates, whom the girls also respectfully addressed as Khalto. I'd heard of her before; she was a well-known political figure in Palestinian society, a prominent leftist and feminist. Khalida immediately struck me as confident and strong-willed. She had previously served as an elected member of the Palestinian Legislative Council (the PA's legislature) and was a longtime advocate for prisoners' rights. A beautiful middle-aged woman with shoulder-length black hair, she had a deep, raspy voice that revealed her years of chain-smoking. This was Khalida's third time in prison, and as with her previous stays, she was serving time under administrative detention.

I knew all about administrative detention, from all the times it had happened to my father. It meant that neither Khalida nor her lawyer knew the reason for her arrest and imprisonment, nor when she'd get out. As is always the case with administrative detention, all they knew was that Israel had a secret file on her that classified her as a security threat. Any "evidence" they allegedly had was never disclosed to her. And so her detention was indefinite. She was initially ordered to serve six months in prison under administrative detention. At the end of that sixth month, they extended it by another six months, and then another four. Having seen my father serve so much time in administrative detention, I intimately understood the agony that comes with such an uncertain sentence.

But Khalida's activism and advocacy for prisoners' rights didn't stop when she herself was imprisoned. On the contrary, she became galvanized. During her previous arrest and incarceration, in 2015 (also under administrative detention), she spearheaded an educational program for the women and girls imprisoned with her. Having realized that the majority of them either had never taken their *tawjihi* exams or were still too young, she used her connections with the Palestinian Ministry of Education and the Commission of Detainees and Ex-Detainees Affairs to begin informally educating her fellow prisoners. In defiance of Israel's prison administration, which bans education for prisoners as a form of collective punishment, Khalida began to teach the various subjects that comprised the *tawjihi* exam, among them business administration, technology, geography, English, and history. She enlisted the help of a couple of other prisoners who had bachelor's degrees to teach the subjects that weren't her forte, like Arabic grammar and math. She and her appointed committee would then create their own *tawjihi* exam to administer to the women and girls and grade them. The completed exams would ultimately be sent to the Ministry of Education. By the end, she would graduate a small cohort of prisoners, who would officially now hold high school diplomas.

Khalida explained to me that Israeli law required prisons to provide a teacher for prisoners like me, under eighteen. She said there used to be a teacher: a Palestinian citizen of Israel who taught the girls Arabic and math. But after she got married, she left her job, and the prison administration never bothered to replace her, despite repeated requests from the prisoners. So, Khalida had stepped in to fill the void, even introducing new subjects that the official teacher wasn't hired to cover. This way, she could adequately prepare all the girls (and whichever women chosen) to complete their schooling for all the *tawjihi* matriculation exams.

"I know it's still unclear how long you'll be here for, Ahed," she said to me. "But to make sure you don't miss any more school, you should start coming to the classes right away."

I nodded. One of my greatest fears at this point was that I'd fall behind on my *tawjihi* studies and not graduate from high school on time.

"I'm also working on putting together a new class for everyone," she said, smiling. "I want to teach you all a course on international law and international humanitarian law, so you truly benefit from your time here by learning your rights and expanding your political consciousness. I'm just waiting to obtain the appropriate books and materials to be able to organize a syllabus and instruct you all properly."

This piqued my interest. For years, I'd dreamed of becoming a lawyer one day to seek justice for my martyred uncle Rushdie, and this felt like the first concrete step toward actualizing that goal. Khalida explained that she had obtained her master's degree in democracy and human rights from Birzeit University, which qualified her to teach such a course. I knew I'd have a lot to learn from her. For the first time in days, I felt a glimmer of hope that something positive might come out of this nightmare.

Khalida told me that classes typically began at 10:30 A.M. and went on until 1 P.M., when we were locked back in our cells. We'd have to stay in our cells until 2:30 P.M., at which point the guards would come back to knock on the walls and conduct a thorough inspection once again. Then there was another, hour-long class from 2:30 to 3:30. This left just a small window of time, from 3:30 until 5 P.M., for us to reserve a spot in the kitchen to make "dinner" or to get some exercise in the yard. But because the yard was very small, I soon discovered that the only real way to achieve continuous movement was to walk around in circles. This not only made you feel like a distressed animal pacing in its cage, but was also very dizzying. Once 5 P.M. hit, the guards locked our cell doors, and we'd be forced to find creative ways to bide our time in our crammed, claustrophobic quarters until the next morning. Then we would wake up and do it all over again.

I HAD BARELY GOTTEN used to the routine of prison when I was dragged out of there and loaded on the dreaded *bosta* to endure a second round of interrogation. The journey again lasted hours, with the driver making the same several stops for prisoner swaps before finally pulling up to the Shaar Binyamin Police Station. Before the interrogation began, I was led into an office belonging to a female officer. When I entered, a male uniformed soldier appeared to be finishing up whatever business he had to do in there. I immediately recognized him as the soldier I'd slapped. Our eyes locked for a moment, and as soon as he recognized me, his facial expression grew angry and he swiftly walked out of the room. I sensed he was ashamed of himself, as he should have been.

"Remove your clothes. I need to search you," the female officer said to me.

I was taken aback. I had already been thoroughly searched when I left the prison and would be searched again when I returned. What right did she have to search and humiliate me there too?

This time, my interrogation was carried out by two men. I felt unsafe alone with them in that small office, but I forced myself to remain as strong as possible and not let myself crack as they barraged me with nonstop questions and made threats against my family. Their questions were, for the most part, similar to the ones I was repeatedly asked in the first interrogation: Why had I done what I did? Who was behind me? And on and on. But these men were notably more aggressive and threatening toward me than the previous interrogator was. They placed a laptop on the desk in front of me and played the Facebook Live video of that fateful moment when I slapped the soldier. They paused the video and asked me to identify who else was in it, which I refused to do. In response, they asked if I'd be happy seeing those people handcuffed as I was. I still didn't reply, speaking only to assert my right to remain silent.

At various points throughout this interrogation, one of the interrogators would look at me with feigned sympathy. He'd shake his head disappointedly and say, "Tsk, tsk, tsk. Look at you, sitting here being interrogated. Look at where you are. Instead of being at home with your family, you're here in handcuffs. What a pity."

I'd start laughing in my head, thinking, *Given everything I've endured in my life—including seeing my relatives killed and maimed by your forces, getting wounded myself as a young girl, having my parents repeatedly arrested, and being denied any semblance of a normal childhood—you want me to feel bad about* this? *The fact that I'm sitting here in handcuffs? That's what I should be upset about?* I was truly amused by his attempts to shame me over something as trivial as wearing handcuffs. That paled in comparison to all the other traumas I'd had to endure in my life.

Whatever reaction he was hoping to elicit, I didn't give it to him. Instead, my expression deadpan, I remained silent, again speaking only to assert my right to remain silent.

After hours of their fruitless interrogation, they threw me into a cell. Not long after, the same interrogator returned and opened the door to my cell. Again, he shook his head with disappointment and said, "Look at you sitting there in handcuffs." As if I had forgotten the fact that I'd been shackled for hours.

I started laughing.

"Okay, I'm in handcuffs," I said, lifting up my shackled hands to drive home the point. "But these aren't important." I went on while smirking. Then I slowly tapped the side of my head with one finger. "What's important is my mind. Sure, you've locked me up in a cell, but don't think that my mind isn't working."

MY OLDER COUSIN NOUR, who appears next to me in the video where I hit the soldiers, was arrested shortly after I was. She was also being interrogated on this day, as was my mother. Nour was eventually put in the same cell as me, and my mother in a cell next to ours. We idled in our cells for hours, making occasional small talk through the bars, but being careful not to discuss anything of substance.

At this point, it had been days since my mother and I were arrested. My mom, who has always been obsessive about hygiene, started venting to us about how disgusting she felt. "I've been wearing the same underwear and socks for days! I can't stand being in these socks anymore! These awful socks!" she exclaimed.

Just as my mother said this, Nour slouched back in the metal chair she was sitting on and placed her hands below the seat. She paused for a second, looking puzzled as her hands felt something beneath the chair.

"Ahed, come look," she whispered.

I lowered my head to see what she was touching. And that's when I saw it: a voice recorder taped to the bottom of her seat.

"Listen. Don't say anything, and just wait," I told her. She nodded.

The Israelis had set us up, placing us together in the same cell and my mom right next to us, within earshot. They were trying to entrap us, thinking we'd be sitting there attempting to get our stories straight, discussing important matters pertaining to our village. I'm sure they assumed we would inadvertently implicate other relatives, who would then also be arrested. We were already being cautious with our words, to avoid falling into any trap they might have set. But after discovering that everything we said was being taped, I wanted to make sure they knew they couldn't outsmart us. So, I began deliberately saying things to spite them.

"You cowardly interrogator. I know you've planted a voice recorder in here," I chanted. "You think you can entrap us by taping us? Don't you know that we've come across these played-out antics before, you foolish interrogator? I suggest you go find yourself another career, because being an interrogator clearly isn't working out for you when you can't even get a confession out of young kids!"

Within moments, guards barged into the cell. They grabbed me and Nour and slammed us up against the wall, patting us down, presumably to see if we had taken the voice recorder. In the grand scheme of things, it was a small and petty act of resistance. But even though it was short-lived, it felt satisfying to know we had sabotaged their plot and given them a piece of our minds on the recording.

Shortly after, the interrogator entered the cell. He fixed his gaze on me for a bit and then grinned. His face appeared triumphant. He was probably thinking that while he had failed to coerce a confession out of me during the interrogation, he must certainly have gotten one on the recording.

Nodding slowly, he looked at me and said, "Excellent . . . Excellent."

"No," I snapped back. "Socks! Socks!" alluding to my mom's earlier comment about her smelly socks.

And with that, I lost it and began to laugh uncontrollably.

Tears streamed down my face, and my sides ached as I practically convulsed. The interrogator and a female officer demanded I stop laughing, but I couldn't. I was hysterical. They had no idea what was so funny, but I knew they'd soon find out.

The following day, I had to be in court again. And when I saw the interrogator sitting with the prosecution, I naturally started laughing again. He took one look at me, and his face flushed with anger. He knew exactly why I was laughing: He had planted a voice recorder in my cell and had still failed to get a confession. All he got was more information about my mother's socks than he ever cared to know.

SOME OF THE MOST tormenting moments during my incarceration were when the Israelis forced me to endure the grueling *bosta* journey for a court date or an interrogation session that never ended up happening. On one such occasion, I was plucked from my prison cell at 2:30 A.M. for another round of interrogation. The *bosta* transported me to the Ramla Prison, where I was taken inside and left all alone in a tiny square room. The room was blindingly white: the lights, the walls—everywhere I looked, I was assaulted with disturbingly bright whiteness. I was already sleep-deprived, considering that I had left my prison cell in the middle of the night, and now the unbearable whiteness made me feel I was losing my mind.

Eventually, they took me to another cell, near the Israeli civilian prisoners. I noticed that there were cameras everywhere. I was all alone in the cell, but was haunted by the loud, cackling laughter of the Israeli prisoners nearby.

Hours later, they transferred me from the Ramla Prison to the Al-Moscobiyya Interrogation and Detention Center, in Jerusalem. But they *still* didn't interrogate me. Once again, they put me in a room all by myself. This room had two cameras on the ceiling pointing right at me. Hours passed, and I wondered what the holdup was while trying not to go crazy. I told them I needed to use the bathroom, and a guard pointed to one, saying, "It's right there." But there were cameras directly above it, so I refused to use it. Instead, I just sat, squirming in physical discomfort, trying my best to hold my bladder until I could relieve myself in private. After seven long hours, they sent me back to Ramla Prison on the *bosta*, and from Ramla back to Hasharon, where I arrived at midnight. I was never interrogated.

On another occasion, I was transported to a court hearing that seemingly everyone but me and the prison system database knew had been postponed. I had heard of this happening to other prisoners. A court date would be scheduled, and the prosecutor would say they were unable to make it. So the hearing would be postponed for a week, but the prisoner's name would remain in the system, and they'd be taken to the court regardless. Once again, I left Hasharon Prison in the middle of the night, suffered the *bosta* ride, and made it to the Ofer Military Court by morning. I waited in the "freezer of death" cell for hours, anticipating being called into court at some point. My teeth chattered, and I shivered from the cell's frigid temperature. The only thing that got me through the wait was the excitement of imminently seeing my family in the courtroom. I missed them terribly, and such rare opportunities to see them breathed new life into me. I knew my dad would shout out words of encouragement to me, which helped me stay strong.

When I heard a guard enter the cell, I jumped to my feet, thinking, *It's finally my turn*. But it was another detainee's turn. This kept happening, over and over again. Each time, I'd stand up in excitement, only to be let down when someone else was taken into the courtroom instead. By 6 P.M., I knew

I was there by mistake and that I didn't actually have a hearing that day. Incidentally, my family knew the hearing had been postponed; the prosecutor knew it had been postponed; and my lawyer knew it, too—everyone except me. I spent a full day waiting for nothing. The hopes of seeing my family were dashed. On the return ride to the prison, I fought back tears and cursed the occupation forces for managing to inflict yet another cruelty.

MY THIRD INTERROGATION WAS the one the entire world saw, because excerpts of it were posted on the internet. My family wanted it to be made public in order to expose how Israel abused Palestinian children and also to provide an example to Palestinian youth of how they should behave while under interrogation. Each time I watch the video, I relive the trauma of all the interrogations I had to suffer through, and the old wounds open back up. Still, I'm glad that the abusive and illegal treatment of Palestinian children at the hands of Israeli forces was laid bare for all to see. Because I've watched and rewatched the parts of this interrogation that are online, I'm able to provide more details here about this particular experience.

In the video, I am once again interrogated by two men without the presence of a woman in the room. One sat behind his desk while I sat across from him. The other interrogator sat at the edge of the same desk, to my left. Knowing that the previous interrogation was scarier and more aggressive than the first, I braced myself for what was to come.

"You know why you're here, but I'm forced to tell you anyway," the interrogator sitting to the side of the desk said in broken Arabic. "It's for when you were in the clashes, when you threw stones, when you were in the protests not allowed by law, when you hit soldiers on previous occasions and on the last occasion. You know that, right?"

I stayed quiet.

The interrogator behind the desk said something in Hebrew, and the second interrogator translated it for him.

"You can speak to a lawyer. You already spoke to one, right?"

I nodded.

"You can speak in private. No one else will overhear what you're saying."

Yeah, right, I thought. But I nodded reluctantly.

They said some things in Hebrew that I didn't understand. And then the interrogator behind the desk began to speak his version of broken Arabic.

"Where do you live?"

I didn't respond.

"Where do you live?" he repeated.

"You know where I live," I said quietly.

"I'm asking you for the purpose of the interrogation."

"I retain my right to remain silent."

"Huh?" he asked loudly.

"I retain my right to remain silent," I repeated.

At times, the two interrogators spoke over each other, simultaneously shouting different things at me. When this was happening, I didn't know whom to look at and tried my best to stare blankly ahead and drown out their voices with my thoughts.

"Do you think you're going to liberate Palestine?" the interrogator to my left asked loudly, while the one behind the desk typed furiously. "Who's going to liberate Palestine? You? Your brother? Your sister? Who? Will Nour liberate Palestine? Will Osama liberate Palestine? Who?!"

I don't even have a sister. But it still pierced my heart each time he mentioned the name of one of my relatives.

"What happened?" the one behind the desk shouted at me. His voice was deeper and his demeanor more intimidating than those of his counterpart. "Whom do you think you're playing tricks on?"

The other interrogator began speaking over him, but his partner overpowered him with his loud shouting.

"Who?" he demanded.

I sat up straight and remained quiet.

"WHO?!" he yelled, his voice crescendoing even louder.

Silence on my part.

"WHO?!" he asked again. He was really losing his cool.

"WHO??" he repeated.

Seeing how unresponsive I was, he tried shifting gears. "If I saw my daughter sitting there in handcuffs . . ." he began. But then he returned to his previous line of questioning. "Who? Tell me who. WHO? WHO?" he shouted.

I kept quiet.

The other interrogator tried speaking to me a little softer, but the aggressive one behind the desk continued to dominate the conversation, raising his voice louder and louder.

"Who? Is your father behind you? Or is it your mother who's behind you?" he barked, leaning over and pointing his finger uncomfortably close to me. "Who? WHO IS BEHIND YOU?!"

I stared straight ahead, avoiding eye contact with him and trying my best to mentally block out his verbal assaults. But truthfully, I was very shaken.

The other interrogator tried out his good-cop act again, speaking to me quietly at first. "Ahed, Ahed," he began, gesturing for me to turn my attention toward him. He sat with his legs spread open and leaned forward so that his face was just inches away from mine. This made me even more uncomfortable. "When I think about my younger sister, I see her in you sitting in front of me right here," he said. "Really. She's blond just like you, and her eyes are just like yours. She's white, just like you! And when she goes to the beach, she looks like a hamburger!" he exclaimed with laughter. "Is that what happens to you, too?"

I turned away from him, cringing at this highly inappropriate and creepy way to be speaking to a teenage girl. But in my mind, I thought, *Beach? What beach? Doesn't he know that we can see the Mediterranean Sea from the highest hill in my village, but can only dream of going? Has he forgotten that, like other Palestinians in the West Bank, we're banned from visiting thanks to his country's laws?*

My mind flashed back to Marah and the days she and I would spend sitting atop that hill for hours, escaping our woes in the village and dreaming up alternative lives, ones where we lived safe and carefree. Oftentimes, we'd stare out at the sea and cry together. We were pained by the unfairness of it all. The sea is so close, yet cruelly off-limits to us. We fantasized about swimming in the glistening blue water, which we assumed was warm, and imagined the sensation of burying our toes in the sand, like we saw in the movies.

The interrogator's attempts at coaxing me into speaking failed. This seemed to anger him even more. "Really," he continued, "tell me how you are in the sun? Like my sister? Red, red, RED?" he yelled.

I said nothing. This prompted the other interrogator to interject. "If you want to stay silent, by all means, go ahead. There are pictures and videos and people and soldiers that can speak on your behalf," he threatened.

They continued competing for my attention, each trying his own tactics to elicit a response from me and talking over the other one in the process.

"I'm from Israel," the angry one behind the desk continued. "I'm from Israel. I'm an interrogator from Israel, and we follow the law like this," he said, extending his hand forward in a straight line. "We obey the law."

I stared at him blankly.

"Israeli law rules the entire area. The whole area is governed by Israeli law. The law of the military. And *you* need to obey the law! You and your entire family!" he scolded loudly.

I stayed quiet.

Then, the "good" cop took another stab at getting me to say something. "Your people probably say there's an occupation because of the government. But I'm not Netanyahu. Am I Netanyahu?"

I shook my head.

"Who am I? I'm from Jerusalem. And I'm a soldier as well. Are you Abbas? No. Right? Right," he said, answering his own question. "We are all human."

Was he asking for my sympathy? This was a strange and ineffective appeal to get me to soften toward him, I thought.

"You don't want to go to jail, right?"

I shook my head.

"Okay. Do you want to go back to Hasharon? To prison?"

I didn't react.

They brought out a laptop and placed it in front of me. Just as they did in the previous interrogation, they played the video from the day I hit the soldiers, the video my mother livestreamed on Facebook. Seeing my relatives on the screen was the most difficult part of the interrogation for me.

"Whose voice is that?" the "bad" cop demanded, pointing to the screen. "Whose voice is that?"

I didn't answer.

"You can hear with your ear, right? Whose voice is that?"

Silence.

"Did you hear it or not? Whose voice is that?!" he asked again, with more aggression. "Who is speaking here?"

"I retain my right to remain silent," I said.

"WHO IS SHE?" he shouted.

I refused to answer.

"Listen to this," he went on, speaking over the audio playing from the laptop. "I'll tell you who's speaking here. It's your mother, Nariman, okay? Narameen?"

"Narameen," the other one affirmed.

"Narameen," he repeated.

"No, Nariman, Nariman, Nariman," said the other one, correcting himself.

"Nariman. And she's telling you all here what to do in the area. Is that true or not?"

I stayed quiet.

"Is it true or not?!"

Silence.

"IS IT TRUE OR NOT?" he shouted.

"I retain my right to remain silent."

"Who are these people?" he pressed, pointing at my relatives on the screen. "Who are these people?! WHO ARE THESE PEOPLE?"

When I refused to tell him, the interrogator to my side leaned his body in front of mine to view the laptop screen. In Hebrew, he began to name who he believed was in the video, answering his colleague's question.

"I see Osama here, I see Nour here. The whole gang. Nour, Nour Tamimi is here," he reported.

"Nour and who else?" the other one asked me.

The interrogator beside me stood up and began writing down names in a notebook while the other one typed furiously on his keyboard. "Nour Tamimi, Marah Tamimi, umm . . . Osama Tamimi, umm . . . Jihad Tamimi—I'm not one hundred percent sure of that, but it's very likely. You have Mahmoud Barakeh Tamimi. I'll tell you where they live in a minute."

My face fell in horror, and my heart began beating faster, as he listed the names of my family members. I could bear the consequences of my own actions, but the thought of any of my relatives being punished for something I had done was my Achilles' heel.

The two interrogators forced me to watch more videos that had been filmed in my village, and demanded I give them names, which of course I did not.

"We'll round up every single one of them," the "good" cop threatened. "You know Nour! You know Marwan! You know Osama! You know Marah! You know them all! We'll take every one of them if you don't cooperate. It's in your hands! They'll talk to us. It's on you!" he shouted.

This went on for what felt like an eternity. My neck and back were painfully stiff from my sitting in the chair in the same position for hours. My wrists were sore from the hand-cuffs. I tried my best to mentally escape from the room as I had in previous interactions, but their barrage of loud questions and endless intimidation made it hard. I summoned all the strength I could to stay calm and not cry in front of them.

Eventually, the video got to the part where I confronted the two soldiers on my family's property.

"Who's hitting the soldier?" the interrogator behind the desk asked. "Me or my daughter? Or his daughter?" he asked sarcastically, pointing to the other interrogator.

"I don't have daughters," the other man replied, laughing. They both laughed and slapped high-fives.

Trying out something new, the daughter-less good-cop in-terrogator started speaking to me in English. "We don't need you to speak," he said and then pointed to me on the screen. "We can go with this, and it's okay."

Then why do I have to endure this torment? I wondered to myself.

"Okay, you want to be a hero?" the interrogator went on. "You're a hero!"

"Where are you here?" the other demanded, pointing again to the video. "WHERE ARE YOU?"

"I don't want to have to bring those children here. Please. Say something, and maybe I won't need to," the "good" cop pleaded. "I don't want to bring the children."

The thought of my cousins and baby brothers imprisoned because of something I had done consumed me with guilt, but I still refused to identify them or say anything. My mind raced with possible scenarios. I told myself that even if they were arrested, they wouldn't stay in prison long. They were merely children, and they had done nothing wrong. But, of course, the occupying forces could do whatever they pleased.

I forced myself not to spiral down that thought pathway; doing so would only break me, and that's precisely what these two men wanted. Instead, I resolved in my head, over and over again, that I would never confess. Even if they brought my dad into that office and killed him in front of me, I wouldn't confess. Even if they tried to chop off my head and tongue, I wouldn't confess.

And after hours of their verbal assaults, intimidation, and sexual harassment, I still didn't confess.

Compared to the interrogations so many other Palestinians had suffered through, mine was mild. I've heard stories of Palestinians, including minors, being tortured ruthlessly at the hands of their Israeli interrogators—blindfolded, badly beaten, tied up in chairs, and placed in horribly painful stress positions for long periods. The accounts of such abuse have long been well documented. I was relieved not to have to endure that. Still, there are no justifications for what those two adult Israeli men put sixteen-year-old me through that day.

FOR MONTHS, IT FELT like I practically lived on the *bosta*, because of how many court dates I had. The physically and psychologically grueling routine of being transported from prison to the court is one to which no one should have to grow accustomed. The amount of time I spent in the actual courtroom at Ofer was negligible compared to the endless hours I spent being transferred around on the *bosta* and then waiting for my turn in the freezer-of-death cell. I had to wear an army green prison uniform each time I went to court, and despite the many layers of clothing I piled on under it, I was always freezing.

It didn't take me long to realize that I was being tried in a kangaroo court and that, like other Palestinians caught up in the Israeli military court system, I never had a real shot at justice. Five days after my initial court appearance, I had another hearing to appeal the court's previous decision to deny me bail and extend my remand. Gaby's appeals on my behalf were rejected, and my remand was extended again. I was growing increasingly frustrated with being awakened in the middle of the night to spend entire days being transported to and from the court only to hear them sentence me to spend more time in prison.

This is what happened four days later, when I returned to Ofer yet again. The prosecutors asked the court once again to extend my detention to give them more time to prepare the charges against me. Gaby told me they were already planning to charge me with assaulting a soldier, harming the security of the area, and—based on what I had said during the Facebook Live video my mother had streamed—incitement.

After I hit the soldiers, I addressed the camera off the cuff, still frazzled by the ongoing tensions surrounding my home, saying, "I hope that everyone takes part in the protests, as that's the only way we'll achieve something, because our strength is in our stones. And I hope that everyone around the world unites so that we can free Palestine. Trump made this decision, and he needs to bear the consequences of any kind of Palestinian response to it, whether it's stabbings, suicide attacks, or stone throwing. We have to do something, and we have to get our story out to the world so that we can achieve something. And, hopefully, that will be to free Palestine."

Gaby informed me that the prosecution was also looking to add other charges, related to past protests in which I had participated. Their request for more time was granted, and my remand was extended for the third time.

With all the trips to and from court, I was getting accustomed to the rapid shutter-click of the cameras pointed my way and to journalists calling out questions to me in the courtroom. But during this latest hearing, I was surprised to see Ahmad Tibi, a Palestinian member of the Israeli Knesset, in the courtroom. Leaning over the wooden railing of the defendant's box, he gave me these words of encouragement and support: "Remember, you're stronger than they are!"

I was humbled that someone as high-ranking as he would come all the way from his 1948 village of Taybeh, north of Tel Aviv, to see me. He later told the press that my mother and I had been arrested only after the footage of my hitting the soldier had started to spread around the world—an admission that Israel was concerned mainly with getting revenge for a humiliating viral video, rather than an actual assault. Tibi pointed out that while Israelis had lost their temper over my slapping a soldier in the face, none of them seemed concerned about the crime the military had committed by shooting my cousin in the head earlier that same day. I was grateful that he was using his platform to draw attention to what had happened to Mohammad.

Four days later, on January 1, 2018, I reappeared in court and was formally indicted on twelve counts, including aggravated assault of a soldier, threatening a soldier, interference with soldiers, incitement, and throwing stones. Half the charges were from alleged incidents that occurred prior to the day I hit the soldier. One charge even dated back more than a year and a half, which raised the question: If those actions warranted an arrest, why wasn't I arrested at the time? Why didn't the soldiers arrest me or Nour or my mom the day I hit them? The only reasonable answer was that my arrest was politically motivated. Israel wanted to make an example out of me. I got confirmation of this soon after when Nour, who was also charged with aggravated assault of a soldier and interference, was released on bail.

The next time I appeared in court was for my own bail hearing. The request for my bail was denied, as was my mother's during her hearing. Gaby argued that international human rights law permits the detention of children only as a measure of last resort and for the shortest appropriate period. She suggested that, rather than be kept in pretrial detention, I could report to a police station outside Nabi Saleh every Friday. The judge refused, saying it was not an "effective alternative." Gaby maintained that I wasn't a security or flight risk and reminded the court that I had never been arrested before. The judge said the fact that I had never been arrested before demonstrated the leniency of the security forces, and he cited previous occasions when I had allegedly attacked soldiers over

the years as evidence that my behavior was "ideologically motivated." Never mind the fact that each time I confronted soldiers, I was outside my own home or near it.

Gaby provided examples of Israeli soldiers who had committed more serious offenses than I but who had been granted
bail. And she criticized the fact that, as a Palestinian minor, I
was subject to a completely different legal system from Israeli
minors, including the settlers who lived in the West Bank. The
military court system, she contended, was inherently discriminatory and denied Palestinians the same protections afforded
to Israeli defendants. Israeli children, for example, got interviewed by a probation officer, who was required to seek out
alternatives to detention. But like other Palestinian children, I
had had no such interview. The denial of bail was just another
example of the unfair double standards Israel applies to Palestinian versus Israeli children. Israel's civil courts deny bail
to Israeli children in only 18 percent of cases. But in cases
involving Palestinian children, the military courts deny bail
70 percent of the time.

In his ruling, the judge ultimately said that he found no
alternative other than to order my detention until the end of
the proceedings, because "the gravity of the offenses of which
[I was] accused does not allow an alternative to custody." This
was laughable. The only real danger I posed was to Israel's
image. Given the charges I was facing, I knew my prison sentence could be long. At this point, I saw no end in sight.

I wasn't aware of it at the time, but the international solidarity behind my case was growing tremendously. I was fortunate that a group of my relatives, family friends, and activists
had teamed up to advocate for me and my mom. They per-
sisted with media outreach, to keep our story in the news.
The hashtag FreeAhedTamimi was trending on social media
globally, and millions had signed a petition calling for my re-

lease. Solidarity marches calling for my freedom and for an end to Israel's practice of arresting and detaining Palestinian children were taking place around the world, including in New York City, Istanbul, Paris, and Madrid. Thirty-eight prominent legal experts from the United States, South Africa, the Netherlands, and various other countries submitted a letter to Israel's army commander calling for my release and criticizing Israel's "separate and unequal system of military detention." I was not the first child to be arrested and detained by Israel, nor would I be the last, but my case seemed to be drawing attention to Israel's abuses in a way that hadn't been achieved before.

Within Israeli society, however, including among its leadership, the attacks and threats against me were only growing more vile. In a BBC interview, Israeli lawmaker Oren Hazan of the right-wing Likud Party argued that "a slap is terrorism," adding, "If I was there, she would finish in the hospital. For sure. No one could stop me. I would kick, kick her face, believe me." Israel's then–education minister and, at the time of this writing, prime minister, Naftali Bennett, said that Nour and I deserved to "finish [our] lives in prison." Shortly after I was arrested, a prominent Israeli journalist named Ben Caspit wrote, "We should exact a price at some other opportunity, in the dark, without witnesses and cameras." It still gives me chills to wonder what price Caspit had in mind, but more than that, I pondered the kind of hatred these grown men must have had in their hearts to write such repugnant things and wish such harm on a young girl. Meanwhile, Israeli settlers from Halamish sneaked into Nabi Saleh in the middle of the night and graffitied the walls of our village: DEATH TO AHED TAMIMI and THERE'S NO PLACE IN THE WORLD FOR AHED TAMIMI.

IT WAS DURING MY lengthy pretrial detention that I marked my seventeenth birthday, on January 31, 2017, behind bars. The girls surprised me with potato chips and some chocolate they had purchased from the canteen. That evening, back in Nabi Saleh, my family threw a birthday party for me at home in my absence. A swarm of media was there to cover it. Palestine TV broadcast the festivities live, knowing that it was one of the only channels we could access in prison. I sat on the edge of one of the bunk beds and watched the celebration with my cellmates, my eyes glued to the screen. My heart lit up when I saw Waed and Abu Yazan and Salam appear. At the front of our house, in the same spot where I had hit the soldiers, candles placed inside empty tear gas canisters had been arranged to spell out FREE AHED TAMIMI. Elsewhere on the ground were dozens of posters with the pictures and names of other women Palestinian political prisoners. The posters were laid out in the shape of a giant peace sign, with candles placed atop each one.

I watched as my family and friends gathered around a huge rectangular sheet cake decorated with a picture of me. The picture was taken during one of the marches in the village. I'm standing in front, wearing a pink shirt with a silver star on it. As they sang "Happy Birthday," I saw Janna fight back sobs and wipe tears from her eyes. It choked me up to see her looking so sad. When a reporter later interviewed her, asking what message she'd like to send me, my cousin defaulted to being the brave Janna the world knew, saying, "Ahed, it's true you're in prison, but we're here celebrating your birthday regardless. Happy birthday and may you be free every year that follows this one!"

Inshallah, I thought.

It felt strange to see everyone at my house without my mom and me there. Even though he spoke eloquently on camera, I could see the pain in my father's eyes. He was now a single dad, left to manage the household affairs, including raising three sons, all on his own. His wife and only daughter would be locked up for God knew how long. Each time I was able to catch a quick glimpse of him in the courtroom, I had grown accustomed to that same pained look in his eyes. He tried to mask whatever he was feeling and appear strong for me, but I understood fully how agonizing it must be for him to see both me and his wife there—in the same military court that had killed his only sister.

Two weeks after my birthday, on February 13, my trial officially began. I entered the courtroom to see, in addition to my relatives, scores of journalists, NGO observers, foreign diplomats, and activists pouring in. But as soon as the judge entered, he ordered everyone but my immediate family out of the courtroom, saying it was for my own benefit, as a minor, that the trial be held behind closed doors.

What a joke, I thought. *If they cared about my benefit or protection to any degree, why did they ensure that their cameras were rolling on the night of my arrest? Probably to appease an angry Israeli public that felt humiliated by my confrontation with the soldiers and to humiliate me.*

Gaby objected to having a closed trial, saying that both my family and I wanted the trial to be open, for all to see. If the judge was concerned about what benefited me, surely he should factor in my and my family's preference. But he didn't, instead insisting that the trial remain closed, most likely because a public trial meant more negative press for Israel. A trial carried out in the dark guaranteed that the world would not continue to see how my rights, like the rights of so many other Palestinian children, were being infringed upon.

Once the session got under way, an Arabic-speaking officer read each of the twelve charges against me. Gaby gave her preliminary statement, questioning the legality of the military court and of the entire occupation. She pointed out that according to the Geneva Conventions, occupation should be temporary, but through facts on the ground—such as the continued expansion of settlements and the attempts to annex more Palestinian land—Israel had shown that it had no intention of its occupation being temporary, thereby making it illegal. The occupation, she contended, should be put on trial, not me. She once again highlighted the injustices of having two separate legal systems applied to Palestinian minors and the children of Israeli settlers who lived on the same land, likening it to apartheid.

Regarding the twelve charges levied against me, Gaby argued that most of them were futile and should be dismissed. The indictment, she believed, was intended to deter me and other Palestinian children from resisting the occupation as I had done. She requested to see the evidence the prosecution had against me, and the prosecution asked for more time. The court was adjourned for a few weeks. We'd reconvene in March, and Gaby would once again fight to have an open session.

A COUPLE OF DAYS before my next hearing, Gaby came to the prison to visit me. She had a plea offer from the prosecutors in hand. "You have two choices," she said. "Either you take this plea deal and serve eight months in prison, or we go through the full trial and you face a much longer sentence. I recommend you take the plea deal." The plea deal, she explained, would require me to plead guilty to four out of the twelve charges brought against me: attacking a soldier, two counts of disrupting a soldier, and incitement. I would also have to pay roughly $1,500 and accept a three-year suspended sentence, which could be activated at any time if I said or did something Israel didn't like. This meant that once I got out, I'd have to tread lightly and be cautious. The time I'd already served was included in the eight-month sentence, meaning I'd likely be released sometime in July.

"I have to think about it," I told her.

I knew that when faced with this choice, virtually all Palestinian defendants accepted the plea deal because it ultimately got them out of prison faster. They knew they wouldn't get a fair trial anyway. It's why Israel's military courts can boast a conviction rate of almost 100 percent. Still, how could I bring myself to plead guilty to any of the charges? I didn't withstand days of harsh interrogation, forcing myself to remain silent for hours, only to later plead guilty. In doing so, I'd be betraying my principles.

I returned to our cell block and consulted my mother, Khalto Yasmeen, and Khalida on the matter. They were all in agreement that I should accept the deal.

"We understand the principle of your not wanting to accept the plea deal," Khalida said. "But it's not worth losing years of your life locked up here when you can make a greater impact out there. Take the plea."

The girls in my cell echoed this advice. They told me to think about my education and my future. They knew I had dreams of becoming a lawyer and that, in order to achieve those dreams, I'd need to be free. I knew what they were saying was true. And now, after my arrest and my experience in prison, getting to know all the girls and women there, my desire to become a lawyer had only intensified. I wanted to get out as quickly as possible so I could advocate for them and stand by them just as they were now standing by me. The concession I'd make by pleading guilty to the charges against me would be worth it in the end, I told myself.

On the day of my sentencing hearing, I walked into the

courtroom with my head held higher than ever. Sure, I had accepted the plea deal despite my principles, but I found comfort and peace in the knowledge that there was now an end in sight. The sooner I got out, the sooner I could do something to make a difference.

A few of my cousins and some friends from school sat in the back of the courtroom. We giggled and gestured to one another, sometimes managing to blurt out a short sentence before an officer of the court shushed us. But we remained undeterred and tried to have as much fun as we could in this debacle of a military courtroom. The court officer finally stood in front of me to block my view of them.

Once the plea deal was presented to the judge and the hearing was concluding, I addressed the courtroom. I decided to speak the only words that needed to be uttered in that setting: "There is no justice under occupation, and this court is illegal."

As the officers whisked me away to the freezer-of-death cell, I managed to shout out to my family and friends, a big grin on my face, "Bye! See you in four months! I love you!"

I'VE ALREADY DRIVEN HOME the point that Israelis and Palestinians are subject to two very different legal systems, the one for Palestinians far more punitive and unfair. But there are two glaring examples of this related to my trial that I have to highlight. The first pertains to Elor Azaria.

Elor Azaria is an Israeli soldier who fatally shot a Palestinian man in Hebron in March 2016. The Palestinian man had already been shot for allegedly planning a stabbing attack against soldiers. He was lying wounded and motionless on the ground when Azaria finished him off with his weapon. The killing was caught on film. A military court sentenced Azaria to eighteen months in prison. He had to serve only half of it due to his "good behavior." Just a few months prior to my own release, he was freed to a hero's welcome. Ultimately, he served only nine months in prison for his crime—just one month longer than my sentence for slapping an armed adult man in the face.

The other example centers on Yifat Doron, and it took place during my mother's sentencing hearing. Yifat is a Jewish Israeli activist and a dear friend of the family. She had been coming to Nabi Saleh every week to join us in the marches and was particularly close to my mother. She was there in the hospital when my Khalo Rushdie died and was standing alongside her when Mama was shot in the leg with a live bullet. I know that our imprisonment was very painful for her.

Like me, my mother took a plea deal that had her serving an eight-month sentence. Soon after my mom was sentenced, Yifat got up from where she was sitting in the back of the courtroom, walked right up to the military prosecutor, and slapped him across the face while shouting, "Who are you to judge her?" But unlike my slapping incident, hers was not caught on camera. She was arrested and, a couple of days later, brought before a civilian, not a military, court in Jerusalem. There, the police requested that she be remanded for five days for obstructing justice and posing a risk to the public. Yifat, who chose to represent herself, didn't object to the police's request that she be kept in custody. Instead, she said, "Concerning the risk, I agree with them that anyone who does not toe the line with your apartheid regime, who thinks independently, must necessarily prove a risk to that very regime." The judge ordered her released anyway.

Unlike me and my mother—unlike all other Palestinians, for that matter—Yifat did not have to spend the months before her trial or the time during her trial in prison. She got out on bail. By hitting a military official, Yifat had proven her point: Even when their crimes are nearly identical to those of Israelis, Palestinians are not punished the same, tried the same, or given the same rights and protections as Israelis. In May 2020, Yifat was sentenced in a civilian court to eight months in prison and ordered to pay a fine of roughly nine hundred dollars.

I LAY ON ONE of the top bunks in the cell, drifting off to sleep. Just then, my cellphone, sitting next to me on the bed, buzzed. I picked it up and saw that Abu Yazan had sent me a text message. I sensed that whatever he had to say was urgent. I tapped the message icon on the screen to open it, but nothing happened. I tapped it again, more aggressively, but it still wouldn't open. I tried turning the phone off and back on again, but the screen remained frozen, displaying that I had one unread message that I couldn't access. I tried closing all the apps on my phone, but nothing I did would allow me to read my brother's message. My heart beat faster, and my hands trembled as I held the phone, desperately trying to see Abu Yazan's message. Tears filled my eyes, and I pleaded to God to reveal the message to me.

And right as the text message was finally opening, I woke up.

It was a bad dream. Cellphones are, of course, illegal in prison. Despite this fact, I had this same dream nearly every night of my eight-month incarceration. Sometimes it was a message from Abu Yazan. Other times, it was from my cousin Mahmoud, or my father, or Marah. And each time, the message would not open. In every dream, I knew a loved one was urgently trying to get ahold of me, to give me an update about something that had happened to my family, and in every dream, I couldn't make contact.

The longing for my family and friends grew more painful with each passing day. I began missing my loved ones so sorely that I would close my eyes to try to conjure their images in my mind. But I couldn't. I'd pour all my focus and concentration into trying to remember the details of their faces and still be unable to. This failure often drove me to tears. How could the faces of the people I loved most in this world be reduced to vague, blurry figures?

It's true that my mother was imprisoned with me, and that her cell was just across the narrow hall from mine, but this hardly gave me comfort. I frequently lamented to the girls how agonizing it was to see my own mother a prisoner, in handcuffs, enduring experiences I wouldn't wish on my worst enemy. My mother raised me to be a strong girl, one who stood up for herself. That's why I've never experienced a greater pain than seeing her so utterly disempowered. It was similar to the pain I felt the year she spent unable to walk or care for herself after Israeli soldiers shot her in the leg—only this time I felt responsible, and my guilt only compounded the pain.

Mama and I deliberately tried to keep space between us, out of sensitivity to the other girls, whose mothers weren't incarcerated with them. The few times my mom would hug or kiss me, we'd notice their eyes fixed on us. You could see in their forlorn faces that they desperately longed for their own mothers. And how could they not? They were children, after all. After recognizing the unfair advantage we had over them, my mother and I became mindful not to do anything that would remind them of their pain. My mom also did her best to serve as a surrogate mother to them. They'd often go to her for a hug or motherly comfort, and even called her Mama.

In prison, you feel almost completely disconnected from the outside world and everyone you left behind. The opportunities to see or correspond with your loved ones are few and far between. The prison authorities don't provide us with phones to call family, and visits are rare and difficult to secure. Families have to apply for visitation permits through the International Committee of the Red Cross, which coordinates with and requires the approval of Israel's intelligence services, but it's the intelligence services that ultimately have the power to approve or deny applications. Those who apply to visit the prison must be immediate family members, and even after being approved, they often have to wait a long time to receive their permits. And because Palestinians are illegally imprisoned within Israel, their families must endure the burdensome trip to the prison, traveling far distances and crossing various checkpoints to reach them.

For the prisoner's part, you don't know ahead of time whether your family has been granted a permit to visit. All you know is that it's a visitation day, so you get yourself ready to see your loved ones—though you may well be disappointed. If someone does manage to come, the prisoner's representative—in our case, Khalto Yasmeen—comes by and tells you your family is there and that you have to come down immediately. Once you finally get to see each other, you're allotted only forty-five minutes for the visit. You meet in a large room split in half lengthwise. Prisoners sit across from their visitors, the two groups divided by a soundproof window. You speak through phone receivers, which often malfunction, forcing you to bang them on the table several times throughout the meeting in a desperate attempt to kick-start them into working again. You're flooded with emotions and must reconcile your conflicting impulses in order to savor every second of the brief time you've been allotted, while also trying to ask as many questions as you can and absorb as much information as possible. You try to ignore the fact that prison authorities are monitoring you, but at the same time, you take care with what you say. You have so many questions to ask. You're trying to concentrate as hard as possible on what your visitors are saying, but you're simultaneously trying to memorize the details of their faces, because you've forgotten them and you don't want to sink into despair the next time you try to conjure up their image in your mind. All the while, the minutes fly by, and you wish time could miraculously freeze.

But before you know it, the visit is over.

You try to hold on to the high you've just gotten from seeing your family for as long as possible, but it's short-lived. The return to your tomb of a cell snaps you back into your grim reality and saps from you all the momentary joy you've just soaked up. You don't know if or when there will be a next visit. Perhaps the next time you see your family will be in court, where you'll have no chance to properly communicate with them.

Corresponding through letters isn't an option, either. Regular mail delivery is one of many luxuries Palestinians don't have under occupation. Most of our houses and buildings aren't numbered, which means incoming mail is usually sent to post offices. But that mail first must be processed, and likely inspected, by Israel, and there's no guarantee if or when it will arrive to its intended recipient. There was no official way that prisoners like me could send letters out. Only the girls from Jerusalem or who lived within Israel had that option. But even then, the letters they'd try to send out or receive from their families would be stuck for months with Israeli intelligence officials, who probably read everything and would sometimes sit on mail for weeks. That's why everyone got so excited when someone was being released—not just because she'd get to go home and be free, but also because we could entrust her with delivering letters to our families. Other than that, we sometimes managed to send letters out with a representative from the Red Cross when they came to visit.

During the eight months both my mother and I served in prison, my father was allowed to visit only twice. The first time he visited us was in March, a few days before our sentencing. He, Abu Yazan, and Salam had finally secured permits to come. It had been nearly three months since I had a face-to-face conversation with any of them. Other than the few words my dad was able to shout out during my hearings, I had had virtually no contact with him, or with anyone from my village, for that matter. I couldn't wait to be able to sit across from him and my brothers, to see their faces right in front of me, and to ask them all the questions that had been building up inside me since the night of my arrest. But when I made my way to the visitation room, I saw only my dad and Salam sitting on the opposite side of the glass, but not Abu Yazan.

"Where's Abu Yazan?" my mom and I asked in unison, each of us anxiously clutching her respective phone receiver.

"They wouldn't let him cross the checkpoint," my dad replied. "He had to turn around and go home."

My mood instantly flipped. What sort of security threat did my little brother pose? A boy his age, traveling to visit his imprisoned mother and sister? The cruelty of imprisoning us inside Israel and then ensuring that our loved ones couldn't visit had never felt so searing. They managed to rob us of our joy even in the rare, transitory moments we were afforded. Beyond feeling angry at this turn of events, I was genuinely worried. Abu Yazan had never traveled such a far distance by himself, and I was stressed wondering how he'd manage to navigate his way back home alone. He was only fourteen. Now, with his absence, all the excitement I had felt in anticipation of this visit was gone. I listened as attentively as I could as my dad updated us on the family and the affairs of the village. I told him about my daily routine and assured him that I was taking my studies very seriously. But the entire time, I struggled to focus on our conversation. I couldn't stop thinking about Abu Yazan or worrying about how he'd get back home on his own. Once again, I wasn't there to protect him.

Aside from struggling with chronic homesickness, I was tormented by the fact that my Israeli interrogators seemed to have followed through on their threats to arrest my relatives. In the weeks following my arrest, many of my family members were rounded up by the military as a form of collective punishment for what I had done and for the global attention it had garnered. In a single night, six of my relatives were arrested in predawn raids. Israel's notoriously racist far-right defense minister justified the arrests by saying, "Dealing with Tamimi and her family has to be severe, exhaust all legal measures and generate deterrence." And so, the occupation forces continued to target and punish my relatives. It got so bad that some of the parents, with the help of local activists, organized teach-ins to prepare the youth in the village for arrest, blindfolding them to simulate the experience. They also carried out mock interrogations and educated them about their rights.

The guilt I felt over being the cause of all this suffering in the village crushed me. And if that weren't debilitating enough, I soon learned that Mohammad, who had barely survived the shot to his head and who was still missing part of his skull, was among the relatives arrested and taken in for interrogation. Despite the fact that he was still recovering from major surgery to his head, he didn't have a parent or lawyer present with him. A senior military commander claimed that Mohammad had "confessed" that "he was injured while he was riding his bicycle and fell off it."

In response to this audacious lie, my family put out a statement saying, "Israel arrested an injured, posttraumatic fifteen-year-old in the middle of the night and got him to lie out of fear of being sent to prison in his condition." My family also released Mohammad's medical records, including the CT scan of his head before surgery, in which the bullet could clearly be seen lodged in his skull. Hadn't Mohammad suffered enough? I had always known the occupation had no humanity or mercy, and still they managed to surprise me with the depths of their callousness.

I'M OFTEN ASKED BY journalists and activists if I regret hitting the soldiers that day, and my answer is always no. I've never said, "I wish I didn't hit them" or "I wish I never went to prison." Although I did spend a lot of time agonizing over the fact that I was responsible for the subsequent arrests and collective punishment inflicted upon my village, I tried my best to maintain a positive outlook toward my circumstances.

After spending a bit of time in prison, I grew to accept that this was the life I'd have to live for a while. I didn't want to waste time dwelling on the past or wallowing in regret or even blaming myself. I realized that, despite all the suffering and hardship I had to endure, life was still moving ahead. I was grateful to be alive and vowed to make the most of my time. The day would ultimately come when I'd be released and would be able to resume my life at home. But until then, I resolved to take advantage of whatever I could within the confines of the prison. Adopting this mentality is the only way you can survive there. Otherwise, you feel the time passing agonizingly slowly. Every hour can feel like a year, and if you don't fill your time doing things and instead just ruminate all day, you'll inevitably crumble. The most dangerous thing you can do in prison is sit there and wallow in negative thoughts.

So, I forced myself to keep busy however I could. Every

few months, a representative from the Red Cross would visit and bring arts and craft supplies for the girls—beads, velvet, glitter, and embroidery tools. It felt like Eid every time we got our hands on these supplies. We'd spend hours making beaded jewelry and then gifting our creations to one another. I learned how to sew and got resourceful with the limited materials at our disposal. For example, we'd wait until the prison administration delivered vegetables, which came in cardboard boxes. Once the boxes were emptied out, we'd cut out pieces to serve as the front and back cover of a notebook. We'd use the velvet the Red Cross brought us and affix it to the cardboard and then decorate it with puffy paint. Then we'd sew in pages. We didn't have proper thread, so instead, we'd pull the threads out of potato sacks and use those. Of course, a needle was considered something holy in prison. Losing one was a tragedy. When the prison administration eventually banned the Red Cross from bringing needles and we lost the one needle we had in our cell, we were devastated.

Oftentimes, the girls in my cell and I would exchange stories. I learned so much listening to their unique life experiences. When I wasn't doing that, I was typically reading a book. Our jailers allowed our visiting relatives to give each prisoner a new book every couple of months, although they often policed which books would be allowed in. I loved self-help books about personal development and growth. The writers' insights about how to grow one's self-confidence and how to navigate life's challenges uplifted me. Anytime a fact from a book struck me, I'd share it with the other girls.

My favorite thing to read was a collection of poetry by Mahmoud Darwish, Palestine's late famed poet, entitled *Jadariyya*, or *Mural*. My go-to poem, the one I'd read anytime I felt depressed or fed up with everything, which was quite often, was called "Nothing Pleases Me."

Nothing pleases me
the traveler on the bus says—Not the radio
or the morning newspaper, nor the citadels on the hills.
I want to cry /
The driver says: Wait until you get to the station,
then cry alone all you want /
A woman says: Me too. Nothing
pleases me. I guided my son to my grave,
he liked it and slept there, without saying goodbye /
A college student says: Nor does anything
please me. I studied archaeology but didn't
find identity in stone. Am I
really me? /
And a soldier says: Me too. Nothing
pleases me. I always besiege a ghost
besieging me /
The edgy driver says: Here we are
almost near our last stop, get ready
to get off . . . /
Then they scream: We want what's beyond the station,
keep going!
As for myself I say: Let me off here. I am
like them, nothing pleases me, but I'm worn out
from travel.

The poem spoke to my soul. It resonated with how trapped I felt physically, mentally, and emotionally and somehow made me feel less alone.

Other times, I'd read a novel and deliver a full synopsis to the girls once I finished. Or another girl would recap what she had just read. Everyone gathered around for our makeshift story time. Once, I was so engrossed in a six-hundred-page romance novel that I devoured it in three days. It was a love story called *You're Mine*. The plot revolves around a guy and a girl who fall in love at a young age. Her family dies when she is young, so his family adopts her. The two essentially grow up together, and everything is beautiful until a war breaks out and the young man is imprisoned. The way the author describes the young man's captivity is so vivid and gripping. The young man keeps a picture of his love in his cell and looks at it all the time. For years, his family has no idea what happened to him and assumes he is dead. Brokenhearted and with the understanding that he will never return, the girl he loves gets engaged to his brother. But our hero eventually escapes from prison! When he reunites with his family, he learns about his brother's engagement to his love and stops wanting to be with her. But his brother backs out of the relationship, acknowledging that she is his brother's original and rightful love.

When they are young, the book's hero constructs a box for his love out of paper. They write notes to each other and put them into the box, swearing never to open it and read what's inside. She wrote, "One day I will marry Waleed. You're Mine." Anyway, at the end of the story, they find the box and open it. Discovering what each wrote to the other, they decide to be together.

It was a beautiful "happily ever after" ending, which was exactly what I needed. I was completely captivated reading it, but also eager to learn how the story ended. While reading, I'd tell the girls, "I can't take this anymore. I want to turn to the last page and see what happens!" They were equally invested in discovering what happened and would say, "No! You can't! Keep reading!"

In prison, we all experienced an absolute drought in terms of romance, and on top of that, we were stuck in one another's faces all day and night. So when a novel like that came along, we had to savor it. Naturally, I told the girls the entire story from beginning to end.

Summarizing books for one another was just one of the ways we passed the time. We had other creative outlets, though. Before we were imprisoned, Noor (a girl who later became one of my cellmates) and I used to listen to a lot of music. Some of the girls in our cell had been imprisoned for three or four years, meaning they weren't up to date on the latest hits. So Noor and I would sit there and perform all the songs we knew, to get them up to speed. If a girl who had just been arrested joined our cell, before asking anything about her case, we'd sit her down and bombard her with questions about all the things that teenage girls cut off from the rest of the world would naturally be itching to know.

"What new songs are out?"
"What's the most popular one?"
"Sing it for us!"
"What's the latest fashion out there?"
"What new buildings have come up in Ramallah?"

The poor girl wouldn't get a break from us.

If we didn't try to keep ourselves constantly entertained, we'd for sure have lost our minds—especially considering the repulsive conditions in which we were living. Hasharon is a very old prison and was infested with cockroaches and mice. We eventually became professional exterminators. Each time a mouse made its way into the cell, one girl trapped it in a corner with a broom while another beat it with a pot or whatever else was at her disposal. For a while, construction was being carried out around the prison, and whatever they were digging up emitted an overpowering pungent sewage-like stench that wafted into our cell and made us all want to vomit. Trapped in our cells and suffering from the odor, we were visited by more cockroaches than ever. I lost count of how many we'd had to kill in a day.

There were, of course, many occasions when tensions among us flared and we'd get into arguments—a natural outcome of cramming so many adolescent girls into a small, poorly ventilated cell. When I first entered the prison, I was one of five prisoners in a cell with only four beds. After some of the girls were released or transferred to another cell because they turned eighteen, I, along with Hadiya, was moved to a new cell with another set of minors. For a while, we were eleven girls in a cell with only six beds, but even just six people would have felt overcrowded given the size of the cell. We would go to sleep together, wake up together, eat together, pray five times a day together, read together, laugh together—everything.

And you could forget about enjoying even an iota of privacy. There were so many bodies in that tiny, sealed-off space that we genuinely felt suffocated. Sometimes we'd even wake up in the middle of the night unable to breathe. Being stuck in what felt like a coffin, with ten other teenage girls in your face day in and day out, was bound to drive anyone crazy. And it was often too much to bear. If one of us was in a bad mood because of it, we all felt it, and the bickering would escalate until we all sat down to mediate or vent.

Other times, we'd hold space for whoever was sad or homesick. When one of us said, "I miss my parents," or "I miss being home," and started crying, we'd sit around her and try to console her, and before you knew it, all eleven of us would be simultaneously weeping and pouring our hearts out about whom or what *we* longed for. This inevitably happened a few times every week.

I'll never forget the time I sat in our cell with a girl named Rama Jaabis. I was telling her about my childhood in Nabi Saleh when she asked me how my uncle Rushdie had been killed. I began recounting the story of how he was shot, describing how I tried to run over to him but couldn't reach him amid all the live bullets the soldiers were firing at me. As I relived those horrific details, I broke into tears. And as I cried, Rama began crying with me. While both of us sat there weeping, the other girls returned to the cell and asked what had happened. As soon as I told them, they began to cry as well. I was moved by their tears and their solidarity. They understood my pain, and their empathy was genuine. Each of us had someone to mourn, someone who had been stolen from us by the occupation. And our collective tears further cemented our sisterhood.

My cellmates not only shared my pain, but also tried to protect me from it. One morning, I woke up a little later than the other girls and asked them to turn on the television.

"It's not working!" one of them quickly replied.

"There's a problem with all the TVs," another clarified. "The prison administration said they'll try to fix it later today."

I got up and told them I was heading to the yard to walk around a bit.

"No, no! Stay here. We want to talk to you about something!"

I sat there as each girl attempted to distract me with a story, each story completely unrelated to the other. Something was definitely up. I managed to escape them at one point and ran to my mother's cell, where I was surprised to find Khalto Yasmeen, Khalida, and a bunch of other women who weren't her cellmates sitting around her comforting her.

"What's going on?" I asked.

"Ahed, they arrested Waed," my mom said.

My cellmates had seen the headline on the news: PRIS-ONER AHED TAMIMI'S BROTHER ARRESTED BY THE OCCUPA-TION FORCES.

I grabbed on to my mom and began sobbing.

"We've been expecting them to arrest any of our family members," she tried to reason with me. "Bassem, Waed, Mohammad, any of them."

I knew what she was saying was true. The military's crackdown on our village after my arrest seemed to have put everyone at risk—especially Waed, whom we knew was wanted and had been regularly sleeping outside the house to evade arrest. It's true that he was older and stronger than me, and had already been arrested before, but I worried about him—about all my relatives—more than I worried about myself. Plus, my immediate family was already going through enough with me and my mother away from them in prison.

Khalida told me to calm down, with no success. All I could do was hug her while I continued to sob. Khalto Yasmeen, pained by seeing me in such distress, held me in her arms and began to cry as well.

Waed was ultimately sentenced to fourteen months in prison for stone throwing. He was still serving his time when my mother and I were released in July. We believe the length of his sentence was retaliatory—revenge for what I had done and the attention it had caused.

DESPITE HOW FRUSTRATED AND emotional we'd often get in prison, we did our best to ensure laughter always mingled with tears. I saw this persistent joy as a form of resistance. When they throw you in prison, the occupation forces want to see you broken and defeated, your spirits as low as the

ground. When, instead, you dare to defy their system of oppression by laughing, it shows them that not even prison will
break you or stop you from caring about your cause. Laughter
sends a powerful message: We're still alive, we're still laughing, and we love life.

One evening, we were brushing our teeth in the cell when
a prison officer named Fuad came in to count us. An exceptionally mean Israeli Druze man, Fuad was tall and over-
weight, with a round face and long eyelashes. His soft voice
belied his meanness, and each time he came around, he'd an-
nounce in a singsong way, "It's time for the count, girls." We
called him Foo Foo behind his back.

When Foo Foo entered our cell, we quickly threw our
toothbrushes down and stood erect for the count, our mouths
still full of toothpaste and covered in white foam. The scene
was hilarious, but we had to force ourselves to be serious and
stand still. The only problem was a girl named Alaa, from
Bethlehem, who was known for her ferocious laughter. Once
Alaa started laughing, her whole body would convulse, and
she'd cackle with her entire being. This was precisely what
happened while Foo Foo was counting us—Alaa couldn't
control herself and burst out laughing. She threw her head
back with the force of it, and when she brought it forward,
she accidentally spat out all her toothpaste, some of it onto
Foo Foo's arm. By the grace of God, he didn't feel it or notice
what had happened. But we all did. As he turned around to
exit the cell, we saw a wad of toothpaste covering his arm
hair.

At this sight, we erupted into uncontrollable laughter.
Minutes passed with some of us doubled over and others
with tears running down their faces. Though we were scared
that news of this would reach Khalto Yasmeen or, worse, the
prison authorities, who might toss us into solitary confine-

ment for our unintended insubordination, we still couldn't stop laughing. Solitary was a terrifying prospect, one we tried to avoid at all costs. Thankfully, Khalto Yasmeen never found out, and even Foo Foo didn't punish Alaa for her outburst or her projectile spitting. We counted our blessings that we never got busted. And every day that followed, we made sure always to brush our teeth *after* the count.

My favorite funny memory, though, was of the prank Hadiya and I carefully concocted. She and I were on the same wavelength in many ways. We're the same age and were the two shortest girls in the cell. Neither of us stressed out much, either. If I thought I had calm nerves, Hadiya was on a whole other level. She was perpetually chilled out. The whole world could be imploding around her, and she'd act like she didn't have a care in the world. We could all be getting scolded by Khalto Yasmeen for laughing too loudly the night before, and Hadiya would laugh it off, saying, "It's no biggie. Just take it easy!" This was Hadiya's unofficial motto for everything: "Take it easy!"

One evening, out of boredom, we started coloring on our faces using the colored pencils given to us by representatives from the Red Cross. Makeup isn't allowed in prison, but glamorizing ourselves (or at least trying to) was one way for us to reclaim parts of our lost teenagehood. We used the black pencil as eyeliner and dipped the red one in water to apply as lipstick. As we were busy getting dolled up, Hadiya said, "Let's play a prank on the guard!"

A huge prankster myself, I immediately signed on to the idea, knowing we had to strike a tricky balance. We wanted to pull off a little prank that would scare the guard and entertain us, but that wouldn't be too bold and land us in solitary. So what did we do? I instructed all the girls to go wild drawing on their own faces with the colored pencils. We dipped them in water and outlined our lips in black and drew on giant raccoon eyes. We also drew on whiskers, to try to look as crazy and terrifying as possible. Sure, we'd spend the next four hours scrubbing our faces to get it all off, but the prank would be worth it.

We then grabbed every article of clothing we could find and draped them over our heads. I told one of the girls to heat up some water, and once it had boiled, we poured it into a pot and placed it on the floor, in the middle of the cell. One of the girls sat hunched over the pot, which now had steam rising from it, and started chanting nonsensical gibberish while flailing her arms to bring the steam closer to her insanely colored face. The rest of us slowly walked around her while chanting in the deepest octave we could hit, *Hummm daa dee, hummm daa dee*, and pounding on our chests. As we chanted, the girl in front of the pot covered her head with a blanket and bent over the steam to inhale it. She did this repeatedly as we chanted and marched around her, pounding our chests.

While we were immersed in our fake séance, the guard came by for the head count as usual. A look of horror came over her face at the sight of us seemingly summoning spirits. She was so scared, she left immediately. It was the first time she didn't count us. When she walked away, we broke out in laughter. It felt like a victory. The prank was satisfying not just because it was hilarious, but because it felt like a small act of resistance. We had once again showed a guard that our spirits would not be broken by this prison. Quite the contrary—we faked summoning spirits just to turn the tables for an instant and make *her* the uncomfortable one for once.

I WILL FOREVER BE grateful for the education I received behind bars—in spite of my jailers' attempts to stop it. They tried to deny us our right to an education and prevent us from understanding our own oppression, but we persevered. We like to say that we made the prison into a school.

One room of our cell block was slightly larger than the cells we lived in, and we converted this into a classroom. There were about a dozen chairs with desks attached to them; we sat on these while being instructed by Khalida. There was also a small dry-erase board. The only problem was that markers were scarce, and the prison authorities rarely kept the canteen supplied with them for us to purchase. So we'd go months without markers. A scarcity in supplies was the norm in our classroom, though. There were nine of us trying to complete our *tawjihi* year in prison, including my mother, who had never graduated from high school. We didn't all have textbooks, so we became accustomed to passing around one book for nine women and girls to share, each of us transferring what she could of the book's contents into her own notebook. Naturally, our notebooks filled up quickly, requiring us to purchase more from the canteen. But these, too, were not always in stock. We suspected that the prison authority deliberately failed to provide them as another method of thwarting our education.

Our makeshift classroom featured a small library, but the prison authority wouldn't permit all the law books we wanted to reach us. In Damon, another prison inside Israel where Palestinians are illegally incarcerated, a new book was allowed in only if it was exchanged for an existing book. But Khalto Yasmeen fought for us to be able to keep every book that entered Hasharon. And because her job as our representative was a full-time one, she used a small corner of our classroom as an office, to take meetings with individual girls or discuss any personal issues that required some privacy.

Studying for *tawjihi* was no less rigorous in prison than it had been in school. Most of our days were spent either receiving instruction in class or studying on one of the beds in our cell. Still, our classes were under constant threat by the prison authorities. Often, while in session, we would see a prison guard walk past the classroom or, in favorable weather, the courtyard, and the next thing we knew, the alarms would go off, forcing us to return to our cells and be locked in there for the rest of the day.

Sounding the alarms seemed to be our jailers' preferred method of interrupting class, but it wasn't the only one. Alleging that the classes were a form of incitement, a charge both offensive and false, the jailers repeatedly threatened Khalida with solitary confinement for teaching us. On top of that, the head guard of our cell block constantly monitored us when we were in class, making no secret of her distaste for our educational pursuits. Eventually, she told Khalto Yasmeen that we were no longer allowed to go into the classroom and that Khalida was no longer allowed to teach us. Khalto Yasmeen responded that either the prison could provide us with a real teacher or we'd keep holding our own classes. We then devised a strategy to reinforce our stance.

Every Thursday, the top boss of the prison made a routine visit to our section to scope out the situation and talk to the representative to see if there were any problems, any protests planned. He was usually joined by an entourage of intelligence and security officials. One Thursday, in anticipation of his visit, we gathered inside the classroom a little earlier than usual. Even though all communication between prisoners and the authorities had to go through Khalto Yasmeen, those of us who were minors were allowed to speak to the authorities on an occasion like this if we were spoken to.

As expected, the prison official came by our class, as it was in session, and asked the minors, "How are you doing?"

"We're not doing well," we told him.

He asked why not. And one by one, each of us explained the circumstances that were impeding our ability to learn.

"Because you're banning education," Manar said.

"Because you don't want Khalto Khalida to teach us, and she's the one who's been teaching us all this time, since you haven't provided a teacher for us, and it's our right to receive an education."

Then it was my turn to speak.

"It's strange to me," I began. "I don't quite understand how mathematics like one plus one threatens Israel's security."

He responded somewhat defensively, assuring us that the prison officials weren't against our education and that we were, in fact, allowed to learn. But we knew it was just lip service. This was confirmed to us soon after, when the head guard of the section came by. When she saw Khalida still teaching us, she ordered all of us out and shut down the classroom. She told us we were no longer allowed to enter it—obviously, something we wouldn't stand for. We all returned to our cells and shut the doors, a collective action known as "shutting down the cell block." It was a method of going on strike we employed to pressure the prison authorities to retract a decision. They knew that refusing to leave our cells was detrimental to our physical and psychological well-being and that if the male Palestinian prisoners caught wind of our strike, they might strike in solidarity. This would ultimately create a big headache for the prison authorities, not to mention earn the censure of the Red Cross. Not leaving our cells meant that no one was shopping at the prison canteen, thereby applying economic pressure on our jailers. Our tools of protest in prison were very limited, but we did what we could.

The prison authorities eventually opened the doors to our cells, but our condition was that if they reopened the cell block, they would also have to reopen the classroom. They responded by saying, "We'll open the classroom, but you're not allowed to enter it."

Everything about the debacle was absurd, from their seeing our education as a form of rebellion, to their paranoia about the classroom, to this last bizarre stipulation. But as Palestinians living under Israeli rule, the arbitrary cruelty of their decisions, which didn't seem informed by any sort of moral or even practical logic, was something to which we were all accustomed.

We ultimately defied them and entered the classroom anyway. And from that day onward, we called it "the classroom of defiance."

After our protest, they stopped threatening to throw Khalida in solitary. But the guards continued to spy on us and hit the alarms when our classes were in session. And we kept studying anyway.

KHALIDA WAS DETERMINED TO establish a course in international law and international humanitarian law. It wasn't easy. For two months, she coordinated with the Commission of Detainees and Ex-Detainees Affairs and a nongovernmental organization called Addameer Prisoner Support and Human Rights Association. (*Addameer* is the Arabic word for "conscience.") They helped her establish the parameters of the course and guaranteed that everyone who completed it would receive a certificate from the ministry that their families could pick up on their behalf. Khalida knew that securing a certificate would validate the course in the eyes of the prisoners and also lift our spirits.

Her next challenge was procuring the books and resources needed to establish the curriculum and creating a syllabus.

Her family managed to get her a book from the Office of the United Nations High Commissioner for Human Rights that outlined all the basic conventions. In order to teach international humanitarian law, Khalida asked the Red Cross to bring in a book that outlined the rights established in the four Geneva Conventions and the rights that applied to criminal courts. Her focus was on teaching us the Fourth Geneva Convention, because it pertained to civilians under occupation, and the Third Geneva Convention, which pertained to prisoners of war.

There was such resounding enthusiasm that thirty-two of the thirty-four women and girls in the cell block at the time enrolled in the course. We had all been born into the occupation; it was the only life we'd ever known. We knew our lives were one endless stream of injustices, but we didn't have the knowledge or vocabulary to articulate those injustices in the language of international law. And so, almost all of us committed to taking this thirty-six-credit course. We met for two hours every Thursday and Friday, one hour for international law and one hour for international humanitarian law. We stuck to that schedule as rigidly as possible, with the exception of classes cut short due to the guards sounding the alarms or when we were on strike and refused to leave our cells.

In the first half hour of each class, Khalida would write the name of the convention we were discussing that day on the board and some main bullet points. We all took notes as she explained the convention and its corresponding articles. In the next half hour, she broke us up into groups of five or six and instructed each group to select an article of the convention to look into further and discuss as a group. Our discussions couldn't be theoretical, though—we had to explain the article through our own lived experience and how we'd been subjected to violations of it. After each group discussed an article using the testimony of one of its members, another member of the group presented the discussion to the whole class. And then the entire class would discuss the article and reflect on their own lives.

We spent two days on the 1987 United Nations Convention Against Torture, not just because it encompassed so much, but also because it was so relevant to abuses we had each suffered at the hands of the occupation. We learned that its full name was the Convention Against Torture and Other Cruel, Inhuman or Degrading Treatment or Punishment and that it was ratified by Israel in 1991. Article 1 of the convention defines torture as "any act by which severe pain or suffering, whether physical or mental, is intentionally inflicted on a person for such purposes as obtaining from him or a third person information, or a confession, punishing him for an act he or a third person has committed or is suspected of having committed, or intimidating or coercing him or a third person, or for any reason based on discrimination of any kind, when such pain or suffering is inflicted by or at the instigation of or with the consent or acquiescence of a public official or other person acting in an official capacity . . ."

I immediately thought about my own interrogation, and my father's, and the interrogation of so many others in my family, and knew they amounted to torture. In our breakout groups, everyone recounted her own story of torture, many revolving around her arrest. For example, one girl representing her group stood up and said, "We talked about the Convention Against Torture looking at Lama's arrest. When she was arrested, the soldiers hit her and later made her take off all her clothes . . ." It was difficult to hear how these women and girls I was growing so close to had each suffered in her own unique way. Still, the prevailing sentiment of the course was one of empowerment. Our discussions were always lively.

We felt genuine excitement analyzing and unpacking aspects of our lives that we hadn't put much thought into before. In doing so, we learned the egregious extent to which Israel repeatedly violated international law.

We focused a lot on the Fourth Geneva Convention, which deals with humanitarian protections of civilians in a war zone or under occupation. I was astounded to learn the various ways Israel had systematically violated its obligations under this convention, including through its use of collective punishment, extrajudicial killing, torture, destruction of property, and population transfer, as in how it enabled and incentivized its citizens to move to settlements in the occupied territory. I could think of countless examples of violations of each of these counts that I had either witnessed myself or seen on the news.

Watching television in our cells, we became glued to news of the Great March of Return in Gaza, a series of demonstrations that had begun while we were attending our classes. Beginning on March 30, 2018, which Palestinians commemorate as Land Day, the besieged people of Gaza had protested weekly along the fence separating them from Israel. They were demanding an end to Israel's crippling air, land, and sea blockade, which had effectively trapped them for over a decade inside the world's largest open-air prison. And they were demanding the right to return to their homes, which Zionist militias had forcibly removed them from to clear the way for Israel's creation in 1948. Seventy percent of Gaza's population are, in fact, refugees.

Israel's response to these demonstrations was deadly. Each week, Israeli snipers opened fire on the protesters, ultimately killing hundreds and wounding thousands over the course of the year-long protests. The scenes of bloodied protesters, journalists, and medics were shocking and heart-wrenching.

In our classes, we had learned that, according to the Fourth Geneva Convention, it was illegal for Israel to target unarmed civilians like this, and that, in so doing, it may have been committing a war crime. My heart broke when I heard about the murder of a beautiful young Palestinian nurse named Razan Al-Najjar. On June 1, 2018, Razan, despite wearing a white coat signifying her status as a medic, was struck by a bullet fired by an Israeli sniper. She had volunteered as a medic at the movement's very first march and saw it as her patriotic duty to tend to her wounded countrymen, even if she had to dodge bullets to do so. She was only twenty years old.

AT THE END OF the course, we each had to write two research papers: one on international law and one on international humanitarian law. This was a daunting task, but Khalida wanted to prepare us for university, where she said it was essential to have strong research skills. Unlike university, though, our resources in prison were scarce, so we had to be innovative. We passed around among our cells the two books Khalida had, copying down facts in our notebooks to use as references for our research, and we scoured our humble prison library for any relevant books that might also assist us. Khalida encouraged us to watch the news as much as possible and note down examples of violations of the conventions or discrimination we had learned about. We were applying the knowledge we were gaining not only to the incidents that had happened to us in our personal lives, but also to news in Palestine that was unfolding in real time.

As we embarked on our respective research assignments, I learned even more about the various forms of discrimination and oppression Israel enacted upon Palestinians. For my classmates from Jerusalem, this included living under the constant threat of Israel revoking their residency permits and forcing them out of their homes. In fact, in March 2018, the Israeli parliament passed a law allowing the interior minister to revoke the residency rights of any Palestinian in Jerusalem on the basis of a "breach of loyalty" to Israel. This was merely one of Israel's many calculated policies and part of a decades-long plan to maintain a solid Jewish majority in the city.

My classmates who were citizens of Israel were able to examine the institutionalized discrimination they faced. Palestinians make up 20 percent of Israel's population, and despite the fact that they live in their own homeland, Israel relegates them to second- or even third-class status. One of my classmates had discovered that more than fifty laws discriminated against the Palestinian citizens of Israel based solely on their ethnicity. Another discussed how government resources were disproportionately directed to Jews, leaving the Palestinians to suffer the worst living standards in Israeli society, with Palestinian children's schools receiving only a fraction of the government spending given to Jewish schools. They also talked about how difficult it was for Palestinians to obtain land for a home, business, or agriculture because over 90 percent of the land in Israel was owned either by the state or by quasigovernmental agencies (like the Jewish National Fund) that discriminated against Palestinians. And they lamented the fact that if they or any of their relatives chose to marry a Palestinian from the West Bank or Gaza, they couldn't pass on their Israeli citizenship to their spouse, thanks to the Citizenship and Entry into Israel Law. Their spouse wouldn't even be able to gain residency status to live with them inside Israel. This meant they'd be forced to leave Israel and separate from their family in order to live with their spouse.

Another of my classmates decided to research the restrictions on freedom of movement that impeded daily Palestinian life. She wrote about the apartheid wall, which, in a nonbinding decision, the International Court of Justice had declared illegal in 2004. We all knew firsthand that the wall cut right through Palestinian towns and villages, dividing communities and separating many farmers from their land. Israel contends that the wall is needed for security, to prevent attacks, but it didn't construct the wall along the pre-1967 Green Line, which is recognized as the boundary between Israel and the West Bank. Rather, the wall was built deep within the West Bank, enabling Israel to annex even more Palestinian land.

The same classmate also wrote about how Israel's many permanent and temporary checkpoints prevent Palestinians from moving around freely and add painful delays to what should be short, direct journeys. She interviewed some of us about our own experiences with checkpoints. I told her about the spontaneous checkpoints the military regularly erect at the entrance to our village and how we'd sometimes sit in the car for hours trying to go to school or work or whatever appointment we had. Another aspect of her research project looked at the identification cards we are forced to carry at all times and present at the checkpoints. She interviewed some of our classmates from the West Bank about how they aren't allowed to go to Jerusalem or any city inside '48 without a permit from Israel, which isn't easy to obtain.

And as we followed the news, we learned that the Israeli government was debating the controversial and racist "Basic" or Nation-State Law, which it ended up passing in July 2018. The law declares that "the right to exercise national self-determination" in Israel is "unique to the Jewish people." It establishes Hebrew as the official language of the country, with Arabic downgraded to "special status." Finally, the law mandates that the state regard "Jewish settlement as a national value" and to "act to encourage and promote its establishment and consolidation." Israeli apartheid was now more official than ever.

I was fully engaged in the course and loved every second of it. By educating ourselves about our rights and protections under international law and persevering despite every attempt to thwart us and derail our studies, we were practicing the most powerful form of resistance. My political consciousness was expanding, and I felt empowered by the knowledge I was gaining. At the same time, it was infuriating. I kept telling my cellmates, "I'm discovering I'm living a violation, not a life!" I devoted my research paper to examining the violations that took place during the period of my arrest, which were many. For example, I learned that it was my right under international law to be told why I was being arrested, but the night the military took me from my home, I wasn't told why. The International Covenant on Civil and Political Rights, which Israel also ratified in 1991, says that all persons, including children, should be given reasons for their arrest at the time of their arrest. Another violation occurred when the soldiers posed with me, a minor, while taking my picture before leading me into the police station. They had no right to humiliate me like that, nor to film my arrest and publish the video without my parents' permission. And then there was the interrogation. Banning my parents and my lawyer from being with me and putting me in a room alone with men and no female officers were all clear violations. The way the interrogators shouted at me, threatened me, and sexually harassed me by commenting on my appearance in order to coerce a confession were all breaches of the Convention Against Torture. The fact that I was held so long in pretrial detention was another violation.

Then there was my trial. I always knew the trial was just

theater and illegitimate, but it was the international humanitarian law course that opened my eyes to the fact that we
were civilians being tried in a military court system that failed
to meet international standards for the fair conduct of trials
and administration of justice. The fact that we were imprisoned in Israel, rather than in the occupied territories in which
we lived and had been arrested, was a blatant violation of
Article 76 of the Fourth Geneva Convention. That same article states that the occupying power is obligated to provide
adequate medical care and special protection for women and
child prisoners, which was not the case. Lama, one of my cellmates, was shot in the leg by an Israeli soldier when she was
arrested. Her lower leg was paralyzed, and she was in constant pain, but Israel refused to provide her the surgery she
needed to recover or to give her any meaningful medical care
at all, for that matter. Several other women and girls in our
cell block had been shot and were seriously injured, yet were
being denied treatment in prison. While less severe, I suffered
frequent stomachaches that weren't properly treated, either.
But medical neglect wasn't the only way the Israeli government hurt us. For an entire month, the prison authorities
banned us from having milk; they wouldn't even sell it in the
canteen. We were young girls and mothers in need of cal-
cium and vitamin D and the other nutrients milk contains—
especially considering how deficient we were in vitamin D
from never seeing the sun.

I also learned more about the Convention on the Rights of
the Child, which says that the imprisonment of children must
be used only "as a measure of last resort and for the shortest
appropriate period of time," as Gaby cited in my trial. Despite
ratifying that convention in 1991 as well, Israel routinely arrests and detains Palestinian children. In fact, each year, between five hundred and seven hundred Palestinian children

are tried in Israel's military courts. The most common charge brought against them is stone throwing, which is punishable by up to twenty years in prison.

One of the more surprising things I learned is that as a population living under occupation, we are granted by international law the legal right to resist through armed struggle. It's protected under the Geneva Conventions, reaffirmed in a 1982 UN General Assembly resolution. The resolution reaffirmed "the legitimacy of the struggle of peoples for independence, territorial integrity, national unity and liberation from colonial and foreign domination and foreign occupation by all available means, including armed struggle."

I thought back to Nelson Mandela and how history often overlooks his full story. Mandela led his movement in a nonviolent struggle, but when the apartheid regime answered with ever more brutal force, he and his party, the African National Congress, took up arms. Mandela always made clear that this was because the regime had left no peaceful road to freedom. Once he was imprisoned, the state demanded that he renounce violence in exchange for his release, but he said no. Only when the regime offered a peaceful road to achieve democratic equality did he finally renounce violence. But the way his legacy has been appropriated conveniently omits this important chapter of his struggle. It amuses me that, as Palestinians, we're always told to be like Mandela while simultaneously being rebuked for resisting.

Flagrantly and in an astonishing number of circumstances, Israel was failing to meet its obligations under international law. The question that everyone in the course inevitably always came back to was: Why was the international community letting Israel get away with it? Khalida explained to us that while it was very important for us to use international law and international humanitarian law as a mechanism to advance our cause for self-determination and equality, we had to understand that our fate ultimately depended on politics. Many politicians around the world were willing to sacrifice the rights of people and turn a blind eye to violations, especially when it came to Israel's occupation. She reminded us that international law had been created by colonial powers and was disproportionately applied to serve their interests. It frustrated me to realize the limitations of international law we faced as Palestinians seeking justice. I now understood that it would never serve as a silver bullet for our cause, given how countries like the United States shielded Israel from any sort of punitive measures. Holding Israel accountable via international law would have to be accompanied by other strategies, like boycotts and divestment.

But this doesn't mean I'm giving up on it. As soon as I learned that an individual can file a complaint with the International Criminal Court, I vowed to do so once I earned my law degree. I want to hold Israel accountable for everything it has done to me. And I want to represent myself in this endeavor, not because I want the spotlight—I know such an undertaking would only expose me to more insults and slander—but because it's important for me to show Israel that we will hold it accountable for even the smallest of crimes. We need to pursue Israel in the courts for every violation it has committed. They need to know that we're in the streets, the schools and universities, the criminal courts, and the press conferences fighting for justice. We need to send them a message that wherever they go, they'll find us doing something to reject their presence on our land.

At the same time, as Palestinians, we have to be honest with ourselves and acknowledge that our problems won't be instantly resolved once we end the occupation. That's why we have to tie our national struggle for liberation to our societal struggle for equality. We must ensure that when we finally do achieve liberation, we're not left with a society that's full of corruption and inequity. It's imperative that we fight for women's rights, to ensure that we have full equality between women and men. We need to get rid of traditional mentalities that judge girls and women through the lens of shame. We also need to fight for better employment opportunities for our youth and find ways to get them involved in the political process. Why should those holding political office be predominantly old men? They've consistently proven themselves incapable and irrelevant. It's time they stepped aside and handed over the reins to a new generation of Palestinian leaders.

This larger vision and strategy for our society was a major lesson I took away from studying under Khalida. My time in her classroom is one of many reasons I've never viewed this chapter of my life as a loss. In prison, I grew in ways that wouldn't have been possible otherwise. In prison, I learned the virtue of patience, something I had always struggled with before. And in prison, instead of putting my own comfort and desires first, I learned how to be in a group and always fight for the interest of the collective.

While I believe I matured years in those eight months, I don't want to paint too rosy a picture of that time. There were many unbearable moments that affected me deeply. One of the hardest was when I saw the *tawjihi* students celebrating the announcement of the results of their exams on Palestine TV one evening. I watched with envy as they marked the biggest milestone of their lives to date. Some hung out the windows of slow-moving cars honking the horn incessantly, waving their fists triumphantly in the air. Others danced the traditional Palestinian *dabkeh* to music blaring in the streets. Fireworks went off everywhere. I wanted so badly to be partaking of that moment with them. I was supposed to be there. I had waited my entire life to don the cap and gown and proudly hold my diploma in my hand. Knowing this was a rite of passage I'd never achieve destroyed me. I turned my back on the girls in my cell and spent the next several hours in bed crying. In an overcrowded cell with zero privacy, I just needed to be alone.

THE ISRAELI EQUIVALENT TO a U.S. parole hearing is the *shleesh*, which translates to "one third." A prisoner gets this hearing when they have completed two thirds of their sentence. They're expected to apologize to the court for their crimes, and if the court deems them worthy, they can have up to a third of their sentence deducted and be released early. For Palestinians, this is a very rare outcome, but many of us roll the dice and attend our *shleesh* hearings regardless. Mine was in June, and because it took place in the prison rather than the military court in Ofer, which required an arduous trip in the *bosta*, I decided to go.

Outside the courtroom, I grew impatient waiting for my turn to be called. I told Haya, a lawyer who works in Gaby's office, that I wanted to return to my cell block to study for my upcoming *tawjihi* science exam and asked her to come get me when it was my turn. On the way to my cell, I stopped by Khalida's cell to say hello and ask her something related to my exam. My mother was sitting with her in the cell, so I joined them for a bit. They were listening to the news on the radio.

No sooner had I sat down than I heard a breaking news alert: Martyr Izz Tamimi killed in Nabi Saleh.

Another family member had been murdered in the village.

He was only twenty-one. I remembered the days when Izz and I would play together in school as young children. He was a shy boy then and remained reserved as a young man. His big dream in life was to build a home next to his parents' and start a family of his own.

I didn't absorb the news of his death right away. I was overcome by a numbness I was all too familiar with by that point, the kind my body and mind defaulted to when awful news suddenly descended. I was in a state of shock. Mama, though, began crying, and her blood pressure shot up so fast that she fainted. It was only when I saw the guards come in to take her to the clinic that I, too, started crying, and once I started, I quickly lost control. I completely fell apart. Screaming, I hit out in front of me, tears rolling down my cheeks. I was already under tremendous stress, studying nonstop for my *tawjihi* exams while dealing with the daily indignities of imprisonment. On top of that, they had arrested Waed just a few weeks prior, in addition to so many other youths from Nabi Saleh. My mind flashed back to Khalo Rushdie. And Mustafa. We'd suffered unspeakable losses and had prayed never to experience them again. Yet here we were again: Another one of us had been murdered by the Israeli army. It was too much to bear.

I learned later that Izz had been shot in the back twice with live bullets while running from Israeli soldiers after allegedly throwing stones at them. The soldiers were positioned with their vehicles at the gas station by the entrance to the village. Izz, who posed no real danger to them, had made it close to the back of the homes where Janna and my Ammo Bilal lived when the bullets struck him. Some of my younger cousins heard the shots being fired and ran out of their homes to see what had happened. When they reached the road, they saw Izz lying on the ground, moving slightly as blood gushed out of him. Samer, who was only eleven, was so traumatized by what he saw that he had nightmares for weeks and wouldn't return to normal for months.

Minutes after Izz was shot, the soldiers approached him, still down on the ground, bleeding. They checked his pulse, but stopped short of conducting any sort of real medical intervention on him, even though he was critically wounded. Nearly a dozen soldiers surrounded him as the life bled out of him. Some of my relatives repeatedly shouted that they wanted to take Izz to the hospital, but the soldiers ignored them. They eventually placed him on a stretcher themselves and took him back to one of their vehicles by the gas station. Meanwhile, other soldiers began firing stun grenades to disperse my relatives, who had gathered to try to help Izz. Eventually, the army allowed a Palestinian ambulance to take Izz to a hospital in Ramallah. Nearly an hour later, his parents learned that he had died.

I was still crying when the guards came to take me back to the hearing. I managed to collect myself before entering the room—though, deep down, I was now seething. Once the proceedings got under way, the prosecutor spoke and then my lawyer Haya spoke a bit. Then she turned to me and told me to stand up and address the court.

I rose to my feet, looked directly at the prosecutor, and smiled. It was a spiteful smile, put on to lead her to believe I was about to apologize—which was, after all, what everyone expected in this hearing. I slowly began speaking.

"I know that this is a hearing where I'm supposed to apologize for what I did . . ." I began. I kept talking, in the hope of getting the reaction I wanted from the prosecutor, the one that said, *She's about to apologize! This girl who captured the world's attention for her resistance is finally going to apologize for what she did.*

"And I know that I'm supposed to apologize to you . . ." I went on.

I had her. My setup had worked. And now she was hanging on my every word, believing a full apology was imminent.

Instead, I suddenly scowled and grew serious. I looked right at the judge and said, "But don't even dream that I'm going to apologize to you. Or to this court. And even if you forced me to attend ten trials like this, don't think I'll ever apologize to you. Because if I apologize to you now, I'd be apologizing to the soldier that killed my cousin an hour ago. I refuse to apologize. And if you think I'm going to say I'll never repeat what I did, you're mistaken. As long as you're occupying our land, I'll do what I did again, and I won't just slap one soldier. I'll slap ten soldiers every time they come to the front of our house. I'll even slap you, if I have to, even if I have to live in prison!"

Before I could finish, the guards ejected me from the court. I was immediately notified that I would not be granted early release, which came as no shock. It pained me greatly that I couldn't attend Izz's funeral or be there to sit in mourning and grieve with my family. The only thing I could do was give the parole board a piece of my mind. In response, they concluded that I felt no remorse for what I had done and that I remained dangerous. I'd have to serve the remainder of my sentence in prison after all.

HOMECOMING

IN THE FINAL WEEKS leading up to my release, I took my *tawjihi* matriculation exams in prison and passed. My mother, who was also in the *tawjihi* course, passed her exams as well. With four children and now in her early forties, she finally completed her high school education. She beamed with pride when she learned her score, filling my heart with joy. The girls in my cell threw an impromptu celebration, singing graduation songs and clapping as we took turns dancing. We wanted to prove to our jailers that not even prison would stop us from achieving our dreams or prevent our success. Education, as always, would continue to be one of our most formidable weapons.

As the hour of my release approached, I grew extremely anxious. The anxiety became so debilitating that I struggled even to leave my cell. I kept staring at my watch—the one Israel gives all prisoners—and counting down the hours and minutes until I got to go home. I became so obsessed with checking the time that the girls eventually took the watch and hid it from me. But my thoughts and fears about how I'd manage to reintegrate into my former life were incessant. I stressed out over how I'd speak to my family and friends. We had been essentially estranged for nearly eight months, with no mode of communication. I'd become an entirely different person during that time, and I worried they wouldn't understand me or connect with me in the same way. *We'll have to get to know each other from scratch*, I thought, which felt daunting.

There were many times during my incarceration when I fantasized about holding some shekels in my hand and going to a café to buy an iced coffee. Dreaming of something as simple as the sensation of coins in my hand was thrilling. It made me conscious of the many things in life that we easily take for granted until they're suddenly snatched from us. I vowed never again to lose sight of my many blessings. Still, as my return home drew nearer, the thought of once again partaking in mundane activities like going to the store or even just walking down the street scared me. It had been so long since I'd done either—or even seen a street or a car, for that matter. Would I be capable of carrying out such basic tasks?

As the days passed, a sense of guilt about leaving my prison family behind began to sink in. They constantly expressed how excited they were for me to go home and listed all the things they wanted me to eat on their behalf: ice cream, shawarma sandwiches, pizza, and so on. I tried to savor my time with them as much as possible, knowing I'd miss them sorely and that, until they, too, were ultimately released, we'd have no way of keeping in touch. To preempt the inevitable longing for one another we'd surely suffer, we wrote letters and stories highlighting some of the favorite memories we'd experienced together. We drew pictures and gifted one another jewelry we'd crafted from the Red Cross materials. I used the velvet notebook I had sewn with cardboard and potato sack strings as a sort of yearbook and passed it around for every girl and woman in our cell block to write me a personalized message. It remains one of my most cherished belongings.

———

I COULD BARELY SLEEP the night before I was released. A mixture of excitement at returning home to my family and guilt for leaving behind the girls kept my mind racing. To add to that, in the two times he was able to visit us in prison, my father informed me that my story had made waves internationally and that I should prepare myself for a deluge of media attention once I was released. That's why, a couple of days earlier, I had sought Khalida's guidance on how to address the press once I got out. I wanted to make sure I'd be able to properly relay the messages of my fellow prisoners to the media. Khalida coached me on how to arrange my thoughts into concise talking points. As helpful as she was, there was no way I could have adequately prepared for what I ultimately encountered.

I expected I'd have the morning to say my goodbyes and have a proper send-off, as prisoners were usually sent home in the early afternoon. But shortly before the 5:30 A.M. head count, a guard came by my cell and said, "Ahed, get dressed." I put on the outfit my family had sent for me to come home in and stood with the rest of the girls for the count. Once it was over, the guard told me it was time to go. I turned to the girls, who wept. They looked at me as if it were the last time we'd ever see each other. Some of them still had over a decade left to their sentences. It pierced my heart to leave them like this, but I held my tears back and hugged them one by one. They told me to stay strong and that they were putting their faith in me to be their voice on the outside.

I left my cell and stood in the narrow corridor dividing the two rows of cells. All the cell doors were closed, but women and girls stuck their hands through their narrow slits, the same slits we'd get handcuffed through before going to court. I walked by each door and held their hands, and we said our goodbyes without actually seeing each other. My mother was with me and also said her farewells to the other women in this manner. When we got to the door of Khalto Yasmeen and Khalida's cell, Khalto Yasmeen asked the guard to open it. The guard complied, and I entered it for the very last time. As I hugged them both, I reflected on the lessons they'd taught me over the past few months. It wasn't just the international law course that had expanded my consciousness. By their examples, Khalida and Khalto Yasmeen had taught me how to be a strong woman who advocated for herself and spoke truth to power. They had helped me understand the critical role women play in our society and in our struggle for liberation. Women make up half our society, and they raise the whole of it. We have to ensure that they're strong and empowered with education and political awareness in order to raise the next generation, who will liberate Palestine.

Both Khalida and Khalto Yasmeen cried as they embraced me and my mother.

"You'll remain our voice and our representative," Khalida said to me. "Don't give in to anyone, and don't let anyone discourage you from reaching your goals. We know who you are and what you're capable of."

"I promise I'll try to make you proud," I assured her. And I meant it.

"Come on; it's time to go," the guard called out to us.

For all the difficulties I'd encountered over those eight months, these final farewells remain one of the most painful memories of my time in prison. It wasn't just that I would miss these girls and women I'd become so close to; it was knowing that the state was working every day to grind them down, demoralize them, and break their spirits. And instead of being allied with them in the fight, bound in our collective care, joy, and resistance, I was stepping away from them and toward my own freedom. Every goodbye felt like a grievous loss. I have not, to this day, recovered from them.

The guard took us to a new cell, where we had to wait until it was time to leave Hasharon Prison—we hoped forever. Once that time came, the guards tried to take away all my personal belongings, including all the letters, art, and jewelry the girls had given me. My mom and I sat on the ground in protest. We told them they could send us back to our cells if they wished, because there was no way we'd agree to leaving without those things. I cherished these mementos from my time in prison—they had become sentimental artifacts from an important chapter in my life story, one that had forever changed me. Plus, I was carrying letters the girls had written to their families, which I had promised to send out for them. Some of the girls hadn't been visited by their parents in over four months, and I refused to let them down. Seeing that we were not relenting, the guards finally agreed to let us take all our things with us.

When Palestinian prisoners are released, Israeli authorities typically drop them off at a checkpoint, where their families excitedly wait to greet them and bring them home. For weeks, I had fantasized about my victory car ride back home, where I'd extend my body out the window and hold up my fingers in a peace sign while taking in the fresh air I had long been deprived of. I expected we'd be dropped off at the nearby Jabara checkpoint, where most prisoners released from Hasharon are taken; the Israeli authorities had even informed my father that that's where we'd meet. But soon after they gave him this information, they changed their plans and told him we'd be dropped off at the Rantis checkpoint instead, about an hour and a half away from Jabara but closer to the village. What ensued were several hours of chaos and conflicting information that ended up sending my father, many of my family members, and dozens of news crews on a wild-goose chase, racing back and forth between the two checkpoints.

Meanwhile, they had shackled my mom and me at our wrists and ankles and blindfolded us in the military vehicle. We weren't allowed to speak to each other, and we had no idea where we were. When the jeep finally stopped moving, the soldiers told me to stand up. They positioned me with my back to the door, took off my blindfold, and began to remove the handcuffs. I could hear a commotion outside the vehicle, people shouting. The soldiers turned me around and opened the door. I stepped out of the jeep, and the first person I saw, other than the uniformed soldiers surrounding the vehicle, was my father. I ran over to hug him, excited to finally reunite. I realized then that we weren't at a checkpoint at all, but rather, at the entrance to Nabi Saleh. For reasons that remain unclear, the soldiers had decided to drop us off at the village. I wouldn't get my joyride after all, but I was happy to finally be home.

In addition to our friends, activists, and countless journalists, everyone in the village was there to give us a hero's welcome. Our friends and family waved the Palestinian flag and held up posters with my face on them. My father draped a kuffiyeh around my shoulders.

What happened next is a blur. I recall the pandemonium of journalists surrounding us, pointing cameras in my face everywhere I looked. People shouted at them to back up, in order to give me and my relatives the space to reunite properly, but they kept closing in on us, each photographer eager to get the best shot. It was in that moment that I truly began to grasp just how big my story had become and how, from this point on, I'd have to step into a role far greater than I had ever imagined.

Even through all the shoving and shouting, Abu Yazan and Salam managed to squeeze their way to me and my dad. I hugged and kissed my younger brothers, who seemed to have gotten so big in the time I was away. The soldiers had, for some reason, waited an additional few minutes to release my mother from the vehicle, sparking a brawl between some of my relatives and activist friends and the many soldiers deployed for the occasion. Emotions and tensions were high, but my mother ultimately finagled her way through to us. The five of us stood together, our arms wrapped around one another. I thought about Waed, who was yet again in prison. I was wearing a bracelet with his name spelled out in beads, which I had made from the Red Cross supplies, so that he could be with us somehow. Our reunion was incomplete without him, our homecoming bittersweet.

The swarm of press that closed in on us was unrelenting, prompting my dad to yell, "Okay, you got your pictures. Now give us space so we can go give our condolences to the family of Izz, the martyr."

It had been over a month since Izz Tamimi was shot dead in the village. Because we had no way to pay our respects to his family while we were in prison, let alone know the full story of his murder, his home was the first place we had to go now that we had been released. We marched in a procession toward his family's house, chanting his name in remembrance and honor of him. We greeted his mother in the backyard of her house, crying as we hugged her, and offered her our condolences. Izz was her youngest son and the apple of her eye. His loss was still a fresh, open wound for her, and her grief was heavy. What should have been a private moment of mourning was interrupted by the press still surrounding us. In an attempt to get them to back off a little, I stood at the entrance of the house and addressed them.

"From the home of this martyr, I say the resistance will continue until we end the occupation. I want to thank everyone who stood by me and who has supported all the prisoners. I hope you'll return at four P.M. for a press conference."

The press conference, my dad told me moments earlier, had already been arranged by the informal committee of relatives, friends, and activists who had done relentless media outreach on my behalf.

I had a bit of time away from the cameras to collect my thoughts and, more important, to hug and kiss all my cousins, whom I was desperate to catch up with. And that's when I saw him: Mohammad, my younger cousin whose near death at the hands of a soldier in December had enraged me to the point of physically lashing out and ending up here eight months later. As we embraced, I felt a surge of emotion overcome me. He looked different now, and I was momentarily unsettled trying to get used to it. The left side of his skull was missing; that part of his head was concave when it should have been round. His left eye drooped, and where the bullet had entered, a big scar slashed the skin above his lip all the way up to his left nostril.

"Welcome home, Ahed," he said, almost shyly. "We all missed you and are so happy to have you back."

"Are you impressed with this all?" I laughed. "I caused all this fuss just for you!"

He giggled and turned a little red.

"It's no big deal," I immediately assured him. "If I had to do it again, I would for your sake. The most important thing is that you're healthy and with us now."

He was with us, but he was no longer the same, as Abu Yazan explained to me afterward. Mohammad's injuries were so debilitating and the experience so traumatic that he was no longer as active or adventurous as he used to be. He had stopped playing soccer and running around with his friends and was now even too scared to set out on the nature expeditions that he and Abu Yazan used to live for. He was too worried he'd get dizzy and faint, possibly sustaining even more damage to his head if he fell. Hearing this tore me up.

After a short visit with family, there were other formalities I had to undertake. We drove to Ramallah, to the presidential compound called the Mukata'a, where former Palestinian leader Yasser Arafat is buried in a mausoleum and where the current president of the Palestinian Authority, Mahmoud Abbas, is headquartered. In accordance with a long-standing tradition practiced by many high-profile Palestinian prisoners once they're released, my mother and I paid tribute to Yasser Arafat by placing a wreath at his tombstone and silently reciting a prayer—Surat al Fatiha, the first chapter of the Quran. I felt a surge of pride and strength as I honored our fallen leader. Although he died when I was still a toddler, I grew up hearing about all the noble sacrifices he made serving the Palestinian cause and how he embodied the national aspirations of his people. He was beloved by Palestinians, and despite being in a position of authority, he always saw himself as one of them, an equal.

After honoring Arafat, I was ushered into a room with his successor, President Abbas, for a meeting I didn't personally care to have. But I put my personal feelings toward him aside and went ahead with the meeting because the girls had entrusted me to convey their demands to him. They wanted me to tell him about the dire conditions in the prison and the various ways in which the prison administration made life there unbearable. They wanted me to tell him about the prisoners who were suffering from their serious injuries and of the few girls struggling mentally to the point of experiencing psychotic episodes, yet who lacked proper medical care or resources. And finally, they wanted him to work toward securing a college-level educational curriculum in the prisons, so that they could continue their studies beyond high school.

Unfortunately, our meeting was brief, just long enough for Abbas to secure a strategic photo op with me. I told him, "This meeting was too short, and I truly hope we can meet again soon. The prisoners have several messages and demands they want me to relay to you." I requested to meet with him another day, but I never heard back.

We managed to escape the press and stopped at an ice cream shop on the way back to the village. I had dreamed about the moment I'd eat ice cream again, but now that it was here, I felt guilty. There was no ice cream in prison. Why should I be enjoying it when the girls couldn't? It felt utterly wrong.

Before the press conference, I had a bit of downtime to catch up with my relatives and try to get some rest, which was pretty much impossible with my adrenaline soaring as it was. I managed to sneak away from everyone for a few minutes and head to my room, where I sat on my bed to try to recenter myself. I had forgotten how soft and bouncy my mattress was, having grown too used to the thin, hard ones that practically broke my back every night in prison.

As I sat there taking deep breaths, my head spinning from the chaos of it all, my dad knocked on the door.

"Come in," I said.

The last time he and I were alone in a room together was on the night of my arrest, when he warned me that the Israeli backlash against me was mounting and that they'd likely come for me. Now he stood in the doorway and studied my face with a different look of concern.

"It's a lot, all this attention," he said with empathy.

"You weren't kidding," I replied.

"Ahed, are you sure you want to continue down this path?" he asked.

"I am. I have to. It's my duty."

After I collected myself, we headed to the press conference, held in the village's central square. Nationalist songs blared from loudspeakers as Palestinian flags fluttered everywhere. A table was set up with at least twenty-five different microphones from various news outlets and three chairs. Behind the table stood a new statue of a masked girl in a school uniform standing on three books and poised to launch a pencil from a giant slingshot. I took a seat between my parents and addressed the more than one hundred journalists huddled around us.

"First I'd like to thank everyone who supported me when I was in prison. I thank everyone who carried out campaigns for my release, and I thank the journalists who are here today and the ones who have been covering my story, because if it weren't for you, we wouldn't have been able to get our voices out to the world. I hope that all the campaigns carried out for me continue for the rest of the prisoners, because the prisons are still full. So, I hope the campaigns continue, and I of course will be working on them alongside you. From here in our village of Nabi Saleh, I want to send my greetings to the people of Gaza who are still participating in the March of Return. And I want to relay the message of the administrative detention prisoner Khalida Jarrar, who sends her support to the people of Gaza and applauds their steadfastness. I want to reiterate the message that Jerusalem is and will always be the capital of Palestine."

It was important for me to stress this, especially considering the fact that I had been arrested amid a wave of protests against Trump's decision to move the U.S. embassy to Jerusalem.

"I just left Hasharon Prison, where twenty-nine female political prisoners remain. Among them are three minors, Lama Al-Bakri, Manar Shweiki, and Hadiya Arinat, as well as the administrative detainee Khalida Jarrar. In addition to that, there are twenty other female political prisoners in Damon Prison. Within these prisons are injured detainees who are serving long sentences.

"The prisoners asked me to relay to you three messages on their behalf. The first is their call for national unity within Palestine. The second is they call on the people of Palestine to remain strong and resilient in our resistance. The third is their request for all Palestinians to stand with the rights of the political prisoners and to call for their release.

"One of my biggest sources of stress in prison was that I thought I'd lose my *tawjihi* year. But I was actually able to complete my *tawjihi* studies with the other prisoners. We called ourselves 'the classroom of defiance' because we were able to challenge and defy the prison administration, which tried numerous times to shut down our class, sounding the alarms and making us return to our cells. They tried every single way they could think of to prevent us from learning. Despite that, we were able to turn this prison full of hardships and oppression into a school. My personal message to you all is that we must tie our societal struggle to our national struggle for liberation. We must boycott, isolate, and pursue Israel as a war criminal.

"I want to thank my mother, who stood by my side and supported me in prison even as she suffered the same violations I did. It's not easy being a mother who has kids that are imprisoned and kids that are home that you can't be with. Despite how difficult that was, she pushed herself to grow even stronger in the face of this occupation that imprisons us and she has been able to use her voice loudly to draw attention to our cause. Finally, I want to say that the power is the people, and that the people will decide the path forward and the way in which we'll resist."

Everyone applauded at the end of my remarks, and I breathed a giant sigh of relief. I told the press that I wanted to take some of their questions, with the exception of the Israeli media, which I said I was boycotting because they consistently defamed my family and our struggle. But really, deep down, I wanted to thank them sarcastically. I wanted to thank them because if it hadn't been for their stupidity—or, perhaps it was their hatred—the world wouldn't know who I was. Israeli media had repeatedly aired the clip of my hitting the soldier, a short excerpt from a long Facebook Live stream, and in so doing, they had made me internationally famous. Whatever their agenda was had totally backfired on them. They had embarrassed their country, not thinking that the whole world would turn against them and stand in solidarity with the Palestinian people. They had tried to make an example out of me, but really, they had only exposed their country as the brutal human rights violator it so unabashedly is.

NOTHING COULD HAVE PREPARED me for the crazy new life I was catapulted into. In those first few hours after my release, I finally began to grasp just how big my story had become. Now that I was out of prison, it felt like the whole world wanted to hear what I had to say. Hundreds of journalists and well-wishers came to my home to greet me and my mother. Our front yard was covered with Welcome Home posters plastered with my and my mom's faces. Tiny Palestinian flags hung from the roof of our house, and roughly one hundred plastic chairs were set up outside to host everyone. I learned that I had been dubbed "the Palestinian Joan of Arc" and had been likened to legendary civil rights activists like Rosa Parks. They called me a lioness. I was being nicknamed "Palestine's icon," a title I was honored to have but of which I didn't deem myself worthy. My younger brothers showed me various artistic tributes from around the world depicting me as a hero. I couldn't believe how many posters, murals, and uncanny cartoon renderings of me there were, all with the same unruly mane of curly blond hair.

I was most moved by a giant mural of my face painted on the apartheid wall in Bethlehem. It was right next to a mural depicting Razan Al-Najjar, the beautiful young nurse who was murdered during one of Gaza's marches. That same section of the wall was where Banksy placed his first few drawings, and right across from it was where he later opened his Walled Off Hotel. I learned that two Italian artists had traveled to Palestine just to paint a mural of me there. When I asked if I could meet them to express my gratitude, I was told that Israeli forces had arrested them for creating the mural.

On that first night back, the swarm of press and visitors finally went home at 2 A.M., and I was able to enjoy the most privacy I had had in eight months. Thrilled to finally have me back, Abu Yazan, Salam, and my cousins Marah, Lana, Sarah, and Bassema decided to throw an impromptu slumber party. We dragged every spare mat we could find into my bedroom and huddled around for some long-overdue catching up. They wanted to know exactly what had happened to me during my interrogation, who my friends in prison were, how we had spent our time—everything. I recapped as much as I could before asking them about everything I had missed out on during my captivity. We had been totally cut off from one another for eight months and had so much to fill one another in on. After hours of nonstop chatter, the seven of us eventually passed out. But we continued to hold those slumber parties as a nightly tradition for a week straight. I wished Waed were with us instead of in prison. His absence was painful.

The next morning, I awoke early enough to get ready for a marathon day of back-to-back interviews that the committee that had worked on my release had lined up with the press. But my stomach was hurting once again, and as soon as I got out of bed, I sprinted straight to the bathroom to throw up. After vomiting up the little food I had eaten the night before plus some bile, I lay clutching my stomach on the bathroom floor and calling out for my mom. She was well aware of the stomach problems I had been having on and off during our time in prison and suggested we cancel the morning's interviews and head to the doctor. I insisted I'd be fine, and after resting for a few minutes, I headed out to the backyard, where the first camera crew was already set up.

That morning, I did nonstop interviews with news outlets from all over the world. They asked how difficult prison was and what violations I had suffered at the hands of the Israeli authorities. They asked what I had learned in my time behind bars. I told them I had gained a better understanding of our cause and of the right way to fight for it and that I had learned the virtue of patience and how to be in a group. They wanted to know what I had missed most. I told them I had missed my family more than anything. And second to that, I had missed being able to look up at the sky and see the sun and moon and stars rather than barbed wire. I had also missed being able to walk down the street unshackled. They asked if my time behind bars had made me more afraid of Israel or had subdued me in any way. I told them that the efforts of the prison administration to kill my spirit had failed. The blow that doesn't kill us only makes us stronger. They asked how I felt about the unprecedented level of my newfound fame. I told them I'd never sought nor enjoyed the limelight, but that it was an honor and a lifelong dream of mine to be able to relay my country's message to the world and see that people cared about Palestine. They asked me how I believed the Palestinian people ought to resist. I told them there were many ways of resisting—whether by writing poetry, speaking out, throwing stones, or making art—but at the end of the day, it was up to the people to decide the right path forward for them. And of course, in virtually every interview, they asked me if I regretted slapping that soldier that fateful day. My answer was always an unwavering no. I didn't do anything wrong that I should regret. The soldier had come to my house; I hadn't gone to his. Not to mention the fact that he was part of the same unit that had shot and nearly killed my cousin just thirty minutes prior.

With each interview I gave, I had to repeat my story—and, in so doing, relive the trauma of my experience over and over again. It wasn't easy to have no recovery period during which to decompress from my time in prison. But I pushed myself to forge ahead solely out of a sense of duty and loyalty to the prisoners I had left behind, my friends at Hasharon, whom I was already missing. I had promised them that I would be their voice on the outside, and I fully intended to honor that promise. So long as they remained shackled and jailed, my freedom would be incomplete.

At times, the survivor's guilt I felt for being free, compounded by the pressure of being in the spotlight, became too much to bear. During one interview, with a correspondent from an Arab satellite news channel, I had started talking about the plight of Palestinian prisoners when I began choking up badly; I couldn't speak for a few moments. When the interview was finally over, I ran to my bedroom and broke down in tears. I kept replaying the moment I had said goodbye to my cellmates, the looks on their faces as the guard shut the door, the tears that welled up in Lama's and Manar's eyes, how Khalto Yasmeen held my hand in hers and said, "Our hope is in you."

In hindsight, I now see that the day I had to say goodbye to them was indeed the hardest of my life. The day Khalo Rushdie died was certainly agonizing and continues to affect me deeply, but at least I can take comfort in the fact that he's now at rest. But the women and girls I left languishing in an Israeli prison were not resting. Nothing has pained me more in my life than leaving them behind. Today, tomorrow, and every day that follows until they're all released, it will continue to eat away at me.

Still, I derived purpose from this pain. As worn down as I began to feel, I knew that staying silent wasn't an option. I had been given a rare platform to advocate for Palestine and its prisoners, and I intended to use it. And so, I agreed to keep doing media interviews and speaking to the delegations of activists and fellow Palestinians who, for weeks, came to our home in Nabi Saleh by the busload. If educating the world about our nation's struggle was my mission in this life, I vowed to carry it out as honorably and as effectively as possible.

It was a stressful adjustment to have to go from not seeing anyone for eight months to suddenly greeting and speaking in front of crowds of people. On top of that, on the few occasions I was able to escape to Ramallah to run an errand or enjoy a brief moment of leisure, I was stopped and asked for selfies every few steps. I was flattered and humbled by the level of attention I was getting, but I struggled to cope with the loss of the anonymity I had once enjoyed. My life had changed so drastically and all at once; it wasn't easy. After all, I was only seventeen years old.

Despite never having a moment to myself during this period, I felt more alone than ever. During the time I was locked up, my closest friend at school, who used to confide in me exclusively, telling me all her secrets, had gone off and found a new best friend. My other friends had similarly moved on. This left me feeling I had no one to talk to. I wanted so badly to pour my heart out to Malak and Lama and the rest of the girls in the prison, but there was no way to communicate with them. I began to slip into a depression, one made worse by the constant sense of guilt I felt for being out while they were still jailed, a feeling that plagued me every waking hour of the day.

If that weren't hard enough, I became the subject of slander and jealousy *within* Palestinian society. Many criticized the fact that I was receiving more coverage and concern than every other Palestinian prisoner, young or old. "Why Ahed?" they asked constantly, pointing out that the time I had served was negligible compared to that of so many others. And they were right: I've always been the first to admit that my experience was but a minor example of the injustices Israel regularly inflicts upon Palestinian youth and Palestinian prisoners and that others have suffered far more than I did. But, in my view, my story was never about me, but rather an example of the lives of so many Palestinians.

Many others singled out my appearance as a blonde with blue eyes as the reason behind the disproportionate level of media coverage I was getting: It all boiled down to white privilege, they suggested. But I was among the first to say that my appearance was a huge reason my case garnered international attention. It enabled white Americans and Europeans to look at me and see their own children. It allowed for a level of sympathy that otherwise might not have been there. And it challenged people's racist stereotypes of Palestinians as all dark, when in fact there is great diversity in our appearance. As a child, I used to look around at my family members and wonder why I looked so different. Why did I have this mane of blond hair that no one else had? After seeing how much the rest of the world fixated on it, I began to think that maybe it was a mask God had given me with which to make a difference.

Still, while my appearance was a big factor, I knew it wasn't the only one. The people who constantly complained "Why Ahed?" likely didn't know all the hardships my village and I had endured, the losses we had suffered. They didn't account for the fact that I'd been filmed confronting soldiers, and even featured in viral videos, since I was a young child; there were plenty more than just that one slap. Nor were they aware that while I was in prison, my father and a team of volunteers put in a lot of effort to communicate with journalists, activists, and leaders around the world to get my story out there. To some Palestinians, I was just a blond girl who hit a soldier once, went to prison, and got famous.

I was hurt by the torrent of insults and rumors flowing my way. There were so many fabricated stories about me all over social media, stories alleging things I never said or gifts I never received, including a new Mercedes-Benz. The level of vitriol shocked me. I was used to being attacked by Zionists, but having my character assassinated by my own people was hard to swallow. I felt horrible, and this only deepened my depression. But before allowing myself to feel completely weak and destroyed, I asked myself: *Where is the Ahed whom Khalto Yasmeen and Khalida educated? Is this the girl they taught? Is this whom everyone in prison put their hopes in?* This gave me the strength to ignore the negativity as much as possible and remain focused on being a voice for the Palestinian cause. I know who I am and what I stand for. People can deny that I suffered in prison, or claim that I don't truly love Palestine and am not doing everything I am for the sake of my people, but it doesn't change the truth.

They can hate me all they want, but any attention they give me will only remind them of the other Palestinians in prison, because I speak about them every chance I get. Once I was released, I repeatedly stressed that there remained 350 Palestinian children jailed by Israel whose detention conditions were worse than mine, considering that many of them had serious injuries. I've also constantly highlighted the plight of women in Israeli prisons. Many people didn't even realize that there were female Palestinian prisoners jailed in Israel. These prisoners are all too often forgotten and overlooked. I told myself that regardless of how polarizing I was to many, at least I put these women and girls on everyone's radar. Even in the negative, there's always something positive.

Still, I received far more love and support from around the world than negativity. I couldn't keep up with the number of speaking invitations from countless countries, in addition to scholarship opportunities to study in the United States, the United Kingdom, Spain, Germany, Brazil, Chile, and India, to name a few. Whatever university I chose to enroll at, there were organizations that had pledged to fund my studies. I was overwhelmed by the number of opportunities suddenly at my disposal, and now that studying law was my main goal, I had a lot to consider. Ultimately, though, after spending eight months away from my family and my village, I decided that remaining in Palestine was in my best interest for the time being. I began applying to the renowned Birzeit University, in the West Bank, which has a well-established law program. I was immensely grateful for the scholarships I received and wished that each one that came my way could be granted to another young Palestinian student. So many others are just as deserving as I, if not more so.

In the meantime, I was invited to take part in a speaking tour across Europe, where I'd be meeting with various human rights organizations, activists, and leaders. I had been out of prison for only a little over a month by the time the tour was scheduled to begin and was already growing a bit weary from the pressure of having to constantly speak. But I knew the level of interest in Palestine—and the solidarity with Palestinians we were seeing—was rare, and I had to seize upon its momentum to further advance our cause.

As my family and I were preparing to embark on our European trip, we got word from a Palestinian Authority committee that liaises with Israeli counterparts that Israel planned to ban me from traveling. There was no legal basis for it to ban me; this was just its latest method of political harassment, an attempt to suppress me and to keep me from continuing to tell my story—their story.

A large international media campaign blasting Israel for banning me from travel became just the latest public relations nightmare for the Zionist state. After a heavy backlash and the threat of my family suing, Israel eventually announced that it had not banned us from traveling abroad, but that I was banned from entering the 1948 territories because I posed a security threat to the state. As soon as we heard this news, my father told us all to hurry up and pack what we could, because he wanted to put their statement to the test immediately.

For Palestinians living under occupation, traveling is yet another area in which Israel exercises control over us, and it is just about as difficult as everything else in our lives. We're not allowed to fly out of the nearby Tel Aviv airport and, instead, are forced to travel from Palestine to Jordan by land, through the Allenby Bridge border crossing. The process is anything but simple and efficient. Though you're traveling only a very short distance geographically, it's nonetheless a tiresome multi-hour journey, one that requires being processed by the

Palestinian Authority; followed by Israeli authorities, who have the ultimate say over whether you can exit and enter; and then followed by Jordanian authorities. Each part of this epic border saga requires getting on a bus, riding, getting out, putting your suitcase through a metal detector, waiting, getting your identity documents stamped, and then getting on to the next bus with your suitcase.

The Israeli side of the Allenby Bridge border crossing is always the most difficult. That's where uniformed soldiers decide whether Palestinian travelers will be able to cross. In most cases, travelers won't know if they'll be able to cross until they get there. If Israel has them placed under a ban, they find out only then. I was already accustomed to this process being exceptionally burdensome for me and my family. Before I was imprisoned, each time we tried to travel, we were singled out and held up on the Israeli side for up to ten hours. Even if we arrived early in the morning, they'd keep us there until nightfall, when no other travelers were left and as the janitor began mopping the floors. Only then would they finally hand us back our passports and other documents and release us, just in time to catch the last bus out to Jordan right before it departed. On the day we set out for Europe, we were relieved just to get through.

The first stop on my freedom tour was France. There, and in every country that followed, I had a packed agenda full of conferences, meetings, speaking engagements, and interviews with reporters that lasted from morning to night. The biggest event I spoke at in Paris was the Communist Party's Festival of Humanity, which featured a vast array of celebrities, from rock stars to rappers. I took the stage on the last day and gave an ad-libbed speech to thousands of cheering supporters about Palestinians' experience of living under Israel's violent military occupation. I talked about the prisoners I had met and their daily suffering, and I reminded the crowd that Jerusalem was and would remain Palestine's capital, irrespective of what Trump said or did. I thanked them for their solidarity and told them how much it meant to my people.

It was one thing to see the amount of international support I had online, but to experience it in real life was unlike anything I ever could have imagined. Walking down the famous Champs-Élysées, I was swarmed by dozens of people who wanted to talk to me and take pictures with me. Some hugged me with tears in their eyes and told me that when they looked at me, they saw Palestine. Others said they had learned about Palestine only through hearing about my story, and now they were committed to doing whatever it took to stand in solidarity with us. They told me my people's cause was now their cause and that they were incredibly proud of me.

I couldn't believe how much I had impacted people. The thousands of enthusiastic supporters I addressed in Greece, Spain, Turkey, Tunisia, and finally Jordan made me feel like I had really accomplished something. For the first time in my life, I saw that people around the world truly cared about Palestine. They cared about the safety of our children, and they demanded an end to the Zionist colonization of our land. We weren't alone. I felt more hopeful and inspired than ever.

The absolute highlight of my tour happened in Spain, where I was honored by the Real Madrid soccer team right before they were scheduled to play a match with Atlético Madrid. I visited the famous Santiago Bernabéu Stadium and was welcomed by the team's manager and former forward Emilio Butragueño. I was beside myself when he gifted me a team jersey with my name on it. While I've always been a diehard Barcelona fan, meeting the Real Madrid team and seeing a real soccer stadium for the first time was a dream come true. And it certainly increased my respect for the team

I had long considered a rival. I couldn't believe that the message of the Palestinian people had reached one of the most famous soccer stadiums in the world. With that visit, my two passions, Palestine and soccer, merged in a beautiful, unexpected way. Israel's foreign ministry spokesman felt otherwise, calling the team "shameful" for having honored me as they did. His government clearly couldn't handle yet more international repudiation.

I couldn't keep track of how many stages I stepped on to, the number of speeches I gave, or the number of interviews I sat down for. As honored as I was to be representing Palestine in such a meaningful way, I was also exhausted. The life of a celebrity was not one I enjoyed. And being abroad only intensified my sadness over being separated from the girls in prison. I kept going only because of the tremendous sense of duty I felt to advocate for them and my country. Soon enough, though, everything started to take a toll on me. Each night, I suffered through the same recurring nightmare. In it, I'd be standing in a crowd, surrounded by people eager to meet me, when suddenly, one of them would lunge forward, grab my neck, and begin to choke me. When I tried to scream, another person would wrap their hands around my neck, suffocating me even more. I pleaded for someone to help me, but everyone just stared at me blankly. No one came to my rescue. In the dream, and in real life, my face would be wet with tears. I'd always wake up crying and unable to breathe. I was a wreck.

I know the nightmares were manifestations of all the pressure I was feeling. They were the natural outcome of my suddenly being in the spotlight, having to repeat multiple times a day the story of my arrest, interrogation, and time spent in prison. There was no space to heal from the trauma. Not even my parents understood how tired I was or that I was deteriorating psychologically. I felt completely alone.

After Europe, we flew to Tunisia at the invitation of President Beji Caid Essebsi to commemorate the thirty-third anniversary of Israel's bombing of PLO headquarters, which killed dozens of Palestinians and Tunisians. At the ceremony, the president gifted me with a statue of a silver dove with an olive branch. Next, we flew to Jordan for more appearances and speaking engagements. That's where the stress eventually caught up with my body, and I had to be hospitalized for three days. A combination of exhaustion and an untreated stomach bug I suspected I had caught from something I ate in prison ultimately broke me down. By the time we made it to Turkey, the final country in our month-and-a-half-long travels, I barely had energy left in me to speak.

Things were no less chaotic when we returned home. The legions of visitors and delegations of activists from around the world continued to visit my home consistently for a year. I never let on that I was still battling a deep depression associated with being out of prison when so many remained there. That's something I suffered silently and privately. But gradually, with time, I started to feel more like myself again. When Waed finally came home nearly a year after my mother and I were released, I felt a huge part of my life was restored. It was the first time in ages that our family was reunited, with all five of us sleeping under the same roof, and it gave me a lot of comfort. I was likewise overjoyed each time one of the women or girls I had served time with in prison was released. I saw Lama Al-Bakri in Hebron, Khalto Yasmeen in Jenin, Hadiya Arinat in Jericho, and Malaak Al-Ghalith and Khalida Jarrar in Ramallah. Seeing them in their own homes, among their loving families, and reminiscing about our days locked up together, was among the happiest times for me.

But, as Palestinians know all too well, every joy is short-lived. In late October 2019, barely nine months after her release from prison, Khalida Jarrar was snatched from her home in the middle of the night and jailed under administrative detention yet again. Her house in Ramallah was surrounded by more than seventy Israeli soldiers who had pulled up in twelve military vehicles. Khalida had been asleep when they ambushed her.

When I read the news on my phone the following morning, I couldn't believe it. It had to be a joke, I thought. I ran to my mother and showed her what I had found. We called Khalida's husband, who confirmed the news of her arrest and detailed the late-night raid that had shocked her entire family. I was devastated. After her last arbitrary twenty-month stint in prison, Khalida deserved to rest. She deserved to spend time with her husband and two daughters and to be able to pursue her life's passions outside a stifling Israeli prison cell. There was no telling how long she'd be locked up this time.

Events like Khalida's third arrest under administrative detention kept me up at night. But during the day, in front of the diverse array of visitors who came to meet me, I mustered all the energy and strength I could to speak to them about my experiences and answer all their questions. I found their presence and their interest in my story both heartening and hopeful. They were proof that the Palestinian struggle was increasingly gaining international support and appeal. Through all my conversations with these visitors, I started to piece together the reasons for this seeming surge in support: First, more people were drawing parallels between the Palestinian struggle and other struggles around the world against militarism, systemic racism, colonialism, and inequality. Second, Israel's routine violence and human rights abuses against Palestinians had been widely documented on social media, thanks to the popularity of smartphones. That has allowed people to draw similarities to the Black American struggle. Black people in the United States have rightfully been complaining about police brutality against their communities for decades, but it took capturing these violent interactions on film, and the videos going viral, for much of the country to realize it had a serious systemic problem. With the struggles of both Black Americans and Palestinians, more people have been forced to pause and recognize that there is something off, something not right.

The rise of the Boycott, Divestment and Sanctions movement was another huge factor behind the internationalization of the Palestinian cause. The BDS movement, which was inspired by South Africa's anti-apartheid movement, was formally launched in 2005 by 170 Palestinian grassroots and civil society groups. The aim is to put political and economic pressure on Israel to respect Palestinian rights and comply with international law. The three goals of the BDS movement are to end Israel's military rule over the Palestinian land it occupied in 1967, full equality for the Palestinian citizens of Israel, and the right of return for Palestinian refugees who were driven out of their homes in 1948. Over recent years, the movement has gained momentum internationally and seen some significant victories, like college campuses divesting their endowments of Israeli companies, corporations ending their business dealings with the illegal settlements, and prominent public figures pulling out of events taking place in Israel. This has been one of Israel's worst fears, so much so that the state launched a vigorous campaign to criminalize BDS through legislation. Its top ally, the United States, has also attacked and criminalized the movement. Since 2014, state and local legislatures and even the U.S. Congress have enacted more than one hundred measures penalizing groups and businesses that boycott Israel. Thirty-two U.S. states have passed anti-boycott laws—this in a country that claims to uphold free speech. In its fierce crackdown on the movement, the United States has followed Israel's lead in dishonestly branding BDS as anti-Semitic. But it's not anti-Semitic. It's anti-Zionist, and conflating the two not only is dangerous, but it dismisses our valid grievances as a population denied our human rights and our rightful land. Once again, as Palestinians, we are punished if we protest violently *and* nonviolently.

But this shouldn't deter us. I'm often asked what I think it will take for Palestine to be free. I'm a firm believer that the international community must boycott Israel and pursue it for war crimes in the international courts. I also believe that the only possible and acceptable resolution at this point is a one-state solution. My vision is for us to live in a single democratic state where everyone is equal, Muslim, Christian, and Jew. Judaism is a religion, just like Islam. It is a different way of worshipping the same God we call Allah, and we respect that. But Zionism is a political ideology that says Judaism is not only a religion, but primarily a nationality—and that it needs a country. Not just any country, but our country, and that it needs this country to be for Jews alone. Zionism has taken our country, where Jews, Christians, and Muslims have lived for centuries, and made it a country that is ruled by and for Jews alone. Zionists' ideology claims that they have the right to take other people's land, to push them out. And I can't accept this. No Palestinian can accept this. No human should accept this. It's not racist to say this—it's the opposite. We need a country where Jews and Christians and Muslims can live together as equals, with the same human rights and democracy. Zionism rejects this vision, demanding that all of Palestine be a "Jewish" state. And some Western countries sympathize with this because of the Holocaust.

We know that Jews suffered terrible, unimaginable crimes at the hands of the Nazis, and all of humanity should stand against such murderous hatred and make sure it's never repeated. But how does that give Zionists the right to push us off our own land to make a country for Jews alone? Why should Palestinians compensate—lose our homeland, our property, our rights, even our lives—for the Holocaust committed by Europeans? We shouldn't have to pay for the crimes of the Europeans against Jews. That's just wrong.

The Jews have suffered, and we have suffered. And we need to find a way to live here in one country, with everyone as equals, not in this apartheid state where Palestinians are forced to live on shrinking pieces of our homeland while the best land is reserved for one group. The world did not accept this in South Africa. Why would they accept it in Palestine?

I also believe that in order for the Palestinians to achieve anything meaningful, we first need national unity and strong leadership that actually inspires and mobilizes the people. We currently have neither. I fault all the Palestinian political parties for this, and I don't pledge allegiance to any of them, despite the respect I have for the roles they've historically played in advancing the Palestinian cause. In more recent times, though, Palestinian parties and leaders have caused us to take ten steps backward instead of one single, meaningful step forward. Too many of our leaders have prioritized their personal interests, whether financial or ego-driven, ahead of the collective interests of the nation. They insist on pursuing a doomed two-state solution that's long been championed by the United States and that consistently puts Israel's interests above ours, when the majority of our people now reject it. It kills me to see those leaders cling to power when there's a generation of bright young Palestinians with fresh ideas and charismatic personalities who could steer the course and advance our cause. So long as we remain without real leadership or unity, we will never be free.

Some see me as an emerging leader, but the truth is, I've never had political ambitions. I know I've been gifted with certain skills and capabilities, but I still have a lot of work to do on myself to further develop and strengthen my personality. I also have a lot to learn. That being said, if the opportunity one day presented itself for me to take on a larger role to serve my people, I would rise to the occasion. In the meantime, I'm committed to my current studies at Birzeit University, where I'm working toward a degree in law. And there are other projects I want to pursue. My time in prison sparked ideas about how we can progress as a Palestinian society. For example, I want to spearhead awareness campaigns in different Palestinian villages, to educate everyone about what to do if they're arrested and how they should conduct themselves under interrogation. I also want to teach other Palestinians what I've learned so far about international law and international humanitarian law and how it applies to our struggle. And most important, I want to work to further empower the women and girls in my society.

Journalists and activists often ask me what I think I've achieved. The cynic in me is quick to say I haven't achieved much. Palestine still isn't free, and our society has a long way to go before everyone is educated and empowered enough to successfully organize and pursue self-determination. We're still not there. Yet, I've been able to teach a lot of people around the world about Palestine, and that is my biggest achievement. I broke through the stereotype held by many about what our conflict is and who its players are. They saw a teenage girl stand up to heavily armed soldiers in front of her home, using just her bare hands and her voice—and saw her serve eight months in prison as a result. They've learned that when it comes to the injustices and repression Palestinians suffer at the hands of Israel, my story was just the tip of the iceberg, and that despite being shot at with live ammunition, we continue to resist nonviolently.

Sometimes, when the weight of everything I have gone through feels too heavy to bear, I escape to the hilltop behind our house to sit in solitude. It's where we played *Jaysh o 'Arab* as children, and where I was standing when I saw Khalo Rushdie fatally shot. Despite the memories and the scars that plot of land will forever bear, it has always been my favorite spot in the world. It's the place where I seek refuge, to get some privacy and clear my mind, and where I always run to when I need to cry or process any of the difficult things I've gone through, including the deaths of my relatives. Since returning home from prison, I've found myself sitting on that hill for hours, trying to catch my breath and make sense of everything I've been through. I often stare out at the Halamish settlement across the road and ask myself when it will be gone. Not just Halamish, but all the settlements where 700,000 Jewish Israelis now live on our stolen land. The violence committed by many of these settlers continues to escalate to frightening new levels, as we witness more of our people being attacked, our buildings vandalized, and our olive trees and farmland purposely set ablaze.

Sometimes, when I'm sitting on that hill, I close my eyes and imagine the day we'll see Palestine free. I imagine how our people will react when that day finally comes. I think some of us might die from elation. How incredible it will feel to live with no more checkpoints or soldiers; no apartheid wall or martyrs to mourn! Our people will finally be united because the separation between the West Bank and Gaza and 1948 will cease to exist. I'll be able to love whom I want and plan for my future without the fear that I might get shot and killed or imprisoned once again. I'll visit Akka as I please and spend an entire day swimming in the sea. One day, I might even save up enough to buy my own charming little stone house overlooking the water. On other days, I'll roam Jerusalem's Old City for hours, eventually joining my favorite old *hajjehs* on the ground, where I'll help them sell their mint leaves and okra as they tell me endless stories about what they've seen in their long lives. Just fantasizing about the day, I'm flooded with such powerful emotions that I can't fathom what I'll feel when it actually happens.

When I open my eyes, I see the Israeli soldiers patrolling the area by the spring on the street below. We're the same age now, me and them, but our lives couldn't be any further apart. I think about the teenage Israeli girls my age serving in Israel's army, and I'm overcome with sadness. Despite the fact that they got to grow up with privileges and freedoms Palestinian children have never known, I truly feel sorry for them. The occupation has brainwashed them, both the men and the women. It threatens to rob them of their humanity and their conscience, and once you've lost those two things, you've lost everything that matters in life.

I try, for a second, to put myself in their place. Military conscription is mandatory for them once they turn eighteen, but I could never imagine myself carrying a gun, raiding a house, or arresting someone my age or younger. Even if you brought before me the very soldier who killed Khalo Rushdie, I would never be able to pick up a weapon and shoot him.

Every day, as I pray for God to free us from the occupation and grant us a future that's safe and prosperous, I also pray for these eighteen- and nineteen-year-olds serving in the army to find their humanity and see the wrongs they're committing, against not just Palestinians, but also themselves. I pray that, just once, they honestly question what they're doing, that they think critically about why they're forced to serve in a military that attacks and kills Palestinians who are simply trying to live on their own land. And while they're at it, I also wish they'd ask us why we as Palestinians are resisting as we are. I want them to educate themselves honestly about the true history of this land and try to hear a Palestinian's perspective and experience. I'm hopeful that if they sat down with a Palestinian and listened with an open mind, they'd understand how they've become complicit in our oppression and would think twice about continuing to do so. Only then will they realize that while the occupation has taken our land, it has taken their humanity, and it continues to spread and wreak havoc within them like a cancer.

But this reckoning with the truth doesn't just fall on Israelis.

By now, you have reached the end of my story, and you, too, have a decision to make. I ask that you try to put yourself in the place of a Palestinian. Imagine that my story is yours and that all this has happened to *your* family, on *your* land. What would you do if your country, the only place your family has known for generations, were occupied by a foreign military? How would you respond if your land were continually being stolen? What would you do if you grew up repeatedly seeing your home raided? Your parents arrested? Your mother shot? Your uncle killed? Try, for just a moment, to imagine that this was your life. How would you want the world to react?

I ask also that you remember your humanity, because that's what will decide what you do when you turn these final pages and close this book. Are you going to stand in solidarity with the Palestinian cause and help in whatever way you can—whether by spreading awareness to others, pressuring your government, or further educating yourself about what's happening? Or will you ignore what you've learned, put this book down, and carry on with your life as usual?

The choice is yours.

As for me, I know I'll see a free Palestine during my lifetime, and I remain full of hope. How could I not? Despite all the ugliness and pain I've endured in my short time alive, I still love life. That fact alone gives me hope. So does witnessing the unwavering steadfastness, or *sumood*, of my fellow Palestinian people. I see that steadfastness in the eyes of the young man whose father was martyred when he was a child and who was later imprisoned himself, but who still insists on living in Palestine. I see it in the persistence of every villager who plants a new olive tree immediately after Israeli settlers set fire to their existing ones. I see it in the smiling faces of the children playing outside with such joy despite growing up in a giant cage. I have hope that those children and their children will have a better life than the one I've lived.

Until that day comes, part of me will continue to live in the free Palestine of my imagination, the one where all our burned olive trees are revived, blossoming and bearing fruit once more. Where Mustafa and Khalo Rushdie arrive home in the evening to join their families at the dinner table, and where Mohammed Abu Khdeir makes it to his Jerusalem mosque safely and in time to perform the *fajr* prayer. Where little Ahmed Dawabsheh is reunited with his parents and baby brother, their burned skin unblemished and immaculate. The four of them are laughing and embracing as they stand beneath the radiant light of two glowing suns.

POSTSCRIPT

I ENTERED 2021 FEELING a general sense of disenchantment. I was in my second year at Birzeit University, studying law, but the Covid-19 pandemic meant all my classes were online. Even though I was already living at home with my family in Nabi Saleh, a ten-minute drive from Birzeit, I missed the daily buzz and excitement of campus life. I yearned to be learning in an actual classroom, instead of my bedroom. But there was no telling when things would return to normal.

At the same time, Israel was receiving global praise for leading the world in vaccinating its population, including settlers like the ones living across the road from our village. But not us. Despite its international obligations as an occupying power, Israel did not initially provide vaccines to the millions of Palestinians living under its occupation, a grotesque display of medical apartheid, and something that only added to my mounting frustration.

Just as I was feeling depressed by the status quo, PA president Mahmoud Abbas made a long-awaited announcement: Palestinian parliamentary elections would finally be held in May. It had been fifteen years since the PA last held elections. Abbas and the PA not only lacked a democratic mandate, but they had grown increasingly brutal in suppressing political opposition and any sort of dissent. Abbas's announcement wasn't a long-overdue concession to Palestinians, who had been demanding elections for years, but an attempt to win favor with the new U.S. administration, which had just come into power. Regardless, the prospect of elections filled many Palestinians with excitement. They were eager to make their voices heard at the polls and to have some say in their lives and futures. An overwhelming 93 percent of eligible voters in the West Bank and Gaza registered to vote.

I wanted to take part in a democratic process, but nothing about how the elections were coming together inspired me to participate. Recent changes to PA electoral laws had made it extremely difficult for people, especially young ones, to run for office. The age requirement for candidates was raised to twenty-eight, and candidates had to pay an exorbitant twenty thousand dollars just to get on an electoral list. I didn't believe anyone on the electoral lists deserved to be in power. None of them put forth a vision or a plan to liberate Palestine. All the candidates felt like more of the same. After so many years of a president who did nothing, Palestinians needed a real leader. I knew these elections wouldn't produce that.

In the end, I didn't have to boycott the elections, because Abbas called them off weeks before they were supposed to take place. He blamed this on the fact that Israel would not allow Palestinians in Jerusalem to vote. His detractors pointed out that he could have applied more pressure to make this happen, and like many other Palestinians, I believed Abbas canceled the elections out of fear that he'd likely lose his grip on power.

As winter gave way to spring, a series of events occurred that put Palestine in the global headlines and reinvigorated me personally. In April 2021, Human Rights Watch released an extensive report that concluded that Israel was committing crimes against humanity, including apartheid. The organization pointed to Israel's overarching government policy of maintaining domination by Jewish Israelis over Palestinians and the grave abuses committed against Palestinians living in the occupied territories. Amnesty International came to a similar conclusion about apartheid in a report it released in February 2022. These reports echoed what Palestinians had been saying for decades. For us, the findings were nothing new. Still, it was validating to see Israeli apartheid being discussed on a global level in such an unprecedented way. I began to sense a shift taking place.

Around the same time that Human Rights Watch released its report, simmering tensions in Jerusalem were once again beginning to boil over. It was during the holy month of Ramadan, and Israeli forces had erected metal barricades around the historic Damascus Gate in the Old City. The gate was a popular spot for Palestinians to gather nightly after breaking their fast and performing evening prayers at Al-Aqsa, but the barricades prevented them from congregating. Palestinians protested this every night, eventually clashing with Israeli police, who were dressed in full riot gear and used horses, stun grenades, and skunk water to disperse them. The protests erupted into sheer chaos as hundreds of right-wing Israelis marched through the Old City chanting, "Death to Arabs." Palestinian medics said one hundred people were injured in the clashes that night.

Israeli police eventually relented and removed the barricades around the Damascus Gate, allowing Palestinians to gather there freely. But tensions continued to escalate, and Israeli forces increased their aggression against Palestinians. On one of the last days of Ramadan, Israeli police stormed the Al-Aqsa Mosque compound and attacked worshippers, firing tear gas and stun grenades at them, even as they prayed *inside* the mosque, our most venerated holy site. I couldn't believe the scenes I saw unfolding on the news. The same grounds on which I had once prayed and to which, for years,

I had been longing to return became a chaotic battle zone. The sheer depravity of the Israeli forces targeting worshippers during our holiest month, on one of our most sacred sites, shocked and enraged me. It seemed their lack of humanity knew no bounds. I cried from the bottom of my heart, desperately yearning to be there with my Palestinian brethren. I wanted to stand up to the Israeli forces and defend our beloved Al-Aqsa and Jerusalem. I hated that Israel made it impossible for me to go.

Elsewhere in occupied East Jerusalem, another battle was taking place, this one in the Palestinian neighborhood of Sheikh Jarrah. Just days earlier, a Jewish settler named Jacob Fauci was captured on camera telling a young Palestinian woman named Muna El-Kurd, who was standing in her own backyard, "If I don't steal your home, someone else will steal it." The video of Fauci, who spoke perfect English with a Long Island accent, went viral. His brazen sense of entitlement to steal a home he knew belonged to a Palestinian family highlighted the decades-long struggle residents of Sheikh Jarrah and other Jerusalem neighborhoods were facing just to remain in their own homes.

In 2009, Israeli settlers forcibly expelled three Palestinian families from their homes in Sheikh Jarrah. Another Palestinian family was kicked out in 2017. And now, an Israeli court had approved the expulsion of six additional Palestinian families, including the El-Kurds. All the families had lived there for decades, but the court sided with Jewish settlers, who claimed that the houses were built on land that Jews owned in the nineteenth century, when the Ottomans ruled Palestine. Of course, the courts would never side with Palestinians, many of whom still had the keys to the homes they were forced out of in 1948, when Israel was created. In fact, the Sheikh Jarrah families were themselves made refugees by Israel in 1948. They settled into the homes in question with the support of Jordan and the United Nations in 1956.

As the families of Sheikh Jarrah awaited a decision about their fate by Israel's Supreme Court, they waged a daily protest in front of their homes, which they were at risk of being kicked out of at any second. Twenty-two-year-old Muna El-Kurd and her twin brother, Mohammed, became the faces of the movement, which quickly garnered international solidarity. The twins posted frequent updates on social media and sat down for countless news interviews. They were articulate, charismatic, and unapologetic, managing to draw attention to the settler colonization and the ethnic cleansing of Palestinians in Jerusalem in an effective and powerful way. They showed that the 1948 Nakba was ongoing. Their efforts made people around the world care about the suffering of the families of Sheikh Jarrah, which very few people outside Palestine even knew about. I had tremendous respect for what they were able to accomplish.

Once again, my heart ached that I wasn't able to go to Jerusalem to stand in solidarity with them. Every day, I'd watch as these families and their supporters' peaceful protests were met with an aggressive crackdown by the Israeli police, army, and armed Jewish settlers. For simply standing outside their own homes and telling the world they deserved to remain in them, the protesters endured tear gas, stun grenades, rubber bullets, skunk water, physical beatings, and arrests. Their movement triggered solidarity protests among Palestinians across the West Bank, in cities within '48, and in Gaza.

Then something happened that escalated the unrest to a whole new level.

Hamas, the ruling party in Gaza, which also has an armed resistance wing, issued a strong warning to Israel: Stop the aggression against the people of Sheikh Jarrah, or pay "a heavy price." Israel didn't heed the warning, and Hamas fired rockets into Israel. After a fourteen-year Israeli-imposed siege meant to weaken Gaza and destroy Hamas, Hamas's rockets had only gotten more precise and long-range. In retaliation, Israel attacked Gaza with air raids, kicking off an eleven-day bombing assault that devastated the besieged territory and its two million residents, who had nowhere to flee because they couldn't leave Gaza and no bomb shelters in which to seek refuge.

This was the fourth Israeli war on Gaza to occur during my lifetime, but it was the first one to take place when I was mature and conscious enough to understand what was happening. During those eleven days, I followed the news obsessively, my phone clutched in my hand every waking hour. Stressed and worried, I barely slept each night. I have friends in Gaza, whom I'd met online, and I felt I was living every second of their nightmare with them. As Israel reduced residential buildings to rubble, leaving tens of thousands of civilians homeless, I messaged my friends constantly to see if they were okay. It was in this period that I truly grasped how difficult their lives were there: There was no safe place to hide, no way for a mother to protect her terrified children as the bombs rained down around them. Every single person in Gaza was just waiting for their turn to die. One friend told me, "I'm not afraid to die. But I'm afraid our house will get bombed while we're in it, and we'll be buried alive under the rubble. I don't want us to die suffocating like that." His words were chilling because many people did in fact die that way. By the end of Israel's eleven-day assault, 260 Palestinians were killed. Sixty-six of them were children. Twelve people in Israel were killed by the rocket fire from Gaza.

As devastating as Israel's war on Gaza and its aggression in

Sheikh Jarrah were, the response they sparked filled me with hope and signaled that things were changing in favor of Palestinians. For the first time in my life, there was a unified uprising by Palestinians everywhere. In Gaza, the West Bank, Jerusalem, *and* inside '48, Palestinians rose up to protest Israeli apartheid rule and the settler violence it imposed on us. My people put everything on the line to stand up for their rights, their dignity, and their freedom. I was most surprised to see Palestinian citizens of Israel mobilize as fervently as they did—something I hadn't witnessed before. They took to the streets to protest their second-class-citizen status and to assert their Palestinian identities in a self-defined Jewish state that actively tried to erase them by calling them "Israeli Arabs." They, too, rallied in support of the families of Sheikh Jarrah and the people of Gaza who were being bombarded. Their rebellion showed the world that the legacy of the Nakba and Israel's system of apartheid were felt by its own "citizens."

The unprecedented solidarity I witnessed was inspiring, and the energy it generated was electrifying. It didn't matter where we lived, what citizenship we held, or what color our ID cards or license plates were—despite Israel's efforts to fragment us, we affirmed that we were one people whose fates were inextricably tied. Our pain was shared. We had a common destiny and a common goal: liberation. On May 18, 2021, our solidarity culminated in the form of a nationwide general strike. Hundreds of thousands of Palestinians in the occupied territories and inside Israel stopped working for the day. We shut down our shops and closed our schools and universities. Many of us took to the streets to demonstrate. I joined a small protest in Nabi Saleh, and when it was over, I drove to Ramallah with my father to participate in an even bigger one there. I felt honored to be part of such a historic moment. The strike didn't have just economic implications. It also sent a powerful political message to Israel and the rest of the world that the Palestinian people were united and that nothing would break our determination to be free. I was more convinced of this than ever.

It wasn't just the events inside Palestine that galvanized me. I was also encouraged by the growing international solidarity with our cause. Massive protests denouncing Israeli apartheid erupted around the world, and they weren't led only by our Palestinian brothers and sisters in the diaspora, who have always stood with us. People of conscience everywhere were no longer remaining silent about Israel's crimes against the Palestinian people. In the United States, for example, Black, indigenous, and various other communities that understood state violence and systematic oppression saw our struggle as an extension of their own. America was still in the midst of a racial reckoning following the police murder of George Floyd, an unarmed Black man. Many Americans realized they could not condemn state violence in the United States and then ignore it when Israel was carrying it out—especially when that violence was funded by their own tax dollars.

During this time, social media was flooded with real-time updates out of Palestine. The hashtags SaveSheikhJarrah and Gaza trended globally. Quick explainers and infographics giving context to what was happening in Palestine were being shared all over Instagram and TikTok. Even traditional American media outlets like CNN and *The Washington Post* seemed to highlight more Palestinian voices than ever. A-list celebrities also spoke out in support of Palestine, something that had long been taboo. And in the U.S. Congress, progressive lawmakers, including Palestinian American representative Rashida Tlaib, introduced legislation to condition U.S. aid to Israel on the latter's upholding human rights.

There was no denying that the tide was turning.

All these developments strengthened my resolve to get my law degree and use it to serve my people. I thought about Khalida Jarrar often. She was still in prison, and this fact alone fueled my drive to make her proud of me and to fulfill the promises I made to her before being released.

In July 2021, something terrible happened. Khalida's thirty-one-year-old daughter, Suha Jarrar, died suddenly in her Ramallah home. My mother and I broke down in tears when we saw the news. We were supposed to run errands in Ramallah, but were too upset to leave the house. Even though Khalida was only a couple of months shy of serving her full sentence, the Israelis refused to allow her to leave the prison for a few hours to bury her daughter. I couldn't imagine the agony she was in as she languished in an Israeli prison cell. This was something from which one could never fully recover.

Suha's death and Khalida's inability to bid her daughter a final farewell were tragic, and yet, they were among the many examples of the daily suffering Palestinians continue to endure under Israel's rule. Regardless of which U.S. president or Israeli prime minister is in power, our lives continue to be difficult. I know that change is gradual and that Palestine won't be freed overnight, but I continue to be motivated by the progress and small victories I see.

In September 2021, news broke that six Palestinian political prisoners had escaped from Israel's high-security Gilboa Prison. They managed to dig a tunnel beneath the sink of their cell using small handmade tools. Having spent time in an Israeli prison cell, and knowing how heavily monitored they are, I was shocked by what they had pulled off. But like Palestinians everywhere, I was ecstatic. The fact that they were able to dig their way to freedom in incredibly difficult circumstances using simple objects showed that Palestinian resistance knew no bounds. Their prison break was a victory for all of us. It filled us with pride and gave us a reason to celebrate. People honked their horns as they drove their cars around town. Women and children distributed sweets, and people sang and danced in the streets. It felt like everyone's spirits were uplifted. Even though the prisoners were all eventually recaptured, two of them were able to evade the Israelis for two weeks and enjoy a brief stint of freedom.

The six escapees shattered the illusion that Israel's security apparatus was as ironclad as the state wanted us to believe. They reminded us that Israel wasn't as strong as the will of Palestinians to stay in their homeland and be free. Nothing built on injustice and might lasts forever. Eventually, the oppressed find a way to liberate themselves.

May we all one day break free from our oppression and imprisonment.

Until then, the struggle continues.

ACKNOWLEDGMENTS

AHED TAMIMI:

Thank you, Palestine, the homeland and the cause that gave my story value and meaning.

Thank you to everyone who helped translate my words into a written text that carries the message of a people who are searching for a homeland. Many thanks to my agent, Alia Hanna Habib, and to my editor, Christopher Jackson, and everyone at One World/Penguin Random House.

I'm immensely grateful to Dena Takruri for embarking on this journey with me and allowing me to share experiences and feelings I've never told anyone. You've lived all of the highs and lows of my life with me with a sense of empathy and camaraderie that I deeply appreciate. From the very first time you interviewed me when I was released from prison, I felt at ease with you in a way I never felt with other journalists. You saw me as a whole person, not just a sound bite, and you genuinely cared about my feelings and what I had to say. I cherish the bond we've forged.

Finally, I thank everyone who reads this book and sees me as I wish to be seen: a freedom fighter.

DENA TAKRURI:

It was fate that I happened to be in occupied Palestine visiting family in the summer of 2018 when Ahed Tamimi was released from prison. At the suggestion of my friend Randa Wahbe, to whom I am grateful, I extended my trip and pitched to my bosses at AJ+ a short documentary about Ahed, her village of Nabi Saleh, and the plight of Palestinian children living under Israeli military occupation. They agreed.

I was fortunate to be one of the first journalists to sit with Ahed after her release. It hadn't even been twenty-four hours since she left the custody of her Israeli captors, but she spoke with astounding poise, clarity, and conviction. It was hard to believe I was speaking with a seventeen-year-old. Despite the fanfare surrounding her, Ahed was remarkably humble and gracious, focused solely on the messages she wanted to relay to the world on behalf of the Palestinian people. I knew I was in the presence of a once-in-a-generation voice—and that our paths had crossed for a reason.

Thank you, Ahed, for trusting me with your story, and for revealing parts of yourself to me that are unknown to most. In the many hours we spent together, you opened up to me about your traumas, joys, hopes, and dreams. You brought me to tears and you made me laugh, but above all, you inspired me. It saddens me that, like so many Palestinian children, you were denied the innocence of childhood. I often reflect on how easily that could have been my life. I hope that by telling your story, we can highlight the brutality of the occupation on generations of Palestinian children, and perhaps even help to finally bring it to an end.

Many thanks to Nariman Tamimi and Bassem Tamimi for your insights, generosity, and hospitality during the significant time I spent in your home. I'm likewise grateful to Jonathan Pollak, Bilal Tamimi, Manal Tamimi, and Nawal Tamimi for your kindness and for all the background you provided me. To Khalida Jarrar: Thank you for sharing your experiences teaching international law and international humanitarian law in the "classroom of defiance" that you made in prison. You are a force.

Writing this book would not have been possible without the invaluable support and feedback from Nadeem Muaddi, Mohammad Alsaafin, Tony Karon, Dalia Hatuqa, Hesham Sallam, Noura Erakat, and Marc Lamont Hill. I cannot express enough my appreciation for your reading the manuscript, letting me bounce ideas off you, and answering my many questions. I'm humbled and honored to call such brilliant minds my friends.

I am incredibly grateful to my AJ+ family for lending me the support and time to go a step beyond our original reporting and work on this book. Thank you to the senior leadership Dima Khatib, Moeed Ahmad, Tony Karon, Shadi Rahimi, and Jonathan Laurence. I'm fortunate to have such wonderful colleagues and friends, including Alessandra Ram and Kate Elston.

Thank you to my amazing agent, Alia Hanna Habib, and everyone at the Gernert Company for all of the help, guidance, and sense of calm you lent this first-time author.

To my trailblazing editor Chris Jackson: Thank you for the respect and care you gave this story and for your belief that Palestinian stories deserve to be told. I'm honored to work with you and everyone at One World/Penguin Random House.

I am immeasurably grateful to my close friends and loved ones whose continuous encouragement and confidence in me kept me going, even during some of the darkest days of the coronavirus pandemic.

To my parents, Sharief and Haifa, and my sister, Lubna: Thank you for believing in me and instilling within me a deep love for our homeland. Mama, I'll never understand how you managed to repeatedly haul two young daughters from San Francisco to the West Bank by yourself, let alone during the

First Intifada, but those early visits shaped me forever. I am forever grateful for all of your sacrifices. To Baba, the best storyteller I know, thank you for always being my number one advocate and fan, and for your boundless optimism that "a book can change the world."

While writing this book, I experienced two tremendous losses that made the pain described in some of the pages all the more palpable, and reaffirmed my commitment to telling Palestinian stories. My maternal uncle, Yahya Tahboub, suffered an untimely death from Covid just weeks before the vaccine became widely available. My Khalo Yahya devoted his youth to struggling to liberate Palestine and was banned by Israel as a result. Dying before ever returning to his beloved homeland made his passing all the more tragic. *Allah yerhamak*, Khalo. May your children and grandchildren visit the free Palestine that you always dreamed of.

Later, when the manuscript was nearly complete, I lost my best friend and favorite person, Amal Khoury, to cancer. Amal was a brilliant and beautiful Palestinian American surgeon who exemplified the strength and fortitude of Palestinian women. She became a surgeon so that she could volunteer in Palestine and treat trauma wounds, like the many Ahed grew up seeing amid the violence of the occupation. Amal touched countless people during her life and would have conquered the world if she'd had more time. She cheered me on every step of the way as I worked on this book, including while I wrote some of the pages on her couch. I'm still struggling to make sense of life without you, Amal, but I'll do my best to fulfill my promise to keep making you proud. I'm eternally grateful for the many years of laughter, love, fun, and advice we shared. You are always with me. I love you, and I miss you so much.

NOTES

CHILDHOOD

3   **It was illegally established** Ben Ehrenreich, "Is This Where the Third Intifada Will Start?," *The New York Times*, March 15, 2013, nytimes .com/2013/03/17/magazine/is-this-where-the-third-intifada-will -start.html.

4   **facilitating the immigration of thousands** Zena Al Tahhan, "More than a Century On: The Balfour Declaration Explained," Al Jazeera, Nov. 2, 2018, aljazeera.com/features/2018/11/2/more-than-a -century-on-the-balfour-declaration-explained.

5   **The partition plan gave 55 percent** "The UN Partition Plan for Palestine," Institute for Middle Eastern Understanding, Nov. 27, 2012, imeu.org/article/backgrounder-the-un-partition-plan-for-palestine.

5   **made up 67 percent** "The UN Partition Plan for Palestine"; Benny Morris, *Righteous Victims* (New York: Vintage, 2001), pp. 184 and 186.

6   **without the ethnic cleansing of 1948** "Plan Dalet: Blueprint for Ethnic Cleansing," Institute for Middle East Understanding, March 8, 2013, imeu.org/article/plan-dalet.

6   **millions of dollars in aid** Alasdair Soussi, "The Mixed Legacy of Golda Meir, Israel's First Female PM," Al Jazeera, March 18, 2019, aljazeera.com/features/2019/3/18/the-mixed-legacy-of-golda-meir -israels-first-female-pm.

6   **donors in the United States** Francine Klagsbrun, "The Pitch That 'Made the State of Israel Possible,'" *NY Jewish Week*, Oct. 10, 2017, jta.org/2017/10/10/ny/the-pitch-that-made-the-state-of-israel -possible.

6   **longest unresolved refugee crisis** "Palestine Remix: Palestinian Refugee," Al Jazeera Interactive, 2014, interactive.aljazeera.com /aje/palestineremix/refugee.html.

7   **supported by international law** "Palestinian Refugees and the Right of Return," American Friends Service Committee, afsc.org/resource /palestinian-refugees-and-right-return.

9   **After six months** "Palestine Remix: Administrative Detention of
        Palestinians," Al Jazeera Interactive, 2014, interactive.aljazeera.com
        /aje/palestineremix/admin_detention.html.

19   **an Israeli court actually ordered** "You Cannot Be Free Without My
        Freedom: The Struggle of Nabi Salih [*sic*]," The Oakland Institute,
        2017, oaklandinstitute.org/you-cannot-be-free-without-my
        -freedom.

20   **settlers threw stones** Ben Ehrenreich, *The Way to the Spring: Life
        and Death in Palestine* (New York: Penguin, 2017).

23   **"a conscientious Nakba"** "You Cannot Be Free Without My Free-
        dom."

23   **number of Israeli settlers** Ali Adam, "Palestinian Intifada: How
        Israel Orchestrated a Bloody Takeover," Al Jazeera, Sept. 28, 2020,
        aljazeera.com/news/2020/9/28/palestinian-intifada-20-years-later
        -israeli-occupation-continues.

24   **meant to separate Palestinians** "Israel & International Law: The
        West Bank Wall," Institute for Middle East Understanding, April 1,
        2015, imeu.org/article/israels-west-bank-wall.

24   **Many protesters were injured** *Against the Wall*, dir. Ayed Nabaa, Al
        Jazeera, 2013, interactive.aljazeera.com/aje/palestineremix/phone
        /against-the-wall.html.

26   **no one from Nabi Saleh** Ala Alazzeh, "Non-Violent Popular Resis-
        tance in the West Bank: The Case of the Popular Struggle Commit-
        tees," Birzeit University, 2011, novact.org/wp-content/uploads
        /2013/10/Non-violent-popular-resistance-in-the-West-Bank-the
        -case-of-popular-struggle-committees-final-July-21-2012.pdf.

THE MARCHES BEGIN

35   **took up a soccer theme** Natasha Roth-Rowland, "Showing Israeli
        Soldiers the Red Card in Nabi Saleh," +*972 Magazine*, May 29,
        2015, 972mag.com/photos-showing-israeli-soldiers-the-red-card-in
        -nabi-saleh/.

39   **it gave Israel full control** "Water Crisis," B'Tselem, Nov. 11, 2017,
        btselem.org/water.

39   **"the most effective, cost-efficient"** skunk-skunk.com/about/.

39   **skunk water's efficacy as a nonlethal** "Who, What, Why: What Is
        Skunk Water?" BBC News, Sept. 12, 2015, bbc.com/news/magazine
        -34227609.

42   **"prisoner of conscience"** "Israeli Authorities Must Release Palestinian
        Prisoner of Conscience in West Bank," Amnesty International,
        Nov. 1, 2012, amnesty.org/en/latest/news/2012/11/israeli-authorities
        -must-release-palestinian-prisoner-conscience-west-bank/.

42   **"Have mercy on us!"** the IMEU, video compilation of some of the

raids, including the one described. "Rare Peek at Nightly Raids of West Bank Village (Nabi Saleh) w/English Subs," YouTube, March 23, 2012, youtube.com/watch?v=vS8Kni8LJZQ.

45   **eyewitnesses to his murder** "Soldier Kills Palestinian Demonstrator Mustafa Tamimi, 28, by Shooting Tear-gas Canister at Him," B'Tselem, Dec. 11, 2011, btselem.org/firearms/20111209_killing _of_mustafa_tamimi.

45   **shot him point-blank** Haggai Matar, "Mustafa Tamimi: A Murder Captured on Camera," +972 Magazine, Dec. 11, 2011, 972mag .com/mustafa-tamimi-a-murder-captured-on-camera/.

45   **must be fired from a distance** Chaim Levinson, "When Israeli Soldiers Kill Palestinians, Even a Smoking Gun Doesn't Lead to Indictments," Haaretz, July 7, 2016, updated April 10, 2018. haaretz.com/israel-news/.premium-when-even-a-smoking-gun -doesn-t-lead-to-indictments-1.5407233.

47   **Jonathan, who lost consciousness** "Israeli Soldiers Clash with Mourners at Funeral of Palestinian Protester," The Guardian, Dec. 11, 2011, theguardian.com/world/2011/dec/11/clashes-at -mustafa-tamimi-funeral.

48   **claims that he hadn't seen Mustafa** Mairav Zonszein, "IDF Closes Probe into Killing of Mustafa Tamimi in Nabi Saleh," +972 Magazine, Dec. 5, 2013, 972mag.com/idf-closes-probe-into-2011-killing -of-mustafa-tamimi-in-nabi-saleh/.

48   **MAG failed to hold** "MAG Closes File in 2009 Killing of Bassem Abu Rahmeh," B'Tselem, Sept. 10, 2013, btselem.org/press_releases /20130910_bassem_abu_rahmeh_killing_file_closed.

48   **out of 739 complaints** "B'Tselem to Stop Referring Complaints to the Military Law Enforcement System," B'Tselem report, May 25, 2016, btselem.org/press_releases/20160525_occupations _fig_leaf.

FORBIDDEN LANDS

51   **world's largest open-air prison** "Gaza Strip: A Beginner's Guide to an Enclave Under Blockade," Al Jazeera, March 14, 2021, aljazeera .com/news/2021/3/14/a-guide-to-the-gaza-strip.

52   **practically any Jewish person** "The Law of Return," The Knesset, knesset.gov.il/laws/special/eng/return.htm.

55   **third-holiest city in Islam** Ziad Abu-Amr, "The Significance of Jerusalem: A Muslim Perspective," Palestine-Israel Journal of Politics, Economics and Culture 2, no. 2 (1995): pij.org/articles/646.

58   **cover or scratch off** Ben Reiff, "The Israeli Right Is Erasing Arabic from Jerusalem, One Street Sign at a Time," +972 Magazine, Sept. 24, 2020, 972mag.com/jerusalem-arabic-street-signs-israeli-right/.

58   **under Israeli military rule** "Quick Facts: Jerusalem," Institute for
       Middle East Understanding, May 4, 2018, imeu.org/article/quick
       -facts-jerusalem.

                        BREAKING THE BARRIER

60   **60 percent of the West Bank** "You Cannot Be Free Without My
       Freedom."
60   **richly endowed with natural resources** "Area C and the Future of
       the Palestinian Economy: A World Bank Study," United Nations,
       Feb. 7, 2014, un.org/unispal/document/auto-insert-202903/.
60   **virtually all Palestinian applications** "Palestinian Building Permits
       'Political,' Admits Israel," *Yahoo! News,* May 3, 2015, news.yahoo
       .com/palestinian-building-permits-political-admits-israel
       -001629371.html.
62   **twenty-two illegal Israeli settlements** Dalia Hatuqa, "'We Are
       Living in a Touristic Prison': Palestinians on Life in the Holy City
       of Bethlehem," *Vox,* Dec. 23, 2019, vox.com/world/2019/12/23
       /21024634/bethlehem-tourism-christmas-west-bank-palestine
       -israel-settlements.
63   **only 13 percent of Bethlehem** Ramzy Baroud, "The Ethnic
       Cleansing of Palestinian Christians that Nobody Is Talking About,"
       Counterpunch, Oct. 31, 2019, counterpunch.org/2019/10/31
       /the-ethnic-cleansing-of-palestinian-christians-that-nobody-is
       -talking-about/.
68   **traveled to other Palestinian cities** Urvashi Sarkar, "Janna Jihad:
       Meet Palestine's 10-Year-Old Journalist," Al Jazeera, April 28, 2016,
       aljazeera.com/news/2016/04/janna-jihad-meet-palestine-10-year
       -journalist-160426132139682.html.
71   **all on video** "Rushdi [*sic*] Tamimi Nabi Saleh," video of Rushdie
       Tamimi moments after he was shot on Nov. 19, 2012, YouTube,
       youtube.com/watch?v=zTmPach1Yjg.
74   **no reason to use live ammunition** Chaim Levinson and Jack
       Khoury, "IDF Probe: 80 Bullets Fired Without Justification in
       Death of West Bank Palestinian," *Haaretz,* Jan. 16, 2013, haaretz
       .com/.premium-army-palestinian-shot-80-times-1.5224816.

                        THE SPOTLIGHT

77   **my confrontation with the soldiers** Video of the confrontation,
       Nokta Grup, "Brave Palestinian Girl Ahed Tamimi vs Soldier:
       Where Is My Brother??????," YouTube, Dec. 24, 2012, youtube.com
       /watch?v=E4FM9WGRWdQ&t=14s.

79   **"Handala was born"** Naji al-Ali, *A Child in Palestine: The Cartoons of Naji Al-Ali* (New York: Verso, 2009).

84   **at least eighty-one youth** Nora Barrows-Friedman, "Israeli Captain: 'I Will Make You All Disabled,'" The Electronic Intifada, Sept. 1, 2016, electronicintifada.net/content/israeli-captain-i-will-make -you-all-disabled/17821.

84   **"I will have all of you walking with crutches"** Ibid.

85   **advocating for dialogue** "Matti Peled," American Friends Service Committee, March 30, 2010, afsc.org/story/matti-peled.

86   **heard one of the officers** Miko Peled, "Why Israelis Must Disrupt the Occupation," The Electronic Intifada, June 12, 2017, electronicintifada.net/content/why-israelis-must-disrupt-occupation /20731.

86   **Israeli forces had killed Saba Abu Ubeid** "Gaza Fisherman Is Second Killed by Israel This Year," The Electronic Intifada, May 16, 2017, electronicintifada.net/blogs/maureen-clare-murphy/gaza -fisherman-second-killed-israel-year.

89   **My dad carried him** Amira Hass, "The Palestinian Family That Fought a Soldier to Save Their Son," *Haaretz*, Sept. 3, 2015, haaretz.com/.premium-the-palestinian-family-that-fought-a -soldier-to-save-their-son-1.5394578.

89   **photos of the incident** Gili Cohen, "Palestinian Women, Children Stop IDF Soldier Detaining a Minor," *Haaretz*, Aug. 28, 2015, haaretz.com/palestinian-women-children-stop-idf-soldier-detaining -a-minor-1.5392534.

89   **fourteen-year-old sister** Lawahez Jabari, "West Bank Teen Ahed Tamimi Becomes Poster Child for Palestinians," NBC News, Sept. 12, 2015, nbcnews.com/news/world/palestinian-poster -child-n425581.

90   **they dubbed "Pallywood"** Editors, "A Perfect Picture of the Occupation," *Haaretz*, Aug. 31, 2015, haaretz.com/opinion/picture-of-the -occupation-1.5393148?lts=1629999856955.

90   **"Shirley Temper," a name** Ehrenreich, "Is This Where the Third Intifada Will Start?"

90   **shout my name** Jaclynn Ashly, "Nabi Saleh: 'It's a Silent Ethnic Cleansing,'" Al Jazeera, Sept. 4, 2017, aljazeera.com/fea tures/2017/9/4/nabi-saleh-its-a-silent-ethnic-cleansing.

91   **suffered third-degree burns** Ido Efrati and the Associated Press, "Ali Dawabshe's [*sic*] Mother Succumbs to Wounds Sustained in West Bank Arson," *Haaretz*, Sept. 7, 2015, haaretz.com/.premium-ali -dawabshe-s-mother-succumbs-to-wounds-1.5396017.

91   **Second- and third-degree burns** Linah Alsaafin, "Maximum Sentence Requested for Jewish Settler in Duma Arson Case," Al

Jazeera, June 9, 2020, aljazeera.com/news/2020/06/09/maximum
-sentence-requested-for-jewish-settler-in-duma-arson-case/.

92   **abducted him drove him** Yair Ettinger, "'We Never Dreamed It
Would End in Murder,' Says Abu Khdeir Defendant," *Haaretz*,
June 3, 2015, haaretz.com/.premium-defendant-in-abu-khdeir
-murder-testifies-1.5369181.

92   **An autopsy later discovered soot** Gregg Carlstrom, "Autopsy Shows
Palestinian Teen 'Burned Alive,'" Al Jazeera, July 6, 2014, aljazeera
.com/news/2014/07/06/autopsy-shows-palestinian-teen-burned
-alive/.

94   **Shamsaan, Arabic for "Two Suns"** Staff Reporter, "Peace Tour by
Palestinian Youth," *Independent*, July 20, 2017, iol.co.za/pretoria
-news/peace-tour-by-palestinian-youth-10383138.

96   **"It's my right to see it"** Dan Williams, "Abbas Hints Has No 'Right of
Return' to Home in Israel," Reuters, Nov. 1, 2012, reuters.com/arti
cle/us-palestinians-israel-abbas-refugees/abbas-hints-has-no-right
-of-return-to-home-in-israel-idUSBRE8A01IL20121101.

96   **"We know too well"** Address by President Nelson Mandela at the
International Day of Solidarity with the Palestinian People, Dec. 4,
1997, archive.nelsonmandela.org/index.php/za-com-mr-s-542.

97   **more than fifty discriminatory laws** "An Overview: Apartheid South
Africa & Israel," Institute for Middle East Understanding, Dec. 9,
2013, imeu.org/article/an-overview-apartheid-south-africa-israel.

97   **elaborate permit and checkpoint system** "An Overview: Apartheid
South Africa & Israel."

99   **revolt that began in Soweto** "The June 16 Soweto Youth Uprising,"
South African History Online, sahistory.org.za/article/june-16
-soweto-youth-uprising.

THE SLAP

103   **giving the country more military aid** Jake Horton, "Israel-Gaza:
How Much Money Does Israel Get from the US?," BBC News,
May 24, 2021, bbc.com/news/57170576.

103   **Obama signed a Memorandum** Alia Chuchtai, "Understanding US
Military Aid to Israel," Al Jazeera, March 8, 2018, aljazeera.com
/news/2018/3/8/understanding-us-military-aid-to-israel.

104   **did not violate international law** Lazar Berman, "No Longer US
Ambassador, David Friedman, Is Sticking to His Sledgehammers,"
The Times of Israel, Feb. 8, 2021, timesofisrael.com/no-longer-us
-ambassador-david-friedman-is-sticking-to-his-sledgehammers/.

104   **UNRWA was set up** F. Brinley Bruton and Lawahez Jabari,
"UNRWA Funding Cut Could Close Palestinian Schools Within
Weeks," NBC News, Sept. 4, 2018, nbcnews.com/news/world

/unrwa-funding-cut-could-close-palestinian-schools-within-weeks
-n905956.

105   **"a long-overdue step"** Alexia Underwood, "The Controversial U.S.
Jerusalem Embassy Opening, Explained," *Vox*, May 16, 2018, vox
.com/2018/5/14/17340798/jerusalem-embassy-israel-palestinians
-us-trump.

130   **felt as if his brain were rolling** "Report of Torture and Ill-Treatment
1994," *Palestine-Israel Journal of Politics, Economics and Culture*,
1994, pij.org/articles/734.

130   **he was never charged** "Exclusive: Interrogation Video Surfaces of
Palestinian Teen Activist Ahed Tamimi," *The Daily Beast*, April 1,
2018, thedailybeast.com/exclusive-interrogation-video-surfaces-of
-palestinian-teen-activist-ahed-tamimi.

138   **Israel classifies all the Palestinians** Chloé Benoist, "Palestinian
Women Haunted by Abuse in Israeli Jails," *Middle East Eye*, Feb. 8,
2018, middleeasteye.net/features/palestinian-women-haunted
-abuse-israeli-jails.

138   **the overwhelming number of children** Alice Speri, "The Homecoming: How Ahed Tamimi Became the Symbol of Palestinian
Resistance to Israeli Oppression," *The Intercept*, July 31, 2018,
theintercept.com/2018/07/31/ahed-tamimi-released-palestine
-child-prisoners/.

142   **Palestinians in the West Bank who are arrested** "The Israeli Military
Court System," Addameer, July 2017, addameer.org/israeli_military
_judicial_system/military_courts.

142   **judges are military officers** Ibid.

PRISON

151   **advocate for prisoners' rights** "Israel Arrests Palestinian Leftist
Figure Khalida Jarrar," Al Jazeera, Oct. 31, 2019, aljazeera.com
/news/2019/10/israel-arrests-palestinian-leftist-figure-khalida
-jarrar-191031071410783.html.

160   **parts of this interrogation** "Ahed Tamimi Interrogation, Dec. 26,
2017," YouTube, youtube.com/watch?v=fyCKd4MhPaM.

169   **past protests in which I had participated** "Israel Extends Detention
of Ahed Tamimi for Third Time," *Middle East Monitor*, Dec. 29,
2017, middleeastmonitor.com/20171229-israel-extends-detention
-of-ahed-tamimi-for-third-time/.

171   **behavior was "ideologically motivated"** Oren Ziv, "Military Court:
Ahed Tamimi and Her Mom to Remain in Prison," *+972 Magazine*,
Jan. 17, 2018, 972mag.com/military-court-orders-the-tamimi
-women-to-remain-in-prison/.

171   **denied Palestinians the same protections** Ibid.

171   **military courts deny bail 70 percent** Bill Van Esveld, "Israeli Prose-
       cutors Throw Book at Palestinian Child Protestor," Human Rights
       Watch, Jan. 14, 2018, hrw.org/news/2018/01/14/israeli-prosecutors
       -throw-book-palestinian-child-protestor.

172   **Thirty-eight prominent legal experts** Jaclynn Ashly, "Ahed Tamimi
       Gets Eight Months in Prison After Plea Deal," Al Jazeera, March 22,
       2018, aljazeera.com/news/2018/03/ahed-tamimi-months-prison
       -plea-deal-180321201412587.html.

172   **"a slap is terrorism"** "Is a Slap an Act of Terror?" BBC News, Jan. 31,
       2018, bbc.co.uk/programmes/p05wqg1f.

172   **"finish [our] lives in prison"** "Israeli Army Arrests Palestinian
       Teenage Girl Who Slapped Soldiers; 'She Should Finish Her
       Life in Prison,'" *Haaretz*, Dec. 20, 2017, haaretz.com/israel
       -news/idf-arrests-palestinian-teen-girl-who-slapped-soldiers
       -1.5629071.

172   **"We should exact a price"** Jonathan Ofir, "'We Should Exact a Price'
       from Ahed Tamimi 'in the Dark,' Israeli Journalist Says," Mondo-
       weiss, Dec. 23, 2017, mondoweiss.net/2017/12/should-israeli
       -journalist/.

175   **Israel had shown** Daniel Estrin and Merrit Kennedy, "Military Trial
       Opens for 17-Year-Old Palestinian Activist," NPR, Feb. 13, 2018,
       npr.org/sections/thetwo-way/2018/02/13/585320714/military-trial
       -opens-for-17-year-old-palestinian-activist.

177   **Elor Azaria is an Israeli soldier** Yaniv Kubovich and Noa Landau,
       "Elor Azaria, Israeli Soldier Convicted of Killing a Wounded Pales-
       tinian Terrorist, Set Free After Nine Months," *Haaretz*, May 8, 2018,
       haaretz.com/israel-news/.premium-hebron-shooter-elor-azaria
       -released-from-prison-after-nine-months-1.6070371.

178   **"Concerning the risk"** Yoav Haifawi, "Why Yifat Doron Slapped the
       Prosecutor at the Tamimi Trial—and Only Spent Two Days in Jail,"
       Mondoweiss, March 29, 2018, mondoweiss.net/2018/03/slapped
       -prosecutor-tamimi/.

179   **eight months in prison** Ibid.

181   **Families have to apply** "Israeli Forces' Transfer of Palestinian Child
       Detainees Amounts to War Crime," No Way to Treat a Child,
       Defense for Children International—Palestine, Jan. 20, 2020,
       nwttac.dci-palestine.org/israel_forces_transfer_palestinian_child
       _detainees_amounting_to_war_crime.

184   **six of my relatives** "Lieberman Imposes Collective Punishment on
       Tamimi Family; Nabi Saleh Declared 'Closed Military Zone,'"
       Samidoun, Jan. 13, 2018, samidoun.net/2018/01/lieberman
       -imposes-collective-punishment-on-tamimi-family-nabi-saleh
       -declared-closed-military-zone/.

184   **defense minister justified the arrests** Ibid.

184 **senior military commander claimed** Robert Mackey, "Israel Extracts 'Confession' from Badly Wounded Cousin of Ahed Tamimi, Jailed Protest Icon," The Intercept, Feb. 26, 2018, theintercept.com/2018 /02/26/pre-dawn-raid-israel-arrests-badly-wounded-cousin-ahed -tamimi-jailed-protest-icon/.

201 **as "any act by which"** United Nations Convention Against Torture, Article 1, "Convention Against Torture and Other Cruel, Inhuman or Degrading Treatment or Punishment," New York, Dec. 10, 1984, p. 1, treaties.un.org/doc/Treaties/1987/06/19870626%2002-38 %20AM/Ch_IV_9p.pdf.

202 **violated its obligations** Zena Tahhan, "Israel's Settlements: Over 50 Years of Land Theft Explained," Al Jazeera interactive, Jan. 27, 2020, interactive.aljazeera.com/aje/2017/50-years-illegal-settlements /index.html.

202 **demanding the right to return** Huthifa Fayyad, "Gaza's Great March of Return Protests Explained," Al Jazeera, March 30, 2019, aljazeera.com/news/2019/03/gaza-great-march-return-protests -explained-190330074116079.html.

203 **it was illegal for Israel** "No Justification for Israel to Shoot Protesters with Live Ammunition," The UN Independent Commission of Inquiry on the 2018 Gaza Protests, United Nations Human Rights Office of the High Commissioner, Feb. 28, 2019, ohchr.org/en /press-releases/2019/02/no-justification-israel-shoot-protesters-live -ammunition.

203 **may have been committing a war crime** "UN Independent Commission of Inquiry on Protests in Gaza Presents Its Findings," press release, United Nations, Feb. 28, 2019, un.org/unispal/document /un-independent-commission-of-inquiry-on-protests-in-gaza -presents-its-findings-press-release.

203 **She was only twenty years old** Sabreen Al-Najjar, "A Year on from the Great March of Return, I Still Mourn My Daughter Razan, Killed in Cold Blood," *The Independent*, March 27, 2019, independent.co.uk/voices/israel-palestine-great-march-return -rouzan-al-najjar-conflict-deaths-a8841996.html.

204 **Israeli parliament passed a law** "Israel Passes Law to Strip Residency of Jerusalem's Palestinians," Al Jazeera, March 7, 2018, aljazeera .com/news/2018/03/israel-passes-law-strip-residency-jerusalem -palestinians-180307153033538.html.

204 **part of a decades-long plan** "Israel: Jerusalem Palestinians Stripped of Status," Human Rights Watch, Aug. 8, 2017, hrw .org/news/2017/08/08/israel-jerusalem-palestinians-stripped -status#.

204 **more than fifty laws discriminated** "Discrimination Against Palestinian Citizens of Israel," Institute for Middle East Understanding,

Sept. 28, 2011, imeu.org/article/discrimination-against-palestinian
-citizens-of-israel.

204   **the Citizenship and Entry into Israel Law** "The Citizenship and
Entry into Israel Law (temporary provision) 5763," The Knesset,
State of Israel, 2003, knesset.gov.il/laws/special/eng/citizenship
_law.htm.

205   **International Court of Justice had declared illegal** "International
Court of Justice Finds Israeli Barrier in Palestinian Territory Is
Illegal," UN News, July 9, 2004, news.un.org/en/story/2004/07
/108912-international-court-justice-finds-israeli-barrier-palestinian
-territory-illegal.

205   **wall was built deep within** "In Pictures: Israel's Illegal Separation
Wall Still Divides," Al Jazeera, July 8, 2020, aljazeera.com/indepth
/inpictures/pictures-israel-illegal-separation-wall-divides-2007080
81141597.html.

205   **"the right to exercise"** Miriam Berger, "Israel's Hugely Controversial
'Nation-State' Law, Explained," Vox, July 31, 2018, vox.com
/world/2018/7/31/17623978/israel-jewish-nation-state-law-bill
-explained-apartheid-netanyahu-democracy.

205   **the law mandates** "Is Israel an Apartheid State?" Institute for Middle
East Understanding, Oct. 4, 2013, imeu.org/article/is-israel-an
-apartheid-state.

206   **all persons, including children** "Children in Israeli Military Detention," report, UNICEF, March 6, 2013, unicef.org/sop/reports
/children-israeli-military-detention.

207   **"as a measure of last resort"** Ibid.

208   **tried in Israel's military courts** "Israel's Detention of Palestinian
Children Is an Outrage to Humanity," Defence for Children International, Sept. 29, 2021, defenceforchildren.org/israels-detention
-of-palestinian-children-is-an-outrage-to-humanity/.

208   **protected under the Geneva Conventions** "Treaties, States Parties
and Commentaries," International Committee of the Red Cross,
ihl-databases.icrc.org/ihl/INTRO/470.

208   **The resolution reaffirmed** Stanley L. Cohen, "Palestinians Have a
Legal Right to Armed Struggle," Al Jazeera, July 20, 2017, aljazeera
.com/opinions/2017/7/20/palestinians-have-a-legal-right-to-armed
-struggle.

208   **but he said no** Michael Parks, "Mandela Rejects S. African Terms
for Prison Release," *Los Angeles Times*, Feb. 11, 1985, latimes.com
/archives/la-xpm-1985-02-11-mn-4278-story.html.

209   **international law had been created** Noura Erakat, *Justice for Some:
Law and the Question of Palestine* (Redwood City, CA: Stanford
University Press, 2019).

209   **an individual can file a complaint** "How Can People Report Crimes
to the ICC?," Justice Hub, Jan. 6, 2015, justicehub.org/article/how
-can-people-report-crimes-to-the-icc/.

213   **shouted that they wanted** Yumna Patel, "Israeli Forces Shoot and
Kill Izz al-Din Tamimi in Nabi Saleh," Mondoweiss, June 6, 2018,
mondoweiss.net/2018/06/israeli-forces-tamimi/.

213   **Nearly an hour later** "Fatally Shot Though Posing No Danger: Israeli
Soldier Shot 'Iz a-Din Tamimi from Behind; He Was Fleeing After
Throwing a Stone at the Soldier," B'Tselem, July 3, 2018, btselem
.org/firearms/20180703_killing_of_iz_a_din_tamimi_in_a_nabi
_saleh.

214   **concluded that I felt no remorse** Yotam Berger, "Israeli Parole Board
Denies Palestinian Teen Ahed Tamimi Early Release," *Haaretz*,
June 7, 2018, haaretz.com/israel-news/.premium-israeli-parole
-board-denies-palestinian-teen-tamimi-early-release-1.6155305.

HOMECOMING

236   **In most cases** "Israel Bars Thousands of Palestinians from Traveling
Abroad; Many Other Don't Even Bother to Make the Attempt,"
B'Tselem, May 15, 2017, btselem.org/freedom_of_movement/2017
0515_thousands_of_palestinians_barred_from_traveling_abroad.

238   **calling the team "shameful"** Uzi Dan, "Real Madrid Hosts Ahed
Tamimi, Palestinian Teen Jailed for Slapping IDF Soldier," *Haaretz*,
Sept. 30, 2018, haaretz.com/middle-east-news/palestinians
/.premium-soccer-club-real-madrid-hosts-palestinian-teen-ahed
-tamimi-1.6514685.

239   **invitation of President Beji Caid Essebsi** "Tunisian President Meets
Palestinian Activist Ahed Tamimi," *Xinhua*, Oct. 3, 2018, xinhuanet
.com/english/2018-10/03/c_137507955.htm.

239   **gifted me with a statue** Mohammed Daraghmeh and Josef Feder-
man, "Palestinian Activist, Ahed Tamimi, Takes Her Cause Abroad,"
The Christian Science Monitor, Oct. 22, 2018, csmonitor.com/World
/Middle-East/2018/1022/Palestinian-activist-Ahed-Tamimi-takes
-her-cause-abroad.

240   **surrounded by more than seventy Israeli soldiers** "Israel Arrests
Palestinian Leftist Figure Khalida Jarrar," Al Jazeera, Oct. 31, 2019,
aljazeera.com/news/2019/10/31/israel-arrests-palestinian-leftist
-figure-khalida-jarrar.

241   **put political and economic pressure** "Here's What You Need to
Know About BDS," BDS, Dec. 7, 2020, bdsmovement.net/news
/heres-what-you-need-know-about-bds.

241   **more than one hundred measures** "What You Need to Know About

BDS," *In These Times,* Nov. 19, 2020, inthesetimes.com/article/bds -west-bank-israel-palestine-anti-boycott-laws-boycott-divestment -sanctions.

241 **Thirty-two U.S. states** "Legislation Targeting Advocacy for Palestinian Rights," Palestine Legal, legislation.palestinelegal.org/.

245 **settlements where 700,000 Jewish Israelis** "Israel's 55-year Occupation of Palestinian Territory Is Apartheid—UN Human Rights Expert," March 25, 2022, ohchr.org/en/press-releases/2022/03 /israels-55-year-occupation-palestinian-territory-apartheid-un -human-rights.

POSTSCRIPT

250 **Human Rights Watch released an extensive report** "A Threshold Crossed: Israeli Authorities and the Crimes of Apartheid and Persecution," Human Rights Watch, April 27, 2021, hrw.org/report/2021 /04/27/threshold-crossed/israeli-authorities-and-crimes-apartheid -and-persecution#.

251 **a report it released in February 2022** "Israel's Apartheid Against Palestinians: Cruel System of Domination and Crime Against Humanity," Amnesty International, Feb. 1, 2022, amnesty.org/en /documents/mde15/5141/2022/en/.

252 **a Jewish settler named Jacob Fauci** "Video Shows Israeli Settler Trying to Take Over a Palestinian House," Al Jazeera English, May 4, 2021, aljazeera.com/news/2021/5/4/if-i-dont-steal-your-home -someone-else-will-jewish-settler-says.

253 **the protesters endured** Mohammed El-Kurd, "Here in Jerusalem, We Palestinians Are Still Fighting for Our Homes," *The Guardian,* July 28, 2021, theguardian.com/commentisfree/2021/jul/28 /jerusalem-palestinians-homes.

AHED TAMIMI is a Palestinian student activist from Nabi Saleh in the occupied West Bank. As a child, she rose to global prominence for repeatedly confronting Israeli soldiers during weekly demonstrations in her village, which resulted in violent attacks on her family, and her imprisonment at the age of sixteen. She has been honored for her courage and efforts to expose Israel's occupation, and is widely regarded as a symbol of Palestine's youth movement. Ahed Tamimi is currently studying international law at Birzeit University and plans to use her degree to advance the struggle for a free Palestine.

Email: TheyCalledMeALioness@gmail.com

DENA TAKRURI is an award-winning journalist who has reported extensively on the Israeli occupation of Palestine, Europe's refugee crisis, tensions on the Korean Peninsula, and other global struggles. She is recognized for her bold and immersive reporting, characterized by speaking truth to power and giving voice to the voiceless. The daughter of Palestinian immigrants, she was born and raised in the United States, yet spent many summers in Palestine. Dena Takruri is currently a senior presenter and producer at AJ+ and has previously worked at HuffPost Live and Al Jazeera Arabic.

Twitter: @Dena
Instagram: @denatakruri
denatakruri.com